THE NEW YORK TIMES
COMPLETE GUIDE TO
Auto Racing

THE NEW YORK TIMES
COMPLETE
GUIDE TO
Auto
Racing

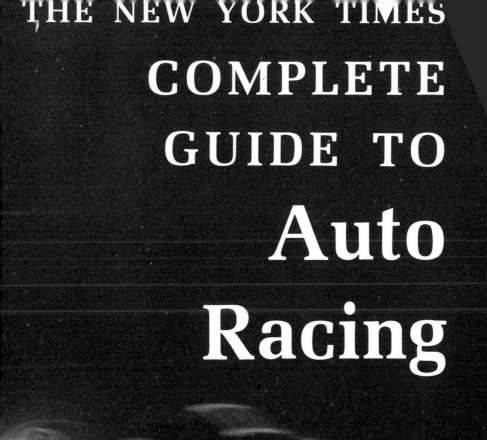

BY JOHN S. RADOSTA

QUADRANGLE BOOKS·CHICAGO

To Vivian

Contents

APPENDICES

Illustration Credits

Jacket and title page—Pete Lyons.

Chapter 1—13, Indiana State Police; 25, John Bishop.

Chapter 2—28, Pete Lyons; 31, Charles McDonnell; 32, Gerald Schmitt; 34 and 37, John Bishop; 41, STP Corporation; 45, Michael R. Sesit; 48, 49, 50, 52 and 53, D. Lynn Justis, United States Auto Club.

Chapter 3—58-59, John Bishop; 60, Cotton Owens Garage; 64, John Bishop; 66, Cotton Owens Garage; 69, Daytona International Speedway; 71, Associated Press; 73, Pete Lyons; 75 top, Michael R. Sesit; 75 center, Dick Jones; 75 bottom and 77, Daytona International Speedway.

Chapter 4—82-83, John Bishop; 89, National Hot Rod Association; 90, Bill Bagshaw; 92, Charles McDonnell; 94, Leslie Lovett, N.H.R.A.; 95 top and bottom, N.H.R.A.; 96 and 97, Leslie Lovett, N.H.R.A.

Chapter 5—98, John S. Radosta; 105, Michael R. Sesit; 109, Gulf Oil Corporation; 111, Pete Lyons; 113 top, Michael R. Sesit; 113 center and bottom, Pete Lyons; 114, Nissan Motor Corporation; 117 and 118, John S. Radosta.

Chapter 6—119, John Bishop; 127, Pete Lyons; 129, Michael R. Sesit; 130, Pete Lyons; 135, Michael R. Sesit.

Chapter 7—137, John Bishop; 141, Barton Silverman, The New York Times; 143, Cameron A. Warren; 144, John Bishop; 146, Volkswagen of America.

Chapter 8—147, Sears, Roebuck; 150, Las Vegas News Bureau; 151, Barton Silverman, The New York Times; 156, Michael Evans, The New York Times; 161, Charles McDonnell; 162, Porsche Panorama.

Chapter 9—164, John S. Radosta.

Chapter 10—190, United Press International.

Chapter 11—198, Michael R. Sesit.

Appendix B—222 left, Michael Evans, The New York Times; 222 right, Pete Lyons; 223 top left, Chevrolet Division, General Motors; 223 top right, 223 bottom and 224 top, Pete Lyons; 224 bottom and 225, Michael R. Sesit; 226 upper left, Barton Silverman, The New York Times; 226 upper right, Leslie Lovett, N.H.R.A.; 226 lower left, Pete Lyons; 226 lower right, D. Lynn Justis, USAC.

Appendix C—227, Michael R. Sesit.

Appendix E—238-39, Charles McDonnell.

Introduction

*I*N MY YEARS of covering auto racing for The New York Times I have never stopped being impressed by the complexity and variety of motor sports. There is something new to learn every season, at every race, and what I learn I pass along to readers of The Times. Much of my reporting is expository: its purpose is to explain, explain, explain—formulas, rules, air foils, politics, construction, economics. And that also is the objective of this book: to attempt to draw a clear picture of auto racing for the reader who is only vaguely familiar with it.

This is why everything in the book starts with fundamentals and emphasizes simplicity. To make life easier for the reader there are abundant illustrations and they are inserted in the text where needed; diagrams are used to clarify what might otherwise be difficult to comprehend. At the back of the book is a commentary on racing language and a glossary; I do not assume you know the meaning of "cubes" or "drift" or "to take a bath"—they are all explained when they first appear and are defined again in Appendix A. Other appendices list champions, car classifications, race clubs and race tracks and help the reader with some basic racing arithmetic.

What I have tried to do is to cover a complicated subject not only as entertainingly but as clearly as possible. I want this book to be a handy reference work; I want it to be useful.

* * *

I like racing, but I am not obliged to like it all. I do not like the chicanery of some of its principals or their wheeling and dealing. I do not like phony races or convenient little accommodations secretly worked out for a favored competitor or promoter.

In a real sense the spectator who pays anywhere from $2 to $40 or $50 to see a race is a consumer and I feel *someone* should look out for his interests. I try to. I am dismayed by what this sport imposes on its loyal cash customers—things like traffic congestion, difficult road access, poor planning, inconvenient and expensive parking facilities. I am repelled by the contempt that some track owners have for their patrons: fans are gouged for ghastly food; they are abused and pushed around by rude rent-a-cops; latrines are disgraceful, and almost nowhere is it possible to be comfortable. Most promoters are reluctant to spend the money it takes to keep spectators informed about the progress of a race either through competent announcers or scoreboards. I am positively bugged by the absence of scoreboards—not just adequate scoreboards but any old scoreboards. And when a good board appears I am happy to lead the cheering.

I believe auto racing cannot validly call itself the "Sport of the Seventies" until it provides amenities for the fans.

There is a good deal of show biz in racing and because of this the reporter is sometimes required to function as a critic. If the production is mediocre, that's the way I call it. I remind promoters and sanctioning bodies that the purpose of criticism is to improve things. Many of the journalists who cover racing have more affection for the sport than the promoters do—in much the same way that the drama critic often has the interests of the theater more at heart than money-oriented producers.

People who are unfamiliar with racing invariably ask: "What about the danger? Don't all these drivers have a death wish?" Few of us who are involved with racing are disposed to practice pop psychiatry, but it is safe to say most of us do not accept the death-wish theory. Danger is an inescapable part of racing but it does not dominate racing. Almost all drivers with whom I have discussed the subject say something like this: "Yes, racing is dangerous, but you can't think about danger all that much, any more than policemen, firemen and pilots do. If you spend time worrying about it, you can't drive well, and then maybe you shouldn't be driving. We know it's there, but we put it in the back of our minds."

Certainly race drivers take all the precautions they should and they are constantly pressing the track owners for safe conditions (safety costs money). But having done all this, they then simply go about their business. Many drivers say they have an understanding with their wives: This is what I want to do more than anything else in the world, and we are prepared for the risks. Most have made financial provisions for their families, and their wives accept the realities.

Some men race for money. Many race because they have a lust for competition. I know several drivers who would race if no money were involved and who compete in everything they do, even away from the track. Some men race because they like the spotlight, the headlines, the glamour and the fun. But whatever their motives, they all agree: Yes, it's dangerous, but that's the way it is.

As for the spectators, there are cynics who believe they come out primarily to see the spills and crack-ups. Perhaps some do but most, I feel, simply prefer to see how close the drivers can get to the "edge."

*   *   *

Nobody knows it all. I do not profess to, nor does this book. Much of the material in it comes from my own notes, reference files and experience. But motor racing is a broad and complicated subject and therefore I have called on friends and associates in the business for data, information, points of view, critiques of my manuscript and most especially for help in assuring accuracy. A letter here, a phone call there, a borrowed file from somewhere else, the use of someone's records—they all add up.

But I am most grateful to several friends who have been magnificently generous with their expertise, assistance—and patience. One is Chris Economaki, my colleague and sometimes my competitor as editor of National Speed Sport News—Chris, who is well informed, a keen observer of the racing scene and blessed with a great sense of humor.

There is Venlo Wolfsohn, a compulsive collector of facts and figures whose data would choke a computer. There is Hunter V. Farnham of the United States Agency for International Development, who once was a slavey on the Grand Prix circuit. The combined interests of these two Washingtonians range all the way from dirt-track midget racing to the most arcane facets of international competition.

Dic Van der Feen, he of the peculiarly spelled first name and former director of public relations at the Sports Car Club of America, has spent hours of his time splitting hairs in the interests of accuracy. Sometimes the ruins of a chapter were sickening to contemplate, but I appreciated his help then as now. The same goes for John Oliveau, executive director of the Automobile Competition Committee for the United States-F.I.A., Inc.

And where would I be without the cool perspective of John Bishop, president of the International Motor Sports Association? In addition to his other talents, Bishop is an able illustrator as well as an inspired doodler during committee meetings and telephone calls. I am delighted that several of his contributions appear in this volume.

William S. Stone, author of that very fine book "A Guide to American Sports Car Racing," gave me some valuable suggestions during the planning stages of this work. And just when I thought I had the job done, he overwhelmed me with reams of comments that were most helpful.

And there is G. William Fleming, former executive director of ACCUS. Bill unknowingly started me on this project one cold winter morning in Stamford a few years ago and he has been unfailingly helpful ever since.

Dozens of race drivers, mechanics, team managers and race officials have given me much of what appears in this guide. They were generous and considerate: if they thought my questions were stupid, they at least put me down gently. I cite one driver with deep affection: the greatest joy of my work in recent years has been my friendship with the late Bruce McLaren, a gentle, kindly man who had a soft voice and a loud laugh and who smiled in a way that suggested he was relishing a little private joke. He gave me hours of his companionship on and off the track. Bruce was killed while testing one of his cars on June 2, 1970. His death has diminished all of us.

There are others to whom I am grateful. In alphabetical order they are:

Tom Binford, former president of the United States Auto Club (USAC); A. Tracy Bird of the Sports Car Club of America (S.C.C.A.); Rod Campbell of Canadian Motoring Consultants; Jim Cook of Jim Cook Associates, Los Angeles; Don Davidson of USAC; Bill Dredge of the STP Corporation; Dr. Frank Falkner of the S.C.C.A.; Jim Foster of the National Association for Stock Car Auto Racing (NASCAR); Bill France of NASCAR; Dustin Frazier of National Speed Sport News; Jim Haynes of the Lime Rock Park road course in Connecticut; Linn Hendershot of USAC; Phil Holmer of NASCAR; James E. Kaser, formerly of the S.C.C.A.; Peter Lyons, freelance writer-photographer; Fred Marik of Professionals in Motion; Brad Niemcek of Carl Byoir & Associates; Wally Parks of the National Hot Rod Association (N.H.R.A.); Jacque Passino, formerly of the Ford Motor Company; Jim Patterson, formerly of the S.C.C.A.; Les Richter of American Raceways, Inc.; John Ross of Canadian Motoring Consultants; Bob Russo of the N.H.R.A.; Jeff Scott of the Columbia Broadcasting System; Bill Smyth of USAC; Nick Storrs of the Northeast Division of the S.C.C.A.; John Timanus of the S.C.C.A.; Miss Patricia Wagner of Barkin Herman Strenski & Franco, Inc., and Ron Zimmerman of the S.C.C.A.

And finally, out of alphabetical order, my thanks to my sister, Mrs. Margaret Abbruzzese, for her painstaking care in the preparation and endless revisions of the manuscript.

New York, April, 1971

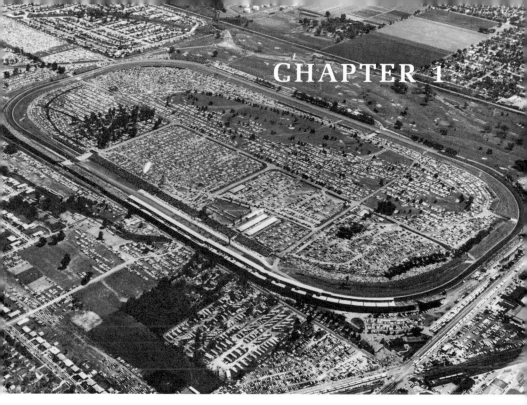

CHAPTER 1

Full house for the Indianapolis 500.

Into the Maze

THE BASIC IDEA of motor racing is simple: to beat the other cars to the finish line.

Beyond that it gets complicated.

There are a multitude of classifications. There is a babel of organizations, each with its own gallery of champions and each authorizing races. There is a confusing overlap as one organization raids the turf of another. There is a mumbo-jumbo nomenclature that puzzles even the old hands. There is fierce competition for race dates because most races are run on Sundays and there aren't many Sundays in the calendar after you eliminate the cold-weather months.

There are road courses, ovals, dirt tracks, paved tracks,

13

airport circuits, hill climbs, night races, sprint races, 24-hour endurance events, 500-milers, quarter-mile drags, races that run rain or shine and races that do not run in the rain.

The fan has to cope with such things as formula, stock, stock block, prototype, sports cars that are not sports cars, stock cars that are not stock cars, piston displacement, double overhead cams, turbocharged and supercharged, blown engines in two different connotations, homologate, scrutineering, contingency awards, sponsors. And nowadays, the inflation of the English language being what it is, any backwater promoter can organize a wheelbarrow sprint and call it a Grand Prix.

There are names like Stewart, Ickx, Hulme, Siffert, Donohue, Gurney, Andretti, Yarborough and Yarbrough, Unser and Unser, Pearson, Foyt, Petty. This is a tightly knit community in which first names, when used alone, are unmistakably identifiable: Jackie, Jacky, Denny, Jo, Mark, Dan, Mario, Cale and LEE Roy (in the Southern intonation, as in PO-lice), Bobby and Al, David (not Dave), A.J. and Richard. (In all the racing world there may be many Richards but there really is only one Richard, and everyone knows you are speaking of Richard Petty. Not Dick Petty: "If my folks wanted me to be known as Dick, they'd have christened me Dick.")

There are other names: Lotus, Lola, Brabham, McLaren, March, Ford, Chevrolet, Javelin, Mustang, Plymouth . . . Trans-Am, Can-Am . . . Sunoco, Shell, Union 76 . . . Riverside, Spa, Monza, Laguna Seca, Mont Tremblant, Darlington, Daytona, Talladega, Indianapolis, Road America, Lime Rock, Ontario, Atlanta. . . . Acronyms like NASCAR, USAC, ACCUS . . . Appendix J, the G.C.R. of S.C.C.A., AA/FD and so on.

For all the complexity of auto racing, millions of Americans are dedicated to it, paying up to $40 to $50 to see a race and traveling hundreds of miles for the privilege. Motor races in the United States attract a paid attendance * of approximately

---

* A note of caution: Accurate attendance figures are exasperatingly elusive. It is part of the game, regrettably, for promoters to inflate attendance statistics. This year's crowd is always greater than last year's—otherwise the track management would look bad. Some promoters, for divers reasons, do not give out attendance figures. They are the honest ones.

50 million a year, second only to horse racing, which has the advantage of pari-mutuel betting.

National Speed Sport News has estimated that even if you *eliminate* from this figure all the attendance at (1) races in the championship division of the United States Auto Club, including the Indianapolis 500; (2) all the Grand National races on the superspeedways of the National Association for Stock Car Auto Racing (NASCAR), and (3) all three professional series of the Sports Car Club of America—even if you eliminate all these events, the remaining attendance still is greater than that of the third spectator sport, baseball.

Racing is expected to continue growing. "The Sport of the Seventies" has become a popular catch phrase.

The annual 500-mile race on the Memorial Day weekend at Indianapolis draws at least 250,000 spectators—that's a quarter of a million people in one enclosure. Daytona claims crowds of close to 100,000. Watkins Glen has reported 110,000, Riverside 80,000. Auto racing is even more popular abroad. In France one event alone—the Twenty-four Hours of Le Mans—has had 400,000 spectators. The Nürburgring in West Germany attracts 200,000 to its big races.* What other sports events come near such figures?

If the experience of European countries is a valid guide, there are three successive steps leading to national achievement in racing—first the tracks, then the drivers and finally the cars.

The tracks we have. In road racing there are superb layouts like Watkins Glen in New York, Riverside and Laguna Seca in California, Road America in Wisconsin (and, across the border, Mont Tremblant and Mosport Park in Canada). Among the oval tracks we have Indianapolis Motor Speedway, venerable but still valuable; Ontario in California, Daytona in Florida, Talladega in Alabama, Atlanta in Georgia, Charlotte and Rockingham in North Carolina, Michigan International in Michigan.

---

*The caveat about American attendance figures is equally applicable to European statistics. European promoters are just as devious as their American brothers.

American drivers rank quite close to the best of Europe's. We have versatile drivers like Mario Andretti, Parnelli Jones, Mark Donohue and A. J. Foyt and specialists like the Unser brothers Bobby and Al, Richard Petty, David Pearson, Cale Yarborough, Lee Roy Yarbrough and Roger McCluskey.

Somehow we still have a way to go with the cars. Engines, yes. Almost exclusively the giant unlimited engines in the Canadian-American Challenge Cup series are American, yet most of the successful cars they push are European—McLaren, Lola, March. The engines at Indianapolis are American Fords and Offenhausers, but there still are Indianapolis cars of European origin—Brabham, Lola, McLaren, Lotus—and some of the American-made units are candid derivations from European designs.

In the Continental Championship road races there have been Chevrolet, Plymouth and Ford engines in British cars with such nameplates as Surtees, McLaren, Lola, Lotus. Only one all-American car has ever won a modern Grand Prix*—Dan Gurney's Eagle-Ford in the 1967 Grand Prix of Belgium. In the world manufacturers championship, Fords won in 1966 and 1967 at Le Mans, but no American car has won at Le Mans since then.

Perhaps the greatest attainment of American racing in this generation is its liberation from what was once an overwhelming European influence. The Indianapolis 500 is Americana itself. Our stock-car contests and our drag meets are utterly indigenous. Our sports-car events retain a few vestigial ties to European cultural influences but there are also home-grown innovations.

The Canadian-American Challenge Cup, completely American in concept and administration despite its name, offers road racing that is up with the fastest in the world. Can-Am races in North America (usually seven in the United States and

* "Modern" in the sense of the World Championship of Drivers, which began in 1950. An earlier all-American car did win the 1921 Grand Prix of France—a Duesenberg driven by Jimmy Murphy.

three in Canada) can hold their own with any of the Grand Prix. (Aside to xenophiles: Sorry about that.)

Another encouraging note: The Sports Car Club of America has developed a racing class called the Continental Championship. Its success is based on the popularity of an open-cockpit, open-wheel (no fenders) race car designated Formula A.* The car is powered by mass-produced V-8 engines with a maximum displacement of 305 cubic inches, or 5 liters—and are those engines guttingling noisy! In just a couple of years Formula A has proliferated in Europe, South Africa, New Zealand and Australia. Overseas this race type is known as Formula 5000—the engine size in limited to 5,000 cubic centimeters (5 liters), the metric equivalent of our 305 cubic inches. The principle difference is that the American Formula A is permitted to use fuel injection, while Formula 5000 cars must use carburetors.

*   *   *

Motor racing is big business as well as show biz. The American automotive industry is reported to be spending something like $50 million a year on "performance and engineering." The tire industry, based in Akron, Ohio, spends millions of dollars developing race tires. Firestone does not subsidize race teams so heavily as it did some years ago, but Goodyear is still in there with its moneybags. Accessory manufacturers—spark plugs, lubricants, fuels, additives, tires, wheels, ignition, everything—are deeply involved in racing. Investors are flirting with the idea of building new tracks. Others are looking for bargains in existing tracks.

Advertisers are sponsoring races, series of races and race teams. Particularly significant is the impact of *nonautomotive* sponsors, including companies involved with toys, soft drinks, men's clothing, cigarettes, toilet seats, beer, whisky, household wax, air travel, variety stores, foods.

Racing has its major and minor leagues, its moguls and

---

*The Continental Championship also includes competition for smaller cars designated Formulas B and C, but these cars do not race against Formula A machines.

bankrupts, successful entrepreneurs and conceited poseurs. It has made its own erratic way without the help of television and without much press coverage (except for accidents). It has managed to prosper on nondescript dirt tracks in the boondocks and on drag strips bulldozed from meadows.

There are four major organizations that sanction* races in this country. They are, in alphabetical order, the National Association for Stock Car Auto Racing, the National Hot Rod Association, the Sports Car Club of America and the United States Auto Club.

Aside from these there are dozens of regional and area groups† that operate their own circuits of specialized competition (midgets, for example, or "supermodified" sprints). There are hundreds of tracks operating independently of any sanctioning club. Some are too penurious to pay sanction fees or to put money into the safety measures required by the sanctioning bodies, but most are independent because there is no need to affiliate. Within the small geographic area of one or two states many operators have formed circuits of three tracks or so that use a common set of rules. Sometimes the cars are of unique local design and really have no other place to run. Independents here and there may skimp on steel guard rails and other safety equipment, but the pressure of insurance rates does force them to be reasonably safe.

All this variety makes for a fair amount of confusion but it also contributes to the strength and health of auto racing. The key is competition. Just as there is competition between the American and National Leagues in baseball, so is there competition between the United States Auto Club and the Sports Car Club of America, between the National Hot Rod Association and the American Hot Rod Association, between the National Association for Stock Car Auto Racing and the Sports Car Club of America, and so on. (Great Britain's motor racing has a strong base because there are more than 50 clubs

*"Sanction" as a verb means to authorize an event. As a noun it is the documentary authority that a promoter purchases from the appropriate organization.
†See Appendix D.

18

conducting races.) Without the spur of competition, the leagues might fall asleep.

You would think all the action in this country could be divided among the four major sanctioning groups along clearly delineated lines. But no, it hasn't worked out that way. There is no powerful cartel that has tried to unify racing into a tidy package. So we do have overlap—or competition:

• The National Association for Stock Car Auto Racing (NASCAR) is absolutely pre-eminent in its field. Yet the United States Auto Club, (USAC) whose primary business is open-cockpit racers, sanctions races for late-model stock cars—and with rules virtually identical with NASCAR rules.

• Until 1968 small "sporty sedans" like Camaro, Mustang, Javelin and Barracuda had run only in road races sanctioned by the Sports Car Club of America. But now NASCAR sanctions races for these cars on oval tracks and road courses. And USAC has also begun running the small sedans on oval tracks—*in the same races* with larger late-model stock cars.

• USAC, whose usual domain is oval tracks, schedules races on road courses, partly in recognition of the growing popularity of road racing. This cuts into the turf of the Sports Car Club of America.

• The outstanding USAC competition racer is the "Indy" car, with its open wheels (no fenders) and a single seat in an open cockpit. In recent years the Sports Car Club of America has challenged the big bad cornhuskers of the Middle West by popularizing its Continental Championship with a Formula A car that looks quite like the "Indy" car.

• NASCAR and USAC have two or three races a year for stock cars on road courses, a radical change from the ovals and another incursion into the S.C.C.A. sphere of interest.

All these overlaps among the major sanctioning organizations are complicated by further competition from the dozens of small race clubs. The sanctioning bodies are unhappy about all the duplication. But motor racing is big business, and when so much money is at stake few of the principals are concerned with the niceties.

*   *   *

Some sports are relatively provincial. Baseball is played in North America, Central America, the Caribbean and Japan. The football we know is limited for all practical purposes to the United States and Canada. Ice hockey and skiing, obviously, have their greatest appeal in lands with cold climates. Cricket, soccer and cross-country bicycle racing are unable to make much of an impression in this country. Other sports— track and field, tennis, golf—are more or less international and have certain common denominators that give them uniformity—though, of course, there are differences of detail in the way they are organized and conducted from one nation to another. But motor racing reaches into most countries of the world and yet is probably more unified than any other field of sport, with the possible exception of the Olympics structure.

Communality is one of the greatest assets of motor racing. Drivers and mechanics who cannot speak one another's language communicate exquisitely. Fans get along with equal ease. A beautiful, fast race car evokes the same sort of admiration in Elkhart Lake as it does at Monza. Certain customs, courtesies, ways of doing things are universal. All this is communality on a person-to-person basis.

Another form of communality covers the organization of racing, the ground rules, specifications, areas of competition, types of equipment.

Enter the Federation Internationale de l'Automobile.

This organization, best known as the F.I.A., is based in Paris. Established in 1904 and initially named the International Association of Recognized Automobile Clubs, it has been called the United Nations of racing and that is not always a compliment—it can be exasperatingly stuffy at times. The F.I.A. is a voluntary association of the national automobile clubs of approximately 70 countries (the number occasionally changes) such as the Royal Automobile Club (Great Britain), the Automobilclub von Deutschland (Germany), Magyar Autoklub (Hungary) and so forth. The purpose of the F.I.A. is to promote an international exchange of ideas, customs, cars, technical information and motor sports.

The F.I.A. is recognized as *the* international authority. Drivers and manufacturers can win *world* championships only by competing in certain international events established by the federation. This is the significance of the phrase "F.I.A. listing." Such listings also enhance the interchange of drivers among the race clubs of this country.

One department of the F.I.A. is responsible for all motor sports, including races, rallies, economy runs and record attempts. This committee is named the Commission Sportive Internationale, known throughout the trade as C.S.I. It draws up and enforces rules (they are written in French, and all disputes are adjudicated on the basis of that language). It also arranges an International Sporting Calendar, establishes the championships and recognizes the eligibility of cars for various categories of competition.

The C.S.I. consists of representatives from 18 countries. Six of them, because they are the great manufacturing nations, are permanent members: Britain, France, West Germany, Italy, Japan and the United States. The 12 others are elected annually from the ranks of the remaining F.I.A. members.

Which brings us now to the United States.

Many countries have a single national auto club that controls motor sports, and that club represents its country in the C.S.I. Not so in the United States. The United States has four major and dozens of minor organizations that sanction auto competition. Therefore we rely on an agency named the Automobile Competition Committee for the United States-F.I.A., Inc. The committee is the permanent representative at the C.S.I. of all American motor-sports interests. Conversely

THE MAJOR RACING ORGANIZATIONS

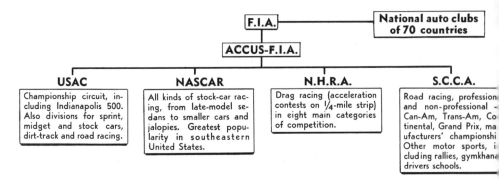

F.I.A.			National auto clubs of 70 countries

ACCUS-F.I.A.

USAC	NASCAR	N.H.R.A.	S.C.C.A.
Championship circuit, including Indianapolis 500. Also divisions for sprint, midget and stock cars, dirt-track and road racing.	All kinds of stock-car racing, from late-model sedans to smaller cars and jalopies. Greatest popularity in southeastern United States.	Drag racing (acceleration contests on ¼-mile strip) in eight main categories of competition.	Road racing, profession and non-professional – Can-Am, Trans-Am, Co tinental, Grand Prix, ma ufacturers' championshi Other motor sports, i cluding rallies, gymkhan drivers schools.

Abbreviations:
F.I.A.—Federation Internationale de l'Automobile
ACCUS-F.I.A.—Automobile Competition Committee for the United States-F.I.A., Inc.
USAC—United States Auto Club
NASCAR—National Association for Stock Car Auto Racing
N.H.R.A.—National Hot Rod Association
S.C.C.A.—Sports Car Club of America

OTHER RACING CLUBS

Names and addresses of other organizati that authorize competition for sprint cars, mid cars, late—model stock cars, formula cars, sr sedans, drag racers and off-road racing cars listed in Appendix D at the back of the book.

it represents the C.S.I. and the F.I.A. in the United States. Because of its unwieldy name, the committee is known as ACCUS, an acronym pronounced ACK-us (or, by some critics, "J'Accus!"). Its headquarters are at 433 Main Street, Stamford, Conn. 06901.

ACCUS is composed of 15 individual members and four club members. Five of the individuals are survivors of the group who founded ACCUS in 1957. Eight are delegates proposed by the four clubs; the two remaining individuals are rather like members-at-large.

The four club members are:

THE UNITED STATES AUTO CLUB, known by its acronym USAC pronounced YOU-sack). Its headquarters are on the outskirts of Indianapolis, at 4910 West 16th Street, Speedway, Ind. 46224. USAC's showpiece is the Indianapolis 500, but it runs many other races for the "Indy-type" car and for stock cars, "pony cars" (Mustang, Camaro) and smaller cars called sprints and midgets. Most of its races are run on oval tracks, some on road courses.

THE NATIONAL ASSOCIATION FOR STOCK CAR AUTO RACING (known by its acronym NASCAR), P.O. Box K, Daytona Beach, Fla. 32015. It races cars that *look* like conventional passenger cars; "stock-appearing" is the accepted characterization. Nearly all of its races are run on oval tracks.

THE NATIONAL HOT ROD ASSOCIATION, 10639 Riverside Drive, North Hollywood, Calif. 91602. Its field is drag racing, an acceleration contest in which cars race one-fourth of a mile from a standing start.

THE SPORTS CAR CLUB OF AMERICA, P.O. Box 791, Westport, Conn. 06880. Its domain is road racing, both professional and amateur, with a variety of cars. It also sanctions hill climbs, highway rallies run under normal, legal rules of the road, and many other types of motor-sports events.

Each of these four clubs conducts an extensive domestic program, sanctioning events under its own rules and supervision. Each designates champion drivers and, in some cases, champion manufacturers.

A sanction is sold by the sanctioning body. The fee ranges from a few hundred dollars to thousands, depending on the value and importance of the event. The sanction authorizes a promoter to organize a race for a given type or types of car recognized by the sanctioning club. It also means the club is extending its name, stature and reputation to the event—no small thing.

Drivers are licensed by the sanctioning clubs. Those licensed by NASCAR or USAC are committed to the season schedule prepared by their racing organization. In effect, therefore, the sanctioning body delivers the talent the promoter wants for his show.

Normally, drivers licensed by one organization do not compete in another league. USAC and NASCAR are quite sensitive about jeopardizing their own races by allowing their drivers to participate in similar races organized by rivals. A

NASCAR or USAC driver can lose his license for competing "outside" without permission.

The Sports Car Club of America, on the other hand, permits its licensed drivers to race anywhere they please. As a matter of philosophy the S.C.C.A. believes in the free interchange of drivers.

Outside the S.C.C.A., however, the circumstances of driver interchange are quite limited. One club can ask another club for permission to invite a driver to run in one of its events, but as often as not the request is turned down. The reasoning is, Why should we cut our own throats? NASCAR doesn't like the idea of one of its drivers' running in a Trans-Am race when NASCAR promoters are putting on races for the same type of car. USAC is appalled at the thought of one of its drivers' racing in the Continental Championship of the S.C.C.A. when USAC promoters already have open-wheel races of their own. NASCAR will not permit one of its drivers to run in a USAC stock-car race because that obviously would be helping the opposition.

Theoretically the F.I.A., as the over-all governing authority, could make driver exchange much easier, but it hasn't worked out that way. Only a few races, those with listings on the International Sporting Calendar, are completely open to drivers from "outside" organizations.

An international listing is valuable because it enables an event like the Indianapolis 500, sanctioned by the United States Auto Club, to invite and exploit a Mark Donohue, who is licensed by the Sports Car Club of America, or a Lee Roy Yarbrough, who normally races under the aegis of the National Association for Stock Car Auto Racing, or from abroad such internationally seeded drivers as Jackie Stewart or Denis Hulme. An international listing makes it possible for the Daytona 500, a NASCAR race, or the Canadian-American Challenge Cup, an S.C.C.A. competition, to invite a Mario Andretti from the USAC sphere. Names like Andretti, Stewart, Yarbrough, Donohue and Hulme are major drawing cards, and they enhance your show if you can get them to race in it.

Restrictions on driver interchange constitute one of the weaknesses of the sport. As it happens, there is a shortage of good drivers and restrictions only aggravate the problem. They limit a driver's earning capacity. They deprive the public of the thrill of versatility, of the opportunity to compare drivers of one league with those of another league. Common licensing—say, from the F.I.A.—would alleviate the exchange problem.

As a general rule few races—and certainly few of the less important ones—have any contact with ACCUS or F.I.A. It is when sanctioning groups want to organize an F.I.A.-listed event that they request ACCUS to arrange the listing on the International Sporting Calendar. Request is a euphemism. Because race dates are among the most valuable properties in motor racing, there is fierce infighting at ACCUS meetings for lucrative international listings. There have been occasions when members have vetoed the listings of one another's races, even the Indianapolis 500, until a compromise could be reached. The veto power was abolished in January, 1970.

ACCUS meetings are held in various parts of the country, but most frequently in New York.

After the United States schedule is established, ACCUS must still negotiate with other countries in order to get it to mesh with the over-all International Sporting Calendar. Aside from reducing conflicts, the practical consideration here is the provision of adequate time for transportation of cars and drivers.

Each year ACCUS arranges for the listing of about 60 United States events on the International Sporting Calendar. When a race is posted on that calendar, international rules take precedence and the event is run under the over-all authority of the F.I.A. and ACCUS. A typical example is the rule requiring that a designated number of cars be produced in a 12-month period for that model to be eligible for certain types of competition. ACCUS inspects documents, dealers' records, serial numbers and other evidence submitted by manufacturers to confirm the number of units produced.

Because of the experience and resources the clubs have in their own specialties, ACCUS assigns them the responsibility of running F.I.A.-listed events, including enforcement of mechanical and safety rules. So ACCUS itself does not organize or sanction competition. It acts primarily as the liaison between an American member club and the international federation.

*   *   *

There is a great division of opinion in the American racing community as to whether the sport should be as diverse as it is. One group wants to bring some order out of what it considers a maddening fragmentation that embarrasses—and perhaps imperils—motor racing. Its members propose formulas that would sort things out in a neat line-up of championships and eliminate all the overlap. This camp includes automobile manufacturers, part of the motor-sports press and presumably a few ambitious individuals who see something in it for themselves if auto racing is centralized.

But there doesn't seem to be much evidence that the public is perturbed by all the diversity. The fan has enough things to annoy him—traffic, difficult road access, poor parking, bad food, dirty latrines, and so on. These are the areas he wants to see improved, and they are more likely to be improved by competitors than by partners in a monopoly.

The fan's interest, moreover, is largely compartmentalized and therefore parochial. Many devotees of oval racing have never seen a road race; if they attended one they would consider it innocuous. The sports-car crowd seldom ventures to the other side of town to see a USAC or NASCAR race. And when they do, they're confused: I know one member of the Board of Governors of the Sports Car Club of America who believes there is an "over-all" winner in the Indianapolis 500.* Joe likes sprint racing, and that's all he is interested in seeing. Harry likes both sprint cars and stock cars, and it disturbs him not at all that two organizations, one in Indiana and the other in Florida, are behind those forms of racing.

There is no reason why it should bother him. Actually, the major leagues have their coordinating entity in ACCUS. As long as ACCUS does its job, there is no convincing case for setting up a "czar" as in baseball and pro football. The danger is that he would homogenize a sport whose strength is its diversity and, in so doing, would stultify it. It is the freedom of competition, the freedom to think forward, that insures the future of motor racing.

*The basis of his naiveté is explained in Chapter 7, Pages 142–44, where races within races are discussed.

CHAPTER 2

"Gentlemen, Start Your Engines"

Indianapolis 500: A. J. Foyt leads a pack out of the first turn into the short straight leading to Turn 2.

*I*T WAS Bill Vukovich, the winner of the Indianapolis 500 in 1953 and 1954, who propounded the successful formula. "Just remember one thing," he advised. "Always turn left." Indianapolis, the capital of Indiana, is often ridiculed as "India-Noplace," a cornfield with traffic lights. "We are approaching Indianapolis," the pilot says over the cabin speaker. "Turn back your watches 15 years." Indianapolis is considered a town where very little ever happens—not even the marvelous annual race known as the Indianapolis 500. Indianapolis Motor Speedway, the track where that race is run on the Memorial Day weekend, is on the outskirts of Indianapolis in the small city of Speedway, Indiana, zip code 46224.

28

There is a good deal of yokelry in the prolonged preliminaries, such as the rendition of "Back Home Again in Indiana" by some stage-struck tenor and the prancing of plump high-school girls in drum majorette outfits. But all this is forgiven the instant Anton (Tony) Hulman Jr., president of Indianapolis Motor Speedway, calls out over the public-address system the traditional "Gentlemen, start your engines." What a noise! Thirty-three brutes coming to life with a roar that shatters the air. Beautiful!

The 500 is one of the world's great sports events. Its blood-tingling start is one of the most exciting of all spectacles—33 cars, closely bunched, scrambling toward the first turn at nearly three miles a minute. The sound of more than 20,000 horse-power—there is nothing like it anywhere on earth. The spectator who doesn't react with a tightening in the pit of the stomach must be in a catatonic trance.

And spectators there are. For business reasons the Speedway never announces attendance figures, but the consensus is that with good weather there are at least a quarter-million people paying up to $39 apiece to jam themselves in around that 2½-mile track. There are close to 220,000 permanent seats in the Speedway and 15,000 more can be installed overnight. There are upwards of 30,000 spectators in the infield. An attendance of 250,000 is more than two and one-half times the size of the Kentucky Derby crowd, enough to make Indianapolis Motor Speedway the most densely populated 537-acre spot in the world.

The fans come from all over Indiana and the neighboring states (it has been uncharitably suggested that they have little else to do). They drive for long hours to reach the Speedway and drive home right after the race. Those who come from greater distances or who want to spend more time at the Speedway camp in the neighborhood in campers, trailers, station wagons and an array of other vehicles. At 6 A.M. of race day, when a cannon booms its signal, they rush harum-scarum through the gates for favorite parking spots, with track attendants scurrying out of the way to save their lives.

Of the thousands who settle in the infield, few can see the racing. Few are interested in progress reports over the public-address loudspeakers (assuming they can hear the announcements over the din of the race cars). Many know nothing about the cars, the drivers, the tactics or the rules. No matter. It is not so much a race they have come to see: This is a pilgrimage like Le Mans—yes, like Le Mans—and it is enough to be there. The infield is a vast cook-out. Mario Andretti, who won in 1969, does not eat before a race and he says toward the end, when he is really hungry, he can smell the grilled meat. It is a gigantic barbecue afloat on an ocean of beer. The beer is carried into the grounds in insulated coolers so big and heavy that two men are needed to tote them. As long as the beer and food hold out, this annual rite of spring is a success.

Motels and hotels more than double their rates at race time and require a minimum stay of three to five days. They are filled, all right, but one has the impression these guests are not fans who have come to see a race out of enthusiasm. Rather, most of them appear to be in town on business, with some professional or commercial identification with the race. Unlike the paying customers in the infield, this is definitely an expense-account crowd.

Besides the 250,000 or more who attend the race, there are thousands of others who pay to see it on closed-circuit television at theaters throughout the country.

None of The Faithful ever refer to "the Indy 500" or even "the Indianapolis 500." All you need say is "the 500," and anyone with any sense will know what you mean.

The 500 is the showpiece of a series of 12 races that count toward the driving championship of the United States Auto Club, which operates out of a small two-story headquarters in Speedway, Ind., just a couple of blocks away from Indianapolis Motor Speedway. USAC's top-of-the-line merchandise has always been called championship racing, but the formal name now is the Marlboro Championship Trail. Philip Morris, Inc., in behalf of its Marlboro brand, sponsors the competition with prizes to drivers in each race and at the end of the season and with assistance to track operators—$300,000 in all. This arrangement is one more illustration of the fact that the sport is increasingly attracting nonautomotive sponsors.

The championship schedule measures drivers' performance by means of a point system that determines the year's champion. Championship racing has a long and continuous history—it began in 1909—and is heavily endowed with prestige and glory. Its main purpose all these years has been to provide the public with good racing competition. A. J. Foyt won the driving championship in 1967 for the fifth time. Bobby Unser won in 1968 and Mario Andretti won in 1969 for the third time. The 1970 winner was Bobby Unser's younger brother Al.

In years past the number of races in the championship series varied from 20 to 25. Beginning with the 1971 season, USAC reduced the number to 12 with the objective of improving the quality of the races; increasing the purses; cutting the teams' costs, and reducing the time pressure on teams that results when too many races are scheduled too close together. All these events, ranging from 150 to 500 miles, are run on paved oval tracks, where the traffic runs counter-clockwise—all turns are to the left.*

The purse and prizes at the Indianapolis 500 are stupendous, and they keep rising every year. In 1970 the total payout was $1,000,002.22, including $205,595 in special awards put up by manufacturers of automotive equipment, accessories and supplies and even nonautomotive products.

At the smaller tracks away from Indianapolis the purses in USAC championship races are more modest. The custom is for the race promoter to pay the drivers a stipulated minimum guarantee, or 40 per cent of the gate if that turns out to be larger than the guarantee. In practice this works out to any-

*On oval tracks, with the races running in counter-clockwise direction, the turns are numbered thus:

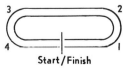

Start/Finish

where from $25,000 for the smaller races to $100,000 for a few big ones plus a share of the television money, if any.

Throughout its history Indianapolis Motor Speedway has been the most important track on the championship circuit, even though it conducts only one race each year. Another 2½-mile plant, Ontario Motor Speedway in Southern California, was opened in the autumn of 1970 with an "Indy-type" 500-mile race. In time Ontario, which is 40 miles east of Los Angeles, may match or even surpass the economic stature of Indianapolis Motor Speedway, which opened in 1909. But whether Ontario will ever command the sentimental affections of a loyal following is something else—there are few who believe the Middle Western corn can be transplanted to such alien ground as Southern California's. The same reservation may be applied to Pocono International Raceway in Pennsylvania, a new track opening in 1971 with still another 500-mile race.

Besides Indianapolis, Ontario and Pocono, the major paved oval tracks for championship races are at Milwaukee; Cambridge Junction, Mich.; Trenton, N.J.; Phoenix, Ariz., and Bryan, Tex.

* * *

Indianapolis 500: Jim McElreath makes a pit stop for fuel and change of right-side tires.

Of all the USAC races it is, of course, the Indianapolis 500 that stands out as the biggest and most colorful. Indeed, USAC probably could not stay in business without the 500. USAC people do not often speak of racing at "Indianapolis"—they speak of racing at "the Speedway." They mention "the Speedway" with the same reverence that Moslems presumably accord Mecca.

The Indianapolis 500 is a race that demands uncommon courage, knowledge and skill. It is one thing, for instance, to drive fast on a solo run in the qualifying trials. But it takes a really exquisite sense of touch to drive in the snarling traffic of a hotly contested race, when cars are running wheel to wheel at 250 feet a second, when perilous contact is a hundredth of a second away.

Drivers say racing down the front straight, from which the grandstand curves around the No. 1 turn, is like going into a tunnel—which makes it difficult to judge the turn. They say the wind is a constant concern, especially when they emerge from the protection of a grandstand into an open area. And most drivers agree that each of the four turns at Indianapolis is sufficiently different from the others to require a different technique—a bump, a slight variation in the banking, and so on.

Temperatures on the track surface rise as high as 145 degrees, and stinking fumes* hang in the air. The drivers endure these conditions lap after lap—200 circuits of the track, 800 left turns—for a bit more than three hours. In their low-slung racers the drivers are in a half-recumbent position. Roaring along the straightaway at more than 200 miles an hour, a driver cannot get a clear view of the track if there is traffic in front of him.

Indianapolis Motor Speedway is more a rectangle than an oval. The two big straights are ⅝ths of a mile long and the two short straights are ⅛th of a mile long. There are four 90-degree turns (left turns, of course), each ¼th of a mile long and slightly banked at an angle of nine degrees.

---

*To some, fragrant perfume!

Although the Speedway is rectangular, the course or "groove" that the drivers follow is oval. As in road racing, there is an optimum "line" a driver can take to extract maximum speed from his car. This means he runs flat-out on the front and back straights, about 12 feet or so from the outer concrete retaining wall. As he approaches a turn at anywhere up to 200 miles an hour, he "backs off" the throttle, perhaps tips the brakes with a light touch, and then dives low into the turn. Coming out of it, he allows the car to drift outward, or arc, extremely close to the retaining wall. Usually he resumes acceleration about halfway through the turn. This sequence is repeated at each of the four turns.

*   *   *

In the 1950's and early 1960's Indianapolis was dominated by the Offenhauser-powered "roadster," a sleek, low-slung departure from the versatile predecessor that had run on dirt as well as paved ovals. The roadsters were lower in profile than the dirt-track cars because the engine and drive train were

The old Indy "roadster."

installed on the left side of the car to establish a favorable weight bias for left-hand turns. This arrangement enabled the driver to sit lower. It also enabled him to sit alongside the drive shaft rather than over it. In this new configuration the drive shaft was at about the level of the driver's hip.

The roadster design was originated in 1952 by Frank Kurtis and subsequently was carried farther by other car builders, notably A. J. Watson. The roadsters pushed the dirt-track cars right out of Indianapolis and became enshrined in public affection. From 1953 through 1963 "Offy" roadsters, as they came to be known, constituted all, or all but one or two, of the 33-car field. The others were the popular and powerful Novis, probably the noisiest race cars that ever ran.

By 1955 most owners were fielding two types of championship equipment—a roadster for the paved ovals and the old-time dirt car for the dirt tracks. Then an irony: the roadster in turn became obsolete while the dirt-track car, which had been forced out of Indianapolis but retained for nonpaved ovals, still survives today.

What killed the roadster was the advent of European rear-engine cars based on the design of Formula One racers running in international Grand Prix competition. The USAC hierarchy in its conservatism reacted predictably: Jack Brabham of Australia and Jim Clark of Scotland were foreigners by definition (indeed, some Indy veterans were so provincial that they had never even *heard* of Brabham and Clark) and their cars were "funny-looking" by common appraisal. Those cars seemed so small and so frail to be challenging the brute strength of the roadsters.

Jack Brabham usually gets the credit for the rear-engine revolution at Indianapolis, since he started it. But Dan Gurney did more for the rear engine because it was he who recognized its potential and who carried the ball.

The story begins in 1961 when Brabham brought in the first threat, a Cooper with a rear-mounted Climax engine. That Cooper-Climax was the only rear-engine car in the 33-car field. With an engine of only 168 cubic inches piston displacement, Brabham had only two-thirds the power of the roadsters, then equipped with Offenhauser engines of 255 cubic inches. Brabham consistently beat the American drivers in the corners but he lost ground on the straights, where power made the difference. Yet the field was reduced by attrition and Brabham hung in there. He finished ninth, which at Indianapolis is rather good.*

This is the end of Brabham's role. After the 1961 race he simply disappears from the picture.

In 1962 Dan Gurney, a Californian who at the time was considered part of the international Grand Prix set, drove a U.S.-built Mickey Thompson Special powered by a rear-mounted Buick engine. Again, as with Brabham in 1961, this was the only rear-engine car in the field. Gurney retired after 92 laps, slightly less than halfway through the race, because of a broken rear-end gear. He placed 20th.

But Gurney had seen enough to convince him that a properly designed rear-engine car could win at Indianapolis. He invited Colin Chapman, the British designer of the Lotus Grand Prix car, to Indianapolis to look at the Speedway set-up.

Chapman said he could build the right kind of car if he could get the right kind of engine. Whereupon Gurney hustled Chapman to Detroit for talks with the top brass at Ford Motor Company. They came to terms: Ford modified the standard 289-cubic-inch production engine into a 255-cubic-inch racing engine. Chapman designed his rear-engine car around it for the 1963 race.

Chapman entered two Lotus-Fords, one for Jim Clark and the other for Gurney. At the same time Mickey Thompson came back with two more rear-engine cars, these powered by Chevrolet engines.

The rear-engine Lotus-Fords, lower and considerably smaller and lighter than the roadsters, were more easily handled and maneuverable because they had independent suspension at all four wheels in contrast to the old-fashioned solid axles of the American racers. They were so agile that they made the roadsters look like ungainly dinosaurs.

Because the engine was positioned just ahead of the rear wheels, there was no need for the conventional (and heavy) drive shaft that extended from an engine up front to the drive

---

*Brabham's car is now on display in the museum of Indianapolis Motor Speedway.

wheels in the back. This made it possible to build a lower car with cleaner aerodynamic lines; it also weighed considerably less.

A few car owners perceived the obvious. One of them is reported to have pointed to his cars in Gasoline Alley and told his cronies, "Gentlemen, you are looking at a million dollars worth of obsolete machinery." Yet the majority of the Indianapolis Establishment, a conservative inner sanctum group of owners, drivers and officials known as the "Indy Crowd," resisted the new design and continued to deride the "funny cars."

Indy revolution, 1963: Jim Clark, driving a rear-engine Lotus-Ford (No. 92), challenges Parnelli Jones' traditional roadster.

They were "funny" until the end of that 1963 race, when Jim Clark ran second in one of the Lotus-Fords, Dan Gurney placed seventh in the other Lotus-Ford, and one of the rear-engine Thompson-Chevrolets placed ninth. Indeed, Clark very nearly won.*

---

*The 1963 race was one of the most controversial ever run at Indianapolis. To this day some fans argue that the winner, Parnelli Jones, should have been black-flagged off the track because his car was throwing oil that endangered other drivers. Clark also was handicapped by his inexperience with the vagaries of Indianapolis officiating and the frighteningly close wheel-to-wheel competition. Experienced Speedway drivers said later that if they had had Clark's car they would have easily walked away from Parnelli Jones.

By the 1964 race 12 cars in the 33-car field had their engines behind the driver—six Fords, six Offys. Clark again came close to winning; this time, while leading the race, he was done in by a thrown tire tread that caused the suspension to fail. In 1965, when Clark finally did triumph in his Lotus-Ford to become the first foreign winner in 49 years, 27 of the 33 cars carried rear engines.

Since then, virtually all the entries—at the beginning of May there are anywhere from 70 to 90 entries from which the field of 33 cars is qualified—have been rear-engined. An occasional eccentric or an unreconstructed diehard shows up with a roadster, and the sentimentalists in the stands cheer him. The last time a front-engine car even qualified was in 1968, and that was for the 30th position in a 33-car field. At the lesser races away from Indianapolis there are a few roadsters milling around but they don't get anywhere.

The comparatively quick transition from roadsters to rear-engine cars might never have happened had it not been for the war of subsidies between the Goodyear and Firestone tire companies. Engine and chassis development is always expensive, but the tire companies, anxious for the promotional and merchandising advantage of having their tires on the winning car, were willing the pay the bills. It is common knowledge that throughout the late 1960's the tire companies owned nearly all the better cars on the track or had heavy investments in them, with the nominal "owners" taking orders from the tire people. The Goodyear-Firestone competition to finance winning cars and teams was lively while it lasted. It has since subsided into more restrained and less extensive methods of support. Nevertheless, Larry Truesdale of Goodyear and Bill McCrary of Firestone, the executives responsible for running the tire companies' racing programs, are two of the most powerful men in auto racing, here and abroad.

As for the Establishment, it just couldn't get over the novelty of the rear engine. Long after the entire field at Indianapolis had committed itself, the impact of the cultural shock lingered. Throughout the late 1960's the track program at

38

Indianapolis Motor Speedway carried the abbreviation "RE," meaning rear engine—this long after the roadsters had disappeared and long after any such distinction was needed. And even after the Speedway program dropped "RE" the abbreviation has persisted in the literature and tabulations of the fringe public relations people at the Speedway. USAC's Yearbook of 1969 carried "RE." As late as 1970 a souvenir program at Trenton, N.J., was characterizing each car in the field as "RE." It was as though passenger cars were still being advertised with self-starters.

Two other departures—turbine power and four-wheel drive—shook the Indy Establishment, though with less lasting effect, in 1967–68. In each case the man who let the cat loose among the pigeons was a stout, rambunctious competitor named Andy Granatelli, president of the STP Corporation. He had grown up in poverty, learning the mechanic's trade by cadging work on the streets of Chicago. He had a passion for innovation and an obsession, based on 18 years of trying, to win the 500.

For the 1967 race Granatelli brought to Indy a magnificent machine he had built in his Paxton shops at Santa Monica, Calif. He called this bright red beast the STP Turbocar. It was a radically designed car with four-wheel drive and a 260-pound turbine engine from Pratt and Whitney, originally intended for use in boats, small planes and helicopters. The engine had few parts to wear out during a race. The turbocar was not rear-engined or front-engined: It was of *side-by-side* construction, with the driver sitting on the right and the engine mounted next to him on the left. Esthetically, the car wasn't much: it bulged and looked clumsy. But because of its strong construction it was considered one of the safest race cars ever built.

Unlike conventional race cars, the turbocar was scarcely audible as it shot by—just a wh-o-o-o-o-sh sound. Rival owners and drivers derisively called it "the airplane" and "the vacuum cleaner." Even the fans ridiculed it. They all stopped laughing when they saw Parnelli Jones, winner of the 1963 race, drive it in practice. It had blazing speed. More important, with the superior traction of four-wheel drive, Jones could take the car wherever he wanted. He did not have to stay in the "groove" that represented maximum efficiency (the fastest way around) for the conventional piston-engine cars. In the turbocar going high or low in the banked turns didn't matter.

By race time everyone suspected Jones was sandbagging, holding back, especially when he qualified for only the sixth place in the starting line-up. That position was no handicap to him. At the start of the race he broke away from his place in the second row and zapped up to the leaders. By the end of the *second turn* he was leading the pack and moving away without breathing hard. (Later Mario Andretti asked Jones, "What took you so long?") At the end of the first lap he was running all by himself. It was a rout. On the 18th lap the race had to be stopped because of rain but the next day, when the race was restarted, Jones simply took off on a leisurely cruise of the Speedway, far beyond the reach of the 32 other cars.

At the end of 490 miles, with 10 to go, Jones was stroking it—that is, taking it easy because he didn't need to push. And then disaster: a $6 transmission bearing broke down, the car rolled to a humiliating stop, and for Jones the race was over.

Now Granatelli was not the first to have brought turbine power and four-wheel drive to the Speedway. He was the first to have made them *competitive,* and that was what perturbed USAC. The club recognized the turbine as an overwhelming threat that overnight could make every other engine in championship racing obsolete. In the fall of 1967 USAC moved abruptly to shackle the turbine. The rules committee voted to reduce its air-intake area from 23.999 square inches to 15.999. In the spring of 1968 Granatelli carried his case to court but lost the suit (he was represented by Richard M. Nixon's law firm).

For the 1968 race Granatelli bounced back with another turbine design with four-wheel drive. The chassis was a Lotus built by Colin Chapman. This car had an air-intake area of the required 15.999 square inches and Granatelli entered three of them. Near the end of the race one, driven by Joe Leonard,

Left: The STP Turbo-car, with a body panel removed to show position of the turbine engine in relation to the cockpit. Below: Parnelli Jones testing the car.

was holding a narrow lead. And again, with victory within grasp, a minor part broke down. This time it was the tiny gear at the end of a $3\frac{1}{2}$-inch fuel-pump shaft, about the size of a ballpoint pen. The car stopped ignominiously on the 191st lap, with only nine laps, or $22\frac{1}{2}$ miles, left to go.*

Despite the mishaps in successive 500's to Granatelli's cars, it was evident that the turbine was overwhelmingly strong. USAC's leaders were taking no chances on having their conventional machines made obsolete. So again in 1968 as in 1967 the club moved to handicap—or "equalize"—the turbine car. This time USAC reduced the air-intake area from 15.999 square inches to 11.999 even though the 15.999 power plant had not won a single race. Granatelli said there was no way of building a turbine engine within such a limitation and he dropped the project—which, of course, was what USAC had wanted.†

USAC moves briskly when it recognizes a threat to its members' investments. Four-wheel drive, augmenting turbine power, also had to be dealt with. Only Granatelli's turbines and one other car in the 1968 entry list were equipped with four-wheel-drive (4-w-d), a system that provides greater speed and safety through more traction. To begin with, USAC all but negated the efficiency of 4-w-d cars by limiting the width of all four wheel rims to 10 inches. On such a rim it was not practicable to mount a tire with a tread of more than 11 inches. In contrast, the conventional racers with two-wheel rear drive were permitted rims of 14 inches on their drive wheels—and consequently, a tire with a tread of between 15 and 16 inches. The effect of all this was to provide the 4-w-d cars with a tire "footprint" four to five inches narrower than that of the con-

* Of Granatelli's two other Lotus Turbocars, one, driven by Graham Hill, crashed; the second, driven by Art Pollard, dropped out for the same reason as Leonard's car—failure of the fuel-pump shaft.

† In January, 1971, USAC's board of directors rejected another innovation, a race car based on what is called the ground-effect principle, similar to Jim Hall's Chaparral 2J (described in Chapter 6, pages 128–29). This time, however, the directors took care to avoid the bad publicity they had suffered in the turbine hassle of 1967–68. In this case the ruling was against a proposal on paper rather than against a car already racing.

ventional racer. The rationale in depriving the 4-w-d of wide tires was that they were being "equalized" with the established two-wheel-drive cars.

Then, to make doubly certain, USAC voted to outlaw four-wheel drive altogether beginning with the 1970 season. It explained the prohibition on economic grounds—that everyone in racing would be forced, in self-defense, to adopt four-wheel drive, and at considerable expense. USAC also rejected the premise that four-wheel drive was "automotive"—it was only for trucks and Jeeps.

*   *   *

The successor to the beloved roadster in the USAC's championship series is known as a championship car or an "Indy" car, the latter being derived from its association with the Indianapolis 500. It is an "open wheel" car, which means there are no fenders covering the wheels. It has a single seat in an open cockpit.

The Indy car is a racing machine slung so low that the driver's line of vision is below the top of the exposed wheels— that is, about 15 or 16 inches above the ground. The rear-mounted engine makes it possible to design the car in the shape of a wedge to present a low profile and therefore minimum drag. To further reduce the frontal silhouette, the driver reclines— not sits—in the cockpit.

Not all cars in a given field look precisely alike—designers have their own individual ideas about streamlining and shape and about where to position components like the water and oil radiators. But the cars must all conform to rigid specifications as to engine size, brakes, dimensions, fuel capacity and safety. The Indy machine has a minimum wheelbase of 8 feet and a maximum over-all length of 16 feet; a minimum tread (width of car measured from centerline of tires) of 3 feet 11 inches and a maximum over-all width of 6 feet 8 inches. It must weigh at least 1,350 pounds dry (without fuel) and without driver.

Today's engines range beyond 700 horsepower. To equalize power in the interest of fair competition, USAC has worked out formulas to control piston displacement according to type of engine. In the following table the measurements to three decimal places are conversions, in American cubic inches, from the metric measurements, in cubic centimeters, required by international racing rules.

Supercharged engines, overhead cams . . . . 161.703 (2,650 cc.)
Supercharged stock-block engines . . . . 203.400 (3,333 cc.)
Nonsupercharged engines, overhead cams . . . . . 256.284 (4,200 cc.)
Stock-block (push-rod) engines . . . . 320.355 (5,250 cc.)

In recent years all but the first of these types have become academic. The power plants most common now are the four-cylinder turbocharged Offenhauser, called the "Offy," and the turbocharged Ford V-8, which is rather like two Offys with a common crankshaft. The Ford and Offenhauser are both specially designed exotic racing engines with overhead camshafts and a displacement of 161.703 cubic inches or, in metric terms, 2.65 liters. They cost about $30,000 apiece and use fuel injectors instead of carburetors.

All engines in current championship racing are turbocharged, a refinement of supercharging. Such engines, in racing slang, are "blown."* A turbocharger is simply a blower that forces more fuel-air mixture into the engine than the engine could normally breathe from the outside atmosphere without help. The added mixture supports the combustion of more fuel, thus providing more horsepower.

The Offy engine is basically the same in design as it was when it was first built under another trade name in 1919. It won 18 consecutive 500's before losing in 1965 to Jim Clark's Ford-powered Lotus. In 1965, 1966 and 1967 cars with normally aspirated (no supercharging) Ford engines finished 1–2–3–4. In

* A "blown" engine has another meaning in racing. In its second context "blown" means that parts of an engine have broken down under the stress of racing—in effect, the engine has been destroyed or seriously damaged.

Al Unser and the Johnny Lightning Special, a P. J. Colt-Ford, in which he won the Indianapolis 500.

1968 a turbocharged Offy won, in 1969 a turbocharged Ford finished first, and in 1970 the winning engine was again a turbocharged Ford. In the 1970 race no normally aspirated engine was able to qualify; every one of the 33 cars in the field had a turbocharged engine—18 Offys and 15 Fords.

The driver of an Indy car chauffeurs what can be termed a rolling fuel tank—he is surrounded by up to 75 gallons of fuel stored in rupture-resistant cells made of strong rubber and called bladders. In general, the fuel is a blend of varying amounts of methanol and nitromethane, but the proportions are a competitive secret. Each chief mechanic has his own recipe.

The suspension system of a race car holds the key to success. It is the means through which the power of the engine is transmitted to the road. In our everyday cars we think of suspension as a system of springs, shock absorbers and torsion bars that absorb jolts and bumps before they are transmitted to the car frame and passengers. But in racing, suspension is not considered in terms of making the driver comfortable. Rather it is important because it carries the power of the engine through the wheels to the ground. Therefore it is essential that the suspension hold the car to the road constantly. A drive wheel that bounces off the ground cannot do its job of moving the car. Similarly, a front wheel that steers improperly is only handicapping the car.

Consequently, the suspension of a race car must be as carefully tuned as the engine itself. It must be adjusted—the track phrase is "set up"—to suit the conditions of the track

45

and the personal style of the driver. By means of fine adjustments based on trial-and-error observation (or the use of certain instruments) during practice sessions, a driver can clip tenths of a second from his lap times.

The stiffness of the antisway bar is easily adjusted. And coil springs; telescopic shock absorbers within the coils; caster, camber and toe-in angles of the wheels; tire pressures and tires themselves—all can be changed to attain the maximum in roadholding and handling.

Wheel rims must be at least 15 inches in diameter. Rim-width maximums are 10 inches for the front wheels and 14 inches for the rear wheels. Rear tires have treads up to 16 inches wide, and from sidewall to sidewall they are about $17\frac{1}{2}$ inches. The front tires have treads of 11 inches and an over-all width of approximately $12\frac{1}{2}$ inches.

Wide tires provide more traction than narrow tires, but there is a point beyond which the wide tire may be self-defeating. Some experts believe today's tires are *too* wide from an aerodynamic standpoint—they call them "barn doors."

The steering wheel, covered with leather to enhance the grip, is held to about a foot in diameter to allow space for the driver's hands to fit inside the cockpit. Steering is so positive and responsive that a half-inch movement of the hands at 165 miles an hour could cause the car to swerve across the track. It is through the steering wheel and the seat of the pants that the driver senses how near his car is to the limit of adhesion—that is, the point at which it will begin to slide sideways.

The driver is required to wear coveralls, socks and gloves of flame-resistant material. Usually he also wears flame-resistant underwear. In addition, he dons a cloth mask to protect his nose and mouth from fire, dust, smoke and bits of debris. This once was a simple bandanna, but most drivers now prefer flameproof fabric. The most recent types of mask resemble the ones that skiers wear.

Helmets must meet rigid standards of protection and must be of approved manufacture. The latest type has a face-

46

piece of very strong clear plastic that obviates the need for goggles. Usually drivers wear earplugs to deaden the roar of engines—their own and the others on the track. Many competitors also wear boxer-type or track shoes with thin soles as an aid to sensitivity on the brake and accelerator pedals. Others wear ordinary sneakers and some Europeans just settle for comfortable old shoes.

*   *   *

The United States Auto Club rearranged its competition schedule beginning with the 1971 season. Aside from the championship series on paved ovals, USAC now sanctions races in five other divisions: (1) road racing, (2) dirt, (3) sprint, (4) midget and (5) stock.

For some years the Championship Trail had included four or five road races for the Indy cars. Now USAC has removed road racing from the championship division and made it a separate class. The objective is to supplant sprint and midget racing as the training ground for young drivers aspiring to race at Indianapolis. In the old days, when front-engine machines were the only cars in championship racing, it made sense to bring drivers up from the sprint and midget ranks. No more. Six years after the rear-engine revolution at Indianapolis, USAC finally recognized front-engine sprints and midgets were illogical as training for the racing of agile rear-engine cars. There are radical differences in the handling characteristics of front-engine and rear-engine cars. The differences in speed are awesome: an alumnus of the sprint car circuit who is accustomed to top speeds of 120 miles an hour on short straights suddenly finds at Indianapolis that he needs to go through the *turns* at 150–160 m.p.h.

The cars used in road racing are quite similar to the Indy machines in appearance. The engine may be one of three types: (1) a stock-production pushrod unit with a maximum displacement of 320.355 cubic inches; (2) a modified stock-block engine with the so-called Gurney or Weslake cylinder heads, maximum size 305 c.i.d.; (3) the all-out Ford or Offenhauser racing engine with double overhead camshafts, limited to 255 c.i.d. and normally aspirated (no supercharging). The engines may use gasoline or methanol or a combination of both, but no nitromethane. The car's wheelbase must be at least 92 inches and the tread may not be more than 80 inches. The body height is limited to 32 inches.

Bobby Unser on the road course of Continental Divide Raceway, Castle Rock, Colo.

Road courses are of varying length, and they are all paved. The principal courses for USAC road racing are Riverside in California; Castle Rock in Colorado; Brainerd in Minnesota, and Indianapolis Raceway Park (which is at Clermont, Ind., and should not be confused with Indianapolis Motor Speedway, which is at Speedway, Ind.).

So it is in road racing now that young drivers build up experience in the rear-engine cars and then shop around in the championship circuit for a "ride"—that is, a job or assignment driving a championship car. As they scramble and struggle

48

through their apprenticeships, these young men work their way toward a single objective—to make it to "the Speedway." Heaven is on the outskirts of Indianapolis.

Dirt-track racing has also been removed from the championship division and made a separate entity. Dirt ovals provide racing as basic as you can get. The sad fact, though, is that the tracks are disappearing for various reasons, including expense of maintenance. USAC hopes to develop a full-scale dirt-track championship program, but this depends on making improvements in the safety of the tracks. For USAC racing the track must be at least one mile long. The most important tracks now active are on the fairgrounds at Springfield and DuQuoin, Ill., Sedalia, Mo., and Indianapolis.

Cars that run in USAC dirt-track races are subject to the same design measurements as the Indy car. The difference is

Mario Andretti churns through a turn in his dirt-track car.

in appearance and suspension. The dirt-track car has its engine up front. The chassis is heavier than the Indy car's. The driver sits high and upright over the drive shaft. These cars are designed to do a specific job: they cover ground on a dirt track faster than the Indianapolis car can.

Sprint cars and midget cars are quite popular, and they will continue to be around a long time. For one thing, they are relatively inexpensive to own and maintain, and they almost

Sprint cars on a dirt track. In foreground, Gary Bettenhausen.

never become obsolete. The favorable economics of this format assures a plentiful supply of drivers.

The sprint car is the classic American racing car. All other open-wheel American cars, over the years, have been versions of the sprints, once called "big cars." Sprint cars look very much like the front-engine cars that run on the dirt tracks but they are smaller, with a minimum wheelbase of 7 feet and a minimum tread of 3 feet 11 inches. As with championship cars, four types of engines of varying sizes are recognized, but for all practical purposes there is only one in common use, a stock-block highly modified Chevrolet engine of 305.100 cubic inches (5,000 cc).

Sprint car racing is highly dangerous, mostly because the cars are driven by aggressive, "hungry" drivers. Another reason it is dangerous is that the cars are running exceptionally fast in a confined area, which increases the chance of contact between the cars.

Some American fans bridle at the thought of a fancy-pants foreigner's being designated the world driving champion. "What's the big deal about Grand Prix?" one of them asks. "I would like to see some of those G.P. drivers handle a sprint car on a half-mile dirt track before I concede they are the greatest since sliced bread."

Everyone to his taste. The field is refreshingly broad. It has something for everyone, which is one of the great strengths of motor racing. The fan quoted above believes sprint racing is the best there is, with competition as basic as it can be. To illustrate the point about the breadth of racing, there are even *different kinds* of sprint racing. Aside from the conventional competition sanctioned by USAC, there are the so-called "super-modifieds" and there are dozens of small sanctioning organizations* with different rules, equipment and policies. And for all the excitement of sprint racing, there are those who believe racing begins and ends with the midgets, which they consider even more fundamental than the sprints. Midget racing makes a superbly exciting show, and the competition is strenuous. Midget racing can be staged indoors—armories, huge auditoriums, the Houston Astrodome and so on—which makes it a convenient winter sport. Again, as in sprint car racing, there is great variety. There are the "TQ" cars (three-quarter midgets) and even quarter midgets. Midget races are sanctioned by USAC and again, as in the case of the sprint cars, by many smaller sanctioning bodies.

* See Appendix D, back of book, for some of the more important ones.

Midgets on the Tri-County Speedway, Cincinnati. Merle Bettenhausen drives No. 69 and Mike McGreevy drives No. 4.

In USAC racing, midget cars are miniature versions of the championship dirt car, with wheelbase limits of 5 feet 6 inches to 6 feet 4 inches. Two types of engines are used, a normally aspirated (nonsupercharged) stock block of 155 cubic inches and a normally aspirated all-out racing engine with overhead cams and a displacement of 114 cubic inches. In the second group the makes include Offenhauser and the highly unusual SESCO—a Chevrolet V-8 that is longitudinally cut in half (SESCO is an acronym derived from the manufacturer's name, Speed Engineering Service Company).

USAC's Stock Car Division sanctions competition for late-model cars only—that is, steel-bodied sedans manufactured in the United States in the three most recent production years. The rules are just about the same as those of the National Association for Stock Car Auto Racing (Chapter 3) with one major exception. The smaller "pony cars," which USAC classifies as Sports Sedans (SS), are allowed to compete with full-size cars. Examples of the smaller machines are Camaro, Mustang, Javelin, Barracuda, Challenger, Firebird. Engine displacement for the SS class may not exceed 5 liters (305 cubic inches) but the rules permit twin carburetors. The minimum car weight is 3,200 pounds. The full-size cars weigh 3,900 pounds and have engines of up to 430 cubic inches displacement. Only one carburetor is permitted.

USAC races pay out close to $4 million a year in purses, posted accessory awards, lap and television money and appearance payments guaranteed the champion of each division. Besides the regular prizes, there is usually more than $100,000 in point-fund money. This is a pool distributed among the leading drivers and car owners of all divisions at the end of the season. The disbursement is based on the number of points the participants have won during the season. The point fund, or kitty, is built up of assessments on each individual race during the season.

*　　*　　*

A USAC stock-car race at Phoenix, Ariz., mixes full-size machines with 305-c.i.d. sports sedans.

The trouble with United States Auto Club racing is the United States Auto Club, a resourceful opponent of the 20th century. The club was hurriedly formed as a nonprofit, member-run organization in 1955 when the American Automobile Association suddenly abandoned the sport of auto racing; until that time a department of the A.A.A. had governed the sport, sanctioning, among other events, the Indianapolis 500 from 1911 onward. From the Triple-A the United States Auto Club inherited much of its personnel and policy—and went backward from there.

USAC's leadership is dominated by conservative car owners. Its officials and stewards are surprisingly old, a geriatric collection of retired mechanics and drivers. The club is the citadel of hard-core complacency, hostile to innovation, provincial inheritor of the Know Nothing tradition, descendant of the yahoos who yelled "Get a horse!" For the True Believers there is no racing other than USAC racing. Few of them ever see races outside the USAC orbit.

USAC's race officiating has sometimes been appalling. Chief stewards have continued to run a race while a fire was burning in the path of the cars; they have continued a race in the rain over the protests of drivers whose lives were endangered; they have reversed decisions and fined drivers and mechanics while refusing to acknowledge mistakes. Sometimes officials are hung up over trivia: they can be more concerned with hounding a mustached driver about "image" than in black-flagging a car that is throwing oil on the track.

Over the years some members have tried to reform USAC with, at best, limited success. The most important of these was the club's long-time president, Thomas W. Binford, a manufacturer of lubricants, a distinguished citizen of Indianapolis, a leader of the Urban League and a prominent figure in civic and human rights organizations. Toward the end of 1968 Binford notified the club's board that he would not run for re-election as president. He was then 44 years old but his tired face and white hair made him look at least 55, possibly because he had been president of USAC for 11 years. Amid the tan Stetson hats, string ties and white cotton socks Tom Binford, Princeton '48 and palpably Brooks Brothers, stood out as USAC's resident anomaly. He was literate, articulate, urbane and a cultured gentleman; he also traveled. As the unpaid president he presided uncomfortably over a club of conservative interests. He overcame great odds to hold the organization together and to win a measure of respect for it. One of his achievements had been to reduce USAC's public ludicrosities to about one a week.

In his memorandum to the board, Binford suggested ways of catching up with the times: "Policies that succeed in one

54

decade," he wrote, "rarely succeed in the next." He urged USAC to "broaden its view" by hiring personnel with experience outside USAC and by studying programs of other racing clubs.

In 1969 USAC made some tentative gestures of cooperation with the Sports Car Club of America on race dates and driver interchange—there was even a hint at the possibility of merger—and then quickly pulled back. Binford has since retired from the presidency, having served the organization well, having done the best any man could. He still is a member of USAC and he also is an individual member of the Automobile Competition Committee for the United States. Technically he is an unaffiliated member of ACCUS, but in Binford the United States Auto Club definitely has a friend in that court.

The automobile industry is conservative; mechanics and drivers are conservative; car owners are conservative. Combine their preterist inclinations and you have a tightly organized community whose basic law is: CONFORM. Penalties for nonconformance are swift and occasionally rather rough. The basic weapon has been the rules change, invoked quickly and sometimes with vindictiveness. An innovation drives the Establishment not to the drawing board but to the rules committee.

Part of USAC's problem is its ambivalence over whether racing is to be considered a test bed for automotive progress or purely a sport. USAC has shied away from the "laboratory" position. During the turbine debate of 1967 one board member put it bluntly: "Just because some joker comes down the street with a new idea, it doesn't mean we have to help him with it." In August, 1968, during the debate on four-wheel drive and the continuing fight over turbine power, the club issued a policy statement that said:

Automotive racing is a spectator sport . . . and any automotive development is a byproduct of the sport, not its original intent.
Yet too often the public has been misled to believe that the primary function of an automobile race is to

aid in the development of automotive products. This is not true. The primary function of a USAC-sanctioned race . . . is to provide entertainment for the fans through close, thrilling competition.

Certainly USAC is proud of the innovations and developments made by the automobile industry through its participation in racing, and they nourish the hope that such progress will continue. But such continued progress will remain a byproduct of the sport, not its original concept.

That policy statement will get you an argument in some quarters of USAC. In contradiction to it is the position of manufacturers who spend millions of dollars perfecting engines, components, tires, lubricants, accessories and equipment for racing. If they go along with the "pure sport" philosophy, that scarcely is evident from the content of the advertisements they address to the public.

USAC's complacency has often been criticized by race drivers, by lesser members, by the racing community outside, by the motor press and by others who see the club as a quaint 19th-century anachronism. Occasionally one can glimpse some movement as the result of such criticism. At the beginning of 1969 USAC announced a few long-range plans for reform. They included correction of the imbalance on its board of directors between "participants" and "nonparticipants"; establishment of a minimum lead time for major changes in engines and chassis; creation of an appeals board to deal with protests against the rulings of race officials.

The most significant change occurred Sept. 1, 1969, when the club, under pressure from the drivers particularly, appointed a full-time, salaried executive director as operating head of USAC. For years it had simply muddled along under elected officers who were unpaid, could not give the club the time it needed and were constantly second-guessed and handcuffed by conservative colleagues on the board of directors.

The appointment of William J. Smyth as executive director

has turned out to be one of the best things that ever happened to USAC, a breath of fresh air. Smyth has had long experience in racing augmented by a successful management stint in the business office of a professional football team, the New Orleans Saints. His first achievement was to bring into USAC headquarters the efficient business administration that the club so desperately needed (he even stopped the penny-pinching staff from making collect phone calls). Smyth improved the quality of championship racing by shortening the schedule to 12 races, all with purses substantially increased over the purses of previous years. He negotiated better deals with promoters, found a $300,000-a-year sponsor for the USAC championship series and lined up television coverage of USAC races. At the same time he created a fine public relations department, which also was urgently needed.

But such progress is relatively minor in comparison with the distance USAC has yet to go. The club is still its own worst enemy. The English poet Osbert Sitwell probably never heard of USAC, but his characterization of Milordo Inglese is surprisingly pertinent to that organization:

His miniature castle was even more heavily fortified
Against the invasive present-day
Than against roaming burglars.

Smyth does not despair. "The impossible," he says, "takes a bit longer."

CHAPTER 3

Stock Car Racing and the "Good Ol' Boys"

THEY TELL the story of the Carolinian, a typical practitioner of his trade in the 1940's, who ran moonshine to the city in his car on Friday night, raced at some unkempt track over the weekend, loaded up with sugar on Monday morning and headed back to the stills in the hills. One Sunday, while leading a race, he was puzzled by an unfamiliar signal from his mechanic in the pits. Then he reasoned it out: some revenuers were waiting to arrest him. So he took the checkered flag, swept through Turns 1 and 2 on what appeared to be a victory lap, then crashed through the fence at Turn 3 onto a country road—and he was home free.

For a long time the hillbilly bootleggers had the advantage over pursuing Government men because they knew the uncharted back roads so well. To equalize the odds, the Government developed some very good machinery. At the same time the local mechanics, fascinated by the ultimate potentialities of a factory-built engine, did some elegant tinkering of their own. Many Southerners will tell you about the speed shop in Spartanburg, Atlanta, Charlotte, Columbia—any Dixie city, it doesn't matter—where two identical sedans are being prepared for this earnest form of racing. One belongs to a moonshiner expanding his delivery fleet; the other belongs to the United States Government.

Moonshining has always been lucrative because it bypasses the tax-collection apparatus. Once, much more than it is nowadays, the delivery of moonshine was a sort of training ground for stock car race drivers. They perfected their skills doing power slides on gravel roads. They learned car preparation, speed, evasion, high-speed U-turns at the PO-lice barriers and secret compartments (still useful on the race track for hidden fuel, if not discovered at tech inspection). The necessary elements were road-holding, stability, stamina, acceleration,

59

braking and—most important—finishing if the leader wanted to avoid the Federal penitentiary.

"Hell, that's where I got my practice," said the late Curtis Turner, one of the great stock car race drivers of some years ago. "You have to run good, otherwise you get caught."

As the mechanics perfected their techniques, and as each hill and valley produced its own hero "lead-foot," local bragging led to match races. In time we had the beginnings of modern stock car racing by those "good ol' boys" who created hot machines and drove them with consummate skill. Men who could scarcely read and write were suddenly the most prosperous in the neighborhood.

Of course, stock car racing is not entirely traceable to bootlegging. The sport owes more to the general life style of Southeastern United States as a whole. As far back as the 1930's the gutsy quality of the "stockers" and even jalopies had caught the Southern fancy. Expansion was inevitable.

It was William H. G. (Bill) France, a gas station attendant earning some extra money in racing, who captured the spirit of stock car racing and developed it, in the late 1940's, into a formal and *respectable* sport—surpassing, below the Mason-

Direct action: Buddy Baker takes a water hose from his crew during a pit stop and arranges his own cool-off.

Dixon Line, pro football, baseball and basketball. In 1971 the over-all prizes in races sanctioned by the National Association for Stock Car Auto Racing should exceed $5.5 million. Purses at NASCAR's Grand National races average $35,000, to which manufacturers' awards must be added. The NASCAR point fund, a sort of kitty distributed among leading drivers at the end of the season, comes to nearly $400,000.

The drivers may still drawl like farm boys but they know how to go about depositing the check from the advertising agency when their business managers are on vacation. They fly their own twin-engine aircraft to the races, make public and television appearances, wear quite mod clothes and operate a variety of business ventures. And although they may not be so adroit on dirt tracks as their daddies were, they handle three-mile-a-minute race cars on the superspeedways with poise and aplomb.

Stock car racing, then, is the world both of the rural dirt track and of the superspeedway. At the latter a ticket may cost $25 or more. It is the world of 30-year-old jalopies with modern engines . . . late models that run 190 miles an hour within inches of one another . . . the awesome roar of 30 to 40 engines in concert . . . the soot of rubber dust and the haze of dust-dust . . . pageants, Confederate flags, the pre-race invocation, hot sun, cold beer, high jinks in the infield . . . beauty queens who seem especially bred (like Beltsville turkeys) to compete for titles . . . Southern politicians who love those gigantic captive audiences.

Stock car racing is also the world of strenuous competition for auto sales, a competition based on the maxim "Win Sunday, sell Monday."

It is a world of incredible speed. At Talladega lap speeds of 200 miles an hour have been clocked. Speed has increased dramatically in the last few years because of three special factors:

(1) More efficient engines that produce greater horsepower without increases in size.

(2) Aerodynamic body design that reduces wind resistance. Occasionally a race car has a bit more slope than its showroom counterpart.

(3) Tires of new compounds that provide greater traction. At present they are about a foot wide. If they were wider the cars would run faster.

Stock car racing is open to steel-bodied cars manufactured in the United States. The greatest crowd pleasers are the cars of the Grand National division, racing versions of late-model Fords, Mercurys, Dodges, Plymouths and Chevrolets. Under the rules "late model" means automobiles from the three most recent production years. Cars classified as Late Model Sportsman, Modified and Hobby are older and less powerful. Still another division is the Grand American Series, open to late-model sedans of the so-called "sporty" type—Mustang, Camaro, Javelin, Barracuda, Challenger, Firebird.

The newest NASCAR class, which began operating in 1971, is for very small American and foreign sedans. This division, called the International Sedan Manufacturers Championship, is open to such cars as Ford Pinto, Toyota Corona, Datsun 510, BMW 2002, Chevrolet Vega 2300, American Motors Gremlin, Fiat 124S. These races are run in conjunction with Grand American programs.

Ostensibly the popularity of stock car racing rests on the resemblance between a spectator's family car and the racer that is blazing around the oval. In fact, though, such resemblance is imagined, because the designation "stock," implying a car available from your friendly neighborhood dealer, is a carny dodge, part of the show biz illusion. It exploits the consumer phenomenon known as "product identification," which manufacturers and race promoters have gone to great lengths to nurture.

The spectator's car and the race car may share the same brand name but the similarity between them is strictly superficial: the racer *looks* like the spectator's Dodge or Ford and that's about it. "Stock-appearing" is a more realistic term. Beneath the hood is a specially prepared racing engine worth more than $6,000. That, after all, is what carries the Pettys, Bakers and Pearsons 200 miles an hour around Talladega. The rest of the car—body, frame, suspension, steering gear, sway bar, brakes—is strengthened for superior performance, endurance and safety. Every bit of unneeded weight is removed.

Actually it isn't product identification that makes stock car racing so popular. The fans are too sophisticated for that. They are as familiar with the distinction between race cars and their own cars as they are with the yelling, dirt, dust, grease, sunburn and indigestion. What they come to see is speed and thrills, and lots of both. There is little in racing that is more exciting than a skillful "draft." A driver gets behind another car and rides its tail around and around: the car in front is breaking through the air, using up fuel and increasing its wear and tear. The driver in the "draft" is getting what amounts to a free ride or a tow. He is getting precisely the same speed as his benefactor—say, 175 miles an hour—at about two-thirds throttle (thus conserving fuel and lessening engine stress). What is so impressive about the draft is that the driver is maneuvering a two-ton machine at 175 miles an hour *within a few feet* of the car in front.

The draft leads to another technique, the slingshot. When the driver wants to pass the car he is drafting, he breaks the suction by moving left or right. The car in front is going flat-out but the drafter, having had the benefit of a tow, has a bit in reserve, enough to pass the lead car. Now out of the air stream, he floors his accelerator and slings past his competitor. There is little the driver in front can do about it—if he wiggles right or left, the drafter matches each movement. The slingshot is used most dramatically on the very last lap of a race, when the No. 2 driver is hounding the leader with a well-executed draft. He slings close enough to the finish so that his rival doesn't have enough time to resume the chase. To see a driver "set up" his man and then sling him is to see a work of art.

Stock car racing is a rough sport and an earthy one and the drivers don't hesitate to bump or "nerf" one another for advantage or position. All this is what the fans want—racing

63

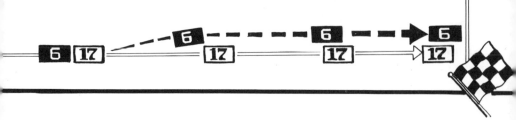

Driver of No. 6 breaks out of the draft and slings past the towing car, No. 17, and takes the checkered flag for the win.

bumper to bumper and wheel to wheel, drafting, slingshotting, close calls, speed in the pit stops and so on.

Yet the sport is more than a mere sport. It is an industry that extends from the board rooms of Detroit to a messy garage where some hopeful youngster tinkers with his race car. The manufacturers have used racing in two ways: as a test bed for technical development and as a sales platform for their merchandise. For various reasons having to do with public relations, insurance and business management, Detroit manufacturers do not race overtly in their own names. What they do is to commission and finance racing teams.

In this country what is commonly called a "factory team"

is really a sort of contractor.* The system is used in stock car racing and also in the Trans-American Championship of the Sports Car Club of America. The team is the nominal owner of the cars it enters in competition. In the spring of 1970 Ford retrenched its racing budget because of the tight economic situation; just before the start of the 1971 season the company announced its withdrawal from all competition except for drag racing, off-road racing and Ford of England's participation in the Grand Prix. Before that, Ford had done its stock car racing through Holman & Moody, the Wood Brothers, Banjo Matthews and Junior Johnson. An old stock car hand, Bud Moore, had been running the Ford Mustang operation in the Trans-Am competition of the Sports Car Club of America. Plymouth has been racing through Petty Engineering, Dodge through Cotton Owens, and so on. (One of the most colorful operators, though rather inactive recently, has been Smokey Yunick of Daytona Beach, Fla., proprietor of "The Best Damn Garage in Town." He worked for General Motors and, briefly, for Ford.)

There is also a relationship called "factory support." Under this arrangement a team receives limited quantities of "pieces" from the factory and a fair amount of technical help.† In addition, factory-supported teams may also collect bonuses from the factories when they win.

All of the factory teams maintain fine garages or shops with dynamometers and other expensive equipment. In these plants the cars are "prepared" for racing, torn down after a race and rebuilt for the next one. The car owners are usually the most expert of mechanics and/or former race drivers. From the

---

* In Europe, however, it has long been the practice for manufacturers to compete openly in their own names with "factory teams" or what the British call "works" teams. Among the prominent examples, past and present, are Ferrari, BRM, Cooper, Lotus, Peugeot, Mercedes Benz. In recent years Porsche has done it both ways: it has maintained a factory team and it has also commissioned a contractor like the Briton John Wyer to run its racing program. And now the Japanese are beginning to compete with factory teams.

†Some factory support is also available to teams of such other stock car circuits as the United States Auto Club, the Auto Racing Club of America and the International Motor Contest Association.

Spark plugs provide valuable information for car builders who, like Cotton Owens, understand their language. Oiliness and color reveal what's going on inside the engine.

manufacturers they receive the basic cars and engines they prepare for racing, together with spare parts and accessories. They make their own special components or "pieces" or buy them from specialists who turn out only wheels, cams, crankshafts and so on.

The car owner is entitled to keep what his team wins in purses and prizes. The race driver may be salaried either by the owner or the factory or he may receive a share of the team's winnings.

The mechanics are the unlettered geniuses of stock car racing. Most have very limited education and few have any training in engineering. Yet they know more about the realities of building and tearing down an engine than the Detroit engineers. They prepare the car in their shops, then "set it up" when they reach the track. During a race they serve in the pit crew. The usual Grand National pit crew includes a very good engine man and a very good chassis man, with each capable of assuming some of the other's duties.

Although factory teams win most of the races and most of the leading positions in races, there still is a modest place for the independents, who operate with their own earnings and whatever money they can raise from sponsors. NASCAR goes to some lengths to keep the independents involved as happily and as permanently as possible, assuring them a share of the year-end point fund and paying purse money far down the list of finishers. NASCAR also covers the independents with an insurance benefit plan. Finally, Bill France makes it a point to help them privately, either out of his own pocket or by conning some equipment from someone who can spare it.

The independents usually buy cars that were used by factory teams in previous seasons. Since they cannot beat the well-endowed factory "hot dogs," they simply stay in the race by husbanding their machinery and waiting for some of the big fellows to knock themselves out. This kind of attrition leaves a few positions open in the top 10. It is a hard way to make a living but there are some drivers who thrive on this regimen.

Race drivers work hard for the big-money superspeedway events. Before such a race they spend three or four days at the track, practicing and testing hour after hour. Frequently a driver goes into the pits to discuss a car's performance and handling with his chief mechanic. A driver needs to know his machine well. It is not enough to tell his crew, "It's handling like a pig." He needs to know enough about engines, suspension and steering to be able to impart intelligent information to the mechanics.

In some respects a 500-mile stock car race is similar in color and atmosphere to the Indianapolis 500. They both offer one of the most thrilling moments in sports—the running start. In the stock car race anywhere from 30 to 40 entrants take their positions (allocated in pre-race qualification runs) behind the officials' pace car and they run two or three slow laps around the oval in double-file formation. This is done to warm up the engines and get the cars as closely aligned as possible, in tightly bunched pairs. The last of these laps is called the pace lap. From his position high above the starting line the starter must satisfy himself that the cars are lined up—in motion, remember—for a safe start. When he thinks they are ready, he radios word to the pace car toward the end of the pace lap. The pace car usually leaves the oval at the beginning of the front straight. From that point on the pace is set by the lead driver, the one "sitting on the pole." The drivers gather speed and rush toward the start-finish line, knowing the starter will wave the green flag as they come close to it. The combined roar of 30 or more engines in full cry is an extraordinary sensation, a supremely exciting moment.

A long-distance race soon settles down to noisy droning for the next two to four hours (depending on the length of the event). The slower cars drop down to the low side of the track, yielding to the quicker ones the faster outside "groove" high on the banks. The pit crews keep charts of fuel and tire consumption and schedule the necessary stops. They also watch their car and driver for any difficulties they can detect from a distance. A crew communicates with its driver by means of short messages inscribed on a "pit board" that is held up at trackside for him to read as he flashes by. Such messages can tell him his position, speed and so on. They can also tell him when to come in for his next pit stop for fuel and tires. Conversely, the driver can alert the crew with hand signals—he will need tires on the next stop, or something is wrong with his brakes, clutch, etc. A few Grand National cars have taken to two-way radio to facilitate communication.

The brightly dressed pit crew members are an attraction in themselves. They are highly trained and have been drilled to function at top speed without wasting a finger of motion. They are able to do incredible repair work under the pressure of competition. A pit stop can be a sort of ballet. Five men—the maximum allowed—swarm around the car, change two tires, pour 22 gallons of gas into the tank and send the vehicle back into the race *in as few as 22 seconds*. Races can be lost or saved in the pits. If a driver has a 45-second lead and needs only 25 seconds for his pit stop, he still retains his lead as he re-enters the race.

68

Daytona 500: A pit stop for fuel and change of right-side tires.

Most pit stops are scheduled but many are made to take advantage of a NASCAR rule related to the yellow caution flag. Whenever there is an accident, like a wreck that strews debris or a blown engine that spills oil, maintenance crews rush onto the track to tidy things up. To insure their safety while they are at work, the yellow flag is waved and yellow electric signal lights flash at trackside. The pace car is driven into the moving stream of race cars and positioned in front of the leader. The other race cars fall into single file behind the leader, maintaining their relative positions. The pace then slows dramatically to one-half the normal race speed. No car may improve its position during the yellow caution period.

The drivers take advantage of this period to hurry into the pits for fuel and tires. Because the field is running so slowly it is possible to rush out again in time to join the procession, pass the finish line and get credit for a completed lap, and then dash into the pits once more. Sometimes, if the yellow caution period is very long, the driver can come in for a change of his right-side tires and then return after a lap for left-side tires—all without relinquishing his position in the pack.

Caution periods also have the side effect of creating another flying start when the green flag comes out again. Some cynics believe this side effect is exploited too obviously at times.

*   *   *

69

Stockers are popular in many parts of the United States but their greatest following is in the Southeast—the Carolinas, Alabama, Georgia, Tennessee, Virginia, Florida. Any town of any consequence in the region has an oval track of sorts, either dirt or asphalt, from a quarter of a mile to a half-mile long. Sometimes it may be the old horse track at the fairgrounds. Critics of the smaller tracks call them "bull rings."

Within the sphere of the National Association for Stock Car Auto Racing is a network of 94 tracks (including a minor-league set-up on the Pacific Coast). These race plants pyramid to a group of so-called superspeedways, the big-time tracks that are at least a mile long. The superspeedways run longer races—in the hundreds of miles—for larger purses. Daytona International Speedway, at Daytona Beach, Fla., considered the mecca of stock car racing, is $2\frac{1}{2}$ miles long. Other big-time tracks, along with their lengths, are:

Alabama International Speedway at Talladega, $2\frac{3}{5}$ miles.
Atlanta International Raceway at Hampton, Ga., $1\frac{1}{2}$ miles
Charlotte (N.C.) Motor Speedway, $1\frac{1}{2}$ miles.
Darlington (S.C.) International Raceway, $1\frac{3}{8}$ miles.
Dover Downs International Speedway at Dover, Del., 1 mile.
Michigan International Speedway at Cambridge Junction, 2 miles.
North Carolina Motor Speedway at Rockingham, 1 mile
Ontario (Calif.) Motor Speedway, $2\frac{1}{2}$ miles.
Texas International Speedway at Bryan, 2 miles.
Trenton (N.J.) Motor Speedway, $1\frac{1}{2}$ miles.

Not all these tracks are committed to NASCAR races exclusively. Several also run races sanctioned by the United States Auto Club and other organizations. Nor are they all exclusively oval tracks. Daytona, Talladega, Michigan and Ontario have infield courses for road races. The most important of these road races is the Twenty-four Hours of Daytona, one of the world manufacturers' championship series (Chapter 5).

The best long-distance Grand National races at the super-speedways attract crowds of 50,000 to 100,000, sometimes in competition with baseball and football games, where admission prices may be considerably lower. The long races run from 250 to 600 miles. The purse and manufacturers' accessory awards in the 1971 Daytona 500 exceeded $200,000, and this total did not include lap prizes. Shorter Grand Nationals are run at the smaller tracks—altogether about 50 a season.

Not all stock car racing is of the glamorous Grand National type. Of the nearly 1,200 races sanctioned each year by NASCAR, close to 1,100 are for the older cars of the Late Model Sportsman, Modified and Hobby Divisions. Stock car racing could not exist without these bread-and-butter races of 10 to 15 miles on Friday or Saturday night at Jackson's Corner. Occasionally the weekly show will feature a larger race for larger purses and a couple of big-name drivers may be induced (by an appearance fee) to compete. When the big names appear, attendance goes up. So do the ticket prices. The smaller races and tracks serve, of course, as a training ground, enabling local drivers to sharpen their skills in competition among themselves and with the visiting stars.

*   *   *

Members of pit crews will do anything to save a few seconds. These three men from different teams, waiting for their cars to arrive, have found a place to store nuts and bolts where they can find them in a hurry.

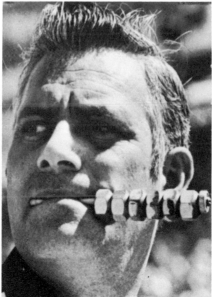

While a considerable share of stock car racing is sanctioned by other organizations, the absolutely dominant presence in this sport is NASCAR—the National Association for Stock Car Auto Racing. NASCAR has a 90-page rule book covering the nuts and bolts of every division. It is full of rigid specifications. Rules are sternly enforced by experienced inspectors to promote safety and frustrate cheating. Mechanics have to be clever indeed to get past the tech inspection with any "goodies," which is what they call illegal devices that improve performance.

Divisions and specs are complex and elaborate. In all divisions the race car must retain the appearance of a stock car—the later the year, the closer the resemblance has to be. The extent of modifications permitted and the model of the car itself determine the division in which a vehicle competes. NASCAR graduates the divisions as follows:

GRAND NATIONAL

Steel-bodied American-made cars of the last three production years. Stock-block engines, with two valves per cylinder, valves actuated by pushrods. One four-barrel carburetor. Engines of up to 430 cubic inches displacement. To keep speeds within safe limits, to equalize competiveness, to reduce costs and to save wear and tear on cars and tires, NASCAR has instituted a system of carburetor restrictor plates that limit air intake—and consequently speed. The size of a hole bored in the plate governs the amount of air intake. Sizes vary from $1\frac{1}{4}$ inches to $1\frac{5}{8}$ inches, depending on the displacement of the engine and the type of its construction (hemispherical-head, tunnel port, porcupine, etc.). Restrictor plates are *not* required for engines of up to 305 cubic inches displacement and for power plants of 306–366 c.i.d. built in the configuration called wedge-type in-line valve engine. Cars with special aerodynamic bodies—such as Plymouth Superbird, Dodge Daytona, Dodge Charger 500, Ford Talladega and Mercury Cyclone Spoiler— may not carry engines of more than 305 c.i.d.

Minimum wheelbase 115 inches, minimum weight 3,900

pounds. No alterations on the body except for safety—rollbar safety cage, hood fasteners, removal of glass, bolting of doors, etc.—but a spoiler (air deflector) of up to $1\frac{1}{2}$ inches in height may be added to the rear-deck lid.

Substantially the same specifications are also used by the Stock Car Division of the United States Auto Club (Chapter 2), but USAC does not require the carburetor restrictor plates.

Daytona 500 of 1971: Richard Petty, the winner in No. 43 (a '71 Plymouth with 426-c.i.d. engine) leads Richard Brooks in an aerodynamic 305-c.i.d. Dodge. Behind them is Donnie Allison in a '69 Ford.

GRAND AMERICAN SERIES

A relatively new division created in 1968, at first called Grand Touring, for "sporty sedans" such as Camaro, Mustang, Barracuda, Javelin, Firebird, Challenger. Like the Grand Nationals, they are late-model cars—that is, from the three most recent production years. Stock-block engines with maximum displacement of 305 cubic inches, with one four-barrel carburetor. Minimum wheelbase 100 inches, minimum weight 3,200 pounds.

Body dimensions and contour must remain intact except

73

for safety changes. Fenders may be reshaped to accommodate racing tires. Spoiler $1\frac{1}{2}$ inches high is permitted.

Grand American cars run on oval tracks except for occasional road races at Daytona, Talladega and Road Atlanta. The Grand American schedule can include as many as 50 races.

This division corresponds to the Trans-American class of the Sports Car Club of America and the Sports Sedan division of the United States Auto Club.

INTERNATIONAL SEDAN MANUFACTURERS CHAMPIONSHIP

Steel-bodied sedans of American or foreign manufacture. For engines with overhead camshafts, maximum piston displacement of 2,300 cubic centimeters. For engines with push-rod-actuated valves, maximum displacement of 4,000 cc. Cars eligible in this class include Alfa Romeo Giulia Super 1600, Gremlin, BMW 1600 and 2002, Chevrolet Vega 2300, Datsun 510, Dodge Colt, Fiat 124 coupe, Ford Pinto 2-liter, Lancia Flavia, Mazda 1800, Mercury Comet, Opel 1900 Kadette, Plymouth Cricket, Saab 99, Toyota Mark II Corona and Volvo 142S.

LATE-MODEL SPORTSMAN

Steel-top sedan types from a 10-year period ending three years before the current season. For example, for the 1971 season, production years 1958–68. Maximum engine displacement 430 cubic inches. One carburetor. Minimum wheelbase 115 inches. Minimum weight 9 pounds for each cubic inch of engine displacement.

MODIFIED

Steel-top sedans from 1935 to a production year ending three years before the current season. For example, for 1971 season, 1935–68. Nearly anything goes: unlimited displacement, rebored blocks, any type of carburetion, fuel injection, superchargers, any fuel.

74

A pair of Alfa Romeos, one of the types eligible for NASCAR's International Sedan Manufacturers Championship.

Modified cars, tightly bunched, head for the starting flag.

Hobby cars, sometimes called limited sportsman, in a night show.

HOBBY (AMATEUR)

Limited to amateurs and novices to give them racing experience and to help them compete at moderate expense. Field is open to cars 10 years old or more, in some cases as much as 25 years old. No multiple carburetors or fuel injection.

To be eligible for Grand National competition, a car must be produced in certain volume: at least 1,000 car bodies of the unit being proposed for competition or a quantity representing one-half the number of franchised dealers of the make, whichever is greater. In practice the upper range works out to more than 3,000 units for the larger manufacturers. The rules also require that at least 500 units of a street-version engine be produced by the manufacturer as a regular production option available for sale to the public; moreover, these units must be sold already installed in the car bodies. (This rule also applies to the Stock Car Division of the United States Auto Club.)

In the Grand American Series the rule is that the manufacturer must produce at least 2,500 units of the car being offered for approval or 1/250th of the previous year's production, whichever is greater. (This rule also applies to the Sports Sedan division of USAC.)

The purpose of these rules, adopted by the Automobile Competition Committee for the United States in 1969, is to encourage competition by cars "more representative" of the automobiles on sale in dealer showrooms. Earlier rules had required a minimum production of only 500 units and had encouraged the use of exotic equipment and racers long known as "funny cars"—meaning cars of spurious credentials that the manufacturers coerced dealers into buying.

In fact, racing stock cars still are "funny" as far as the public is concerned. If at a stock car race you have a pit or garage area pass that gets you close enough to the entries for a careful look, you will find almost no resemblance between the race cars and the commercial versions of those vehicles. The point is that the "production" car that is homologated—which means submitted for approval in a racing class—is only a base car, a point of departure from which a race car can develop.

The theory behind this minimum-production business is that you too can buy a showroom car and develop it into a racer—if you have the money, the equipment, the talent and the expert technical advice from the factory. This same congenial fiction also prevails in the Trans-American Championship of the Sports Car Club of America.

*   *   *

Today's stock-car racing has antecedents other than the Blue Ridge moonshiners, casual match races and early meets in dusty fields. There is also Daytona Beach on the Atlantic coast in northern Florida. As far back as 1902 that long strip of hard-packed sand was being used for speed tests, and among the pioneer names associated with it are Sir Malcolm Campbell, Barney Oldfield, Alexander Winton, R. E. Olds, Ralph De-Palma, William K. Vanderbilt. The speed-test era ended in 1935 when Campbell ran his Bluebird at a speed of 276.82 miles an hour over a measured mile.

Another era began March 8, 1936, with a race for stock automobiles. The course was 3.2 miles long and consisted of

Marshall Teague in one of the old-time beach racers. The hood is secured with rope. Tape protects the chrome and paint and the chrome border of the windshield from sand-blasting—after all, these were family cars that were driven home after the race. There were no special wheels; you simply removed the hub caps and went racing.

the beach for one stretch and a parallel asphalt road for the other. Turns were bulldozed through the dunes to connect the two straights. That sand and asphalt course was used for stock-car racing for the next 20 years.

During those two decades formal courses were being built elsewhere, mostly in the South. There was almost no organization and the sport was growing at a pace that was getting out of hand. The prospects of profit attracted mechanics who developed cheating into an art. Drivers and promoters encouraged the mechanics. The promoters themselves cheated by not giving the public what they had promised and skipping town with the gate receipts, leaving bills and drivers' purses unpaid. No one concerned himself much with safety or enforcement of what rules there were. There was no supervision, no direction, no organization. The condition of the sport was chaotic.

Although other men had long recognized the need for tightening inspection and promotion procedures, Bill France was the first to do something about it. As a race driver dating from the 1930's he had seen enough of the confusion and stealing. He knew that promoters, drivers and car owners had to have an organization that would encourage bigger purses, enforce rules and safety standards and above all give the sport some respectability. He issued an invitation to a meeting at the Streamline Hotel in Daytona Beach and 18 men responded on Dec. 14, 1947. Within two months NASCAR was incorporated. The first NASCAR race was held Feb. 15, 1948, on the old Daytona beach-and-road course. All the races that year on that course and on six tracks were for modified cars—beefed up sedans and coupes.

The first Grand National for late-model stock cars, promoted by Bill France Enterprises, was run June 19, 1949; it was a 150-miler on the $\frac{3}{4}$-mile dirt track of the old Charlotte Speedway.

There were eight other Grand Nationals that year, 1949. NASCAR was well on its way, and hard work and steady effort strengthened its position. The first "superspeedway" especially built for NASCAR races—high-banked turns and a paved surface 1⅜ miles long—was opened in 1950 at Darlington, S.C., by a group of businessmen. NASCAR's first 500-miler was run there. It succeeded despite a fog of pessimism. Few had believed the race cars could last 500 miles. Few had believed fans would travel to the limit of nowhere, at "the sorry Hartsville Road property" that wouldn't even grow decent cotton.

Bill France has been president of NASCAR since midwifing it in 1948. Despite the second word of its name, NASCAR is really more a private business enterprise than it is an "association" of members. France is the majority stockholder. He also is president of Daytona International Speedway, an excellent $3 million track he opened in 1959; of Alabama International Motor Speedway at Talladega, a $5-million-plus track that went into operation in 1969, and of several other enterprises within the NASCAR orbit.

The affairs of NASCAR and of France's tracks are directed from a modest two-story air-conditioned building outside the Daytona Speedway. These affairs blend so smoothly into each other that the naked eye can barely discern where one ends and the other begins.

For the last few years NASCAR personnel have been referring to the president as "Bill Senior" in recognition of the constantly rising importance of Bill France Jr., the very competent executive vice president of NASCAR, who has been learning the business since his teens. Bill Junior, who was born in 1933, has even done a short stint of race driving and is the race director at most major NASCAR events. He is reported to run more of the everyday business of NASCAR than Bill Senior does and obviously he is the man who will some day succeed the founder. A younger son, Jimmy, joined the management staff in 1971 after completing his hitch in military service.

Another valuable member of the organization is Linn Kuchler, vice president and competition director. But for all the ability and influence of Bill Junior and Kuchler, the unassailable fact is that Bill Senior is the overwhelming figure in stock car racing, an ingenious, aggressive and almost universally admired promoter. Bill France *is* NASCAR. Occasionally a new situation crops up that is not clearly covered in the rule book. In his quietly pragmatic way he settles the problem single-handedly with no fuss, issuing one of his "instant loose-leaf" rulings. It may be the outgrowth of a quid pro quo accommodation with this manufacturer, some Southern sweet-talk with a protesting competitor, a concession here, a promise there, some genial back-scratching, some diplomacy, some hard-headed adamancy. The carburetor restrictor plate, imposed in 1970 and carried to elaborate embellishment in 1971, is the most recent example of France's capacity to improvise something to cope with a pressing situation. In this case the problem was cars that had become too fast for the tracks and tires they were running on; there was also the exasperating frequency with which costly engines were breaking down under the stress of racing.

As a person France is genial and gracious, with an honest smile and pleasant voice. Tall, heavy but not fat, he is more than 60 years old and has little gray hair to show it. He can still drive a race car when he feels like it and is qualified to fly the company's twin-engine aircraft. France has had little formal schooling but is excellently self-educated. He is articulate, knowledgeable, and comfortable in any company.

He runs a tight ship. Very little is done around NASCAR or his tracks without his approval.

He is immensely powerful. He can suspend a car owner or mechanic or driver any time he wants to and for as long as he pleases. If he decides to withhold a sanction from a race track, that track would do well to ponder other uses for its real estate. Some years ago France put down an ill-planned effort by drivers to form a labor union. He suspended the leader, Curtis Turner, from 1961 through 1965, during some of Turner's best driving years.

Of course this kind of power invites a counterforce. By the summer of 1969 the drivers had made it clear they were impatient with what they considered NASCAR's paternalism, that they resented having so little voice in NASCAR affairs.

Richard Petty, one of NASCAR's all-time great drivers, took the lead in organizing a quasi union called the Professional Drivers Association. As Motor Trend magazine noted at the time, Petty was "taking the professional athlete out of the grip of the they're-only-dumb-athletes-and-have-to-be-taken-care-of syndrome and putting them into the position where they belong—as a vital, organizing part of the sport. It's rather like the monkey rebelling against the organ grinder."

The Professional Drivers Association was better thought-out than Curtis Turner's bungling effort had been. It was organized with about 40 of NASCAR's leading drivers, and the drivers were advised by the same lawyer who represented the players of the National Basketball Association.

Petty said at the inception of the P.D.A. that the drivers wanted better insurance benefits, a retirement plan and bigger purses (including a share of television proceeds). They also wanted safety improvements. The drivers were disgruntled, too, about having to waste time, energy and expense money by competing at small country-town tracks where purses had not increased significantly from the minor-league levels of ten years earlier. And there were little things: "Daytona stages the most prestigious race of the year with their 500-miler in February," said Petty, "but that track has no lounge or rest room or anything for the drivers. The only facilities we have there have been given to us by the accessory firms who constructed shops in the garage area. We shouldn't have to depend on outsiders."

Any item that raises costs worries the track owners. That's one thing. But it is quite another thing when higher costs are forced by pressure from drivers—obviously they can keep on pressuring for more. Track owners on the NASCAR circuit have been positively chilled by the big talk of higher purses, shares of TV income, retirement funds, insurance benefits, safety improvements and the like. Nor are the promoters of the small tracks cheered by the inclination of the big-name drivers to pass up the "bull ring" races and concentrate on the superspeedway events.

Actually, more than the surface issues of purses and safety

are involved in the creation of the Professional Drivers Association. Its establishment may turn out to be the beginning of a power struggle between the promoters and the performers. The drivers are insisting on a voice in the way the racing business is conducted. The conservative NASCAR organization is reacting vigorously to this threat, which NASCAR sees as going beyond mere unionism.

Drivers' big names are the prime attraction in racing. If the superstars can exploit their leverage, they will not settle for the status of members of baseball or basketball teams. They will shoot for, say, the strong position that professional golfers enjoy. Conceivably driver organization could spread to the other racing clubs, such as the United States Auto Club and the Sports Car Club of America. (Already in USAC the drivers have succeeded in getting the club to schedule fewer races and bigger purses.)

Part of the time Bill France Senior fights the P.D.A. openly, even vituperatively. Part of the time he acts as though the P.D.A. does not exist. It is still too early in the game to guess the eventual outcome. But given the colorful personalities involved and the high stakes, the battle may turn out to be as interesting as any auto race.

CHAPTER 4

Funny Cars
Are Serious Business

The Wonderful World
of Drag Racing

A KALEIDOSCOPIC ARRAY of exotic vehicles ranging from the unimaginable to the incomprehensible gathers every weekend at hundreds of locations throughout North America for one of the more extraordinary aspects of motor sports—drag racing. This is a bewilderingly complicated sport, yet all of the sound and fury, fumes and fragrance, engineering and chemistry are channeled toward one simple objective; to see how quickly a machine can travel one-fourth of a mile—1,320 feet, or about four and a half city blocks—from a standing start.

The paying fans total about eight million a year at meets sanctioned by the National Hot Rod Association and the American Hot Rod Association and at independent tracks. They cheerfully accept a broiling sun and 90-degree temperatures or the penetrating chill of an evening to watch their "instant sport" through an eye-smarting smog of burned rubber and fuel.

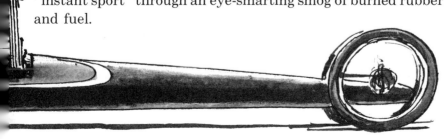

Among the 75,000 spectators at a pro football game, few are interested in buying footballs, but at a drag meet—and, for that matter, any auto race—just about everyone is a customer of the automotive industry. Detroit has moved into drag racing with money, know-how, innovation and sophistication, and factory teams are now common.

Most fans are in their early 20's, with approximately a high school education and occupations they describe as "technical" or "mechanical," but there are also enthusiasts who happen to be college professors, physicists, engineers, physicians, airline pilots and so on. They all like noise and gadgets. They say their cars are less than three years old and are chosen on the basis of performance. There are differences, of course, in their preferences. Some like stock cars, others come to see the funny cars. But nearly everyone loves the underdog. Let him reach the top today and next week they'll be cheering his opponents.

In this fanciful world of color, odors, noise, excitement and ingenuity, both tee shirts and race cars are emblazoned with the likes of "You Lose," "Ladies First" (displayed by a woman contestant), "Polish Airlines," "Stormin' Norman," "Let It All Hang Out," "Tiny Tantrum," "Head Hunter," "Fords Kill Chevys" and "For Sale." Drivers are known as The Snake, Big Daddy, The King, The Mongoose. Cars are named Hawaiian, Freight Train, Black Plague, Terrified.

It scarcely matters that a race is over in about seven seconds of smoke and burning rubber. "The best runs," says a typical fan, "are the ones you can't see at all." Says another: "The noise isn't so bad. The trick is to keep your mouth open."

Cars lurch off the starting line so quickly that sometimes their front wheels lift into the air, and the rear tires spin and burn. When a pair of 1,000-horsepower fantasies leap forward with bright yellow flames shooting from their exhaust headers, with an explosion of sound, plumes of smoke and a dazzling burst of acceleration—either you dig it or you aren't living.

Drag racing has no resemblance to stock car or sports car racing. Everything about it, from its equipment to its language, is special. To the uninitiated, drag racing is an unreal world, rather like a cult with an ethos of its own. It's heady stuff.

Wally Parks, president of the National Hot Rod Association, the founder of organized drag racing, says the sport draws more participants with their own machinery than any other form of racing. The semi-pro and amateur competitors spend enormous amounts of their own money building and preparing their cars (some cost $20,000 or more) and the prizes they win seldom match their expenses. No one seems to mind much. A tinsel trophy is token enough of having run that quarter-mile quicker than the other guys. Here the important thing is to compete just for the thrill.

At the same time it is noteworthy that the National Hot Rod Association offers more than $2 million in cash prizes; the American Hot Rod Association and the independents add at least another million dollars. This kind of money places drag racing high among motor sports.

The true dragster, whatever the size of his bank account, constantly strives for perfection. Whether he is Big Daddy Don Garlits with a $15,000 monster or a teen-ager tweaking a bit more horsepower from his Volkswagen, the goal is one and the same—to cover a fourth of a mile of asphalt, from a standing start, faster than anyone else in his class. Driving isn't all that matters. Much more time is spent in construction, modification, tuning and preparation of the vehicle. Each year the National Hot Rod Association accommodates more than half a million contestant entries and Parks sees "something for everybody" in drag racing. "It's for the hobbyist," he says. "It's big business, science, challenge and crusade. It represents people doing things they like to do."

*   *   *

Drag racing started in the late 1940's. It prospered after World War II, when mechanically minded kids began matching Model A frames with 1932 Ford roadster bodies, then stuffing in a V-8 engine and tacking on heavy-duty suspension and oversize rear wheels.

They also kept the neighbors awake at night and killed a few of their number by racing on public roads and streets. Wally Parks and others, including police authorities, did something to civilize this activity by organizing drag meets on unused airport runways. Usually the runways were one-half to three-fourths of a mile long. Experience showed that a quarter-mile was about the limit that a driver could safely accelerate and still manage to stop before running out of runway. So the quarter-mile became the sport's established standard.

Of course there still are thousands of youngsters who drag one another from the stop lights or on relatively empty suburban streets. They are a public menace comparable to the hoodlums who give motorcycling a bad name. The sport of drag racing, for its own protection, tries as a matter of policy to entice the bad guys in from the streets and channel all their energy and aggressive competitiveness into supervised meets.

Some time ago a young fan, in a letter to The New York Times, stated his case in socio-economic terms. He emphasized "the good aspects of drag racing, such as how a teen-ager is kept off the streets because he is working on his car instead of murdering some old lady in the park or pushing dope. The drags benefit the nation's economy, mechanics are produced and are well needed. . . ."

Although drag racing appeals primarily to the young, its popularity is spreading. The reason is that drag racing is often very exciting. The lingering impression of a drag meet is the assault on one's senses—the shattering noise of screaming engines, the ground-shaking speed (you really feel it in your bones), the odor of exotic fuels, the sight of smoke billowing from tires ("slicks") that stink as they burn. A public-address system adds to the racket with rock music and witless chatter. The fans like it that way.

* * *

Individuality finds its fullest expression in drag racing. The most impressive evidence is the astonishing spectrum of vehicles seen at any drag meet. They range from stock factory cars juiced up in home workshops to the hand-built, stupefyingly expensive all-out dragsters. The variety of designs and combinations is infinite and some startling performers come from some surprising sources. Imagination is about the only limit.

Individuality is one reason the National Hot Rod Association recognizes more than 100 classes of cars (the number varies slightly from year to year). The classes are determined by such criteria as over-all weight, weight divided by engine displacement, weight distribution, allowable modifications and even aerodynamic characteristics. (A smaller organization, the American Hot Rod Association, has approximately 300 classifications, and its members do not seem to consider such refinement overdone.) A purpose of this multiplicity is to make competition as equitable as possible.

Some entries resemble normal automobiles either vaguely or precisely while others are comparable only in the sense that they have four wheels. Indeed, some have *six* wheels, the last two being small ones extending from the rear to prevent the cars, with their tremendous torque, from tipping over backward. In the upper regions of competition no one pretends these machines are cars. The frames and wheels exist merely to carry a driver and an engine down a quarter-mile strip in the shortest possible time. Here, then, is where you see every conceivable size and shape of motor vehicle.

Vehicle? Consider the most spectacular of them all, the elongated "rail job" or "slingshot." This fantasy has a pair of enormous rear wheels with tires 13 to 15 inches wide, a mammoth engine of unlimited size, a driver's safety cage and two long chassis rails connecting up front with a pair of spindly bicycle wheels. The engine, usually a supercharged Chrysler or Ford, can generate up to 1,500 horsepower. What is amazing here is that you have 1,500 h.p. pushing a vehicle that weighs only 1,200 pounds or so.

These superdragsters, designated AA, can cover a quarter mile in less than seven seconds, reaching 230 miles an hour by the end of the dash. They need a parachute, sometimes two, to slow them down. The driver wears an aluminized safety suit and breathing mask that make him look like the Governor of Outer Space in a Grade B movie.

The cars can be "fuelers" or "gassers." The quicker ones are the fuel dragsters, which burn not gasoline but a mixture of methanol and nitromethane. "Liquid horsepower," "pop" and "go-juice," these sophisticated blends are called. Some mixtures cost $5 or more a gallon, and a fuel dragster may consume two to three gallons in a fourth of a mile. The engine churns up 1,500 h.p. and yet it cannot even start itself—it needs to be push-started by a truck. The "slingshot" is so highly specialized that it cannot do anything more than race 1,320 feet in a straight line.

Only slightly slower—say, 200 miles an hour—is the gas dragster. It is similar in appearance to the fuel dragster but runs on commercial gasoline.

Below these AA monsters is a downward range of machines that includes funny cars, stock family cars and "altereds" (drag racers, to repeat, have a language of their own).

Funny cars are serious business, possibly the class that is growing fastest in popularity. They are wolves in sheep's clothing in that their hot engines are concealed beneath innocent-looking fiberglass bodies that resemble the bodies of production cars, but they are specialized machines, only a trifle slower than the rail dragsters and more difficult to handle. Their highly modified, supercharged engines run on esoteric fuel blends. Superficially they look like a Detroit "muscle" car but their body shells of fiberglass, hinged to the chassis, are molded in one piece (no doors, no side windows); the car can be opened, clam-like, to expose the mechanical innards. Often the driver, for better weight distribution, sits about where the back seat of a normal passenger car would usually be.

As with the rail dragster, the power-to-weight ratio is highly unusual: up to 1,500 or 1,600 horsepower pushes a vehicle weighing less than 2,000 pounds at *200 miles an hour*. In contrast a typical family sedan weighs about 3,800 pounds and carries a 300 h.p. engine that has difficulty managing 100 m.p.h.

The funny car was not created rationally. It sort of hap-

Don Prudhomme, "The Snake," blasts off the starting line in a Plymouth-powered Funny Car.

pened. A few years ago mechanics and drivers were overreaching themselves in modifying their store-bought stock cars, like substituting for the regular body a fiberglass one molded from a stock Mustang, or moving the driver's seat to the rear, and so on. The cars were disapproved for failure to conform with competition regulations. Officials and fans came to characterize them as "funny cars." But they caught on and there was so much demand to see them in action that a separate class had to be created. Today the funny car is respectable.

Then there are the altereds, in which just about anything goes. These are the real hot rods, the seemingly ludicrous rigs that once were roadsters, coupes or whatever. They look homemade but on the drag strip they can be surprisingly sophisticated. Many have engines five to ten times more powerful than their original equipment.

In the 1970 season the National Hot Rod Association introduced a new category, the Pro Stock Eliminator, for all-out professional racing. It is enthusiastically supported by Detroit and by race promoters because it exploits product identification—that is, it backs up the spectator's own choice of a Ford, Chevrolet, Plymouth, etc., for personal everyday use.

The class is limited to American production cars of the

three most recent model years. The category is designed to provide more muscle for the "muscle" cars. The original engine type must be retained as a base, but liberal modifications are permitted so long as the engines burn pump gasoline, are nonsupercharged and use no more than two four-barrel carbu-

Enormous torque of the Dodge Hemi Challenger sends Bill Bagshaw's Pro Stocker, "Red Light Bandit," leaping off the start line. Pair of casters mounted at rear prevents the car from tipping over backward.

retors or four two-barrel carburetors. The steel body shell must be kept, but entrants are allowed to lighten over-all weight by substituting plastic components for the original steel hoods, deck lids and front fenders.

For equitable competition a certain ratio is required—seven pounds over-all weight to each cubic inch of engine displacement. As the minimum weight is 2,700 pounds the engine size works out to 385 cubic inches. That's a lot of engine for such a light car and it means some fast times on the drag strips. A car of 3,500 pounds, which is not unduly heavy, can take a 500-cubic-inch engine, which is a whopping size. A standard 427-inch engine can be stuffed into a car of slightly less than 3,000 pounds. The important thing is that all cars use the same engine-to-weight yardstick.

All entries in a drag meet are designated by code-letter combinations like AA/FD, A/S, A/MP, F/SA, L/S, C/MP,

I/SA and nearly a hundred others. The purpose is to classify the cars into major divisions and sections.

*   *   *

The usual format of a drag meet is competition between pairs of machines on a straight strip of asphalt or concrete. A drag meet is run like a tournament, with winners meeting winners. The tournament-style eliminations are what make it possible to accommodate the hundreds of entries at each meet.

The drag strip is about as wide as a four-lane highway. Beyond the finish line is a shutdown area a half-mile or more in length that provides the driver with enough space to slow his car to manageable speed. A road parallel to the race strip leads back to the staging area and pits. Spectators are protected from runaway cars by rows of steel guard rails, wide grass areas.

Victory is based on elapsed time (abbreviated e.t.), the number of seconds a car needs to run the quarter-mile, which is calculated instantly by electronic timepieces. The paired racers break the beams of photoelectric cells at the start and finish lines, providing precise timing to the thousandth of a second. At the finish line a signal light goes on in one lane or the other to tell the spectator who won.

A drag racer builds up speed as it runs downcourse and it reaches its maximum speed at the finish line. To measure that terminal velocity a speed trap is installed at the end of the drag strip. The trap is 132 feet long, with photoelectric beams positioned 66 feet before and after the finish line. The electronic clocks there provide a reading in miles per hour refined to the nearest hundredth of a mile. That speed is announced over the public address system but only as a gee-whiz point of interest, a conversation piece. It has no bearing on the result—the winner, to repeat, is determined by elapsed time.

The start signal is flashed by a computer-like device called the Christmas Tree, a tall pole installed in the center of the track about 20 feet downcourse from the starting line. The tree carries two vertical panels of white and colored lights, one for each of the paired competitors.

There are nine lights on each panel. The first two are small white bulbs that burn steadily after they light up. The first, called "prestaged," indicates to the driver that his front wheels are getting close to the electronic beam on the starting line. The second, called "staged," signals that the wheels are in precisely the right position. It means don't move any farther!

The next five lights are larger lamps of amber, designed to flash from top to bottom in sequence. When the staged lights of both competitors are burning, the starter presses a button to actuate the sequence of five amber lights. The sequence terminates in either a green light for "Go!" or a red light for "Foul."

Each amber light flashes on a half second after the preceding one, giving the driver a total countdown of 2.5 seconds. The rhythm never varies. Therefore each driver can pace himself to anticipate the green light that follows the five ambers. This takes practice, experience and a delicate sense of timing. If a driver reacts to the green an instant quicker than his opponent, the advantage is his. But if he jumps the green signal (like a New York taxi driver) by so much as a fraction of a second, a red light flashes on instead of the green to signal a foul—and he is disqualified. There is a cruel efficiency to this elimination system, which penalizes anything short of perfection in man and machine. Last week's hero can be this week's bum.

Cars that are evenly matched start "heads up"—that is, the green lights flash on simultaneously. Unevenly matched cars start with handicaps, which means one car gets its green light earlier than the other. This is how the system works: national elapsed-time records are maintained for every car class. The difference between such records determines the handicap. For example: the record quarter mile for Class X may be an e.t.

92

of 11.77 seconds and for Class Y an e.t. of 14.10 seconds. When Class X and Class Y cars meet at the start line the difference of 2.33 seconds is "dialed" into the Christmas Tree computer. The slower car is the first to receive the sequence of amber lights leading to the green light; 2.33 seconds after it gets the green light the green signal goes on for the quicker car.

The first car may take a substantial lead because of its head start, but this usually is equalized as the race progresses toward the finish. When handicaps are stretched to as much as three or four seconds the big excitement in the grandstands is "Will he catch up?" and "Can he hold him off?"

The car running closer to its national record has the better chance to win. Theoretically, if both cars are running right on their national records, they will reach the finish line in a dead heat (it rarely happens). In any case, handicap races are usually thrilling.

Cars are raced in pairs in staccato sequence. The traffic is controlled by experienced track stewards skilled in directing the flow of vehicles out of the staging area, in proper pairs, up to the starting line. This keep-'em-moving traffic direction is impressively efficient, close to show biz.

*   *   *

Some drag meets are run on a "cups or bucks" system in that each contestant chooses whether he will compete for trophies and fun or run for cash and other awards. The competition in the money category, of course, is much stiffer.

Prizes (and money) in a drag meet would not spread very far if they had to be divided among the winners of 100 or more classes. So the practice is to thin out the field in preliminary heats. After the early heats the class winners are clustered into eight brackets called "eliminators." (In drag racing "eliminate" means to beat competitors; the losers are eliminated.) The best machine in each of the eight divisions is called the "top eliminator." Almost invariably the top fuel eliminator is the best in the show.

In National Hot Rod Association racing, four of the categories are grouped as professional eliminators, the other four as sports-racing eliminators. The professional eliminators race heads-up and the others with handicaps.

This is the breakdown:

GROUP I—PROFESSIONAL

TOP FUEL ELIMINATOR

These are the top-of-the-line fuel-burning dragsters, the "rail jobs" or "slingshots," the sport's special breed of acceleration vehicle. For brute power and extravagant performance these big machines are the most spectacular in the show, with e.t.'s of less than seven seconds and speeds in the 225 m.p.h. range. They cost anywhere from $10,000 to $30,000. They are permitted any kind of modifications to engines, drive trains, chassis, etc., as long as they meet safety regulations. They are even permitted to use *two* engines. As their name implies, they use only fuels, the esoteric alcohol blends.

These cars are designated AA/Fuel Dragsters or AA/FD.

At major National Hot Rod Association events the field for this category is made up of the best 32 (in some cases 16 or 8) elapsed-time qualifiers out of all the AA/FD entries.

Top Fuel and Top Gas Eliminators look alike. This one happens to be the Top Gas Eliminator driven by Gordon Collett in the Gatornationals at Gainesville, Fla.

TOP GAS ELIMINATOR

This category, designated AA/GD (for gas dragster), is the same as the top fuel eliminator except that the cars, again "rail jobs" or "slingshots," must use commercial gasoline (contents of the tanks are checked at the end of every run). The tire smoke is not quite so dramatic as the top fuelers' but the acceleration is nearly as breathtaking—these cars can do 200 miles an hour from that standing start.

FUNNY CAR ELIMINATOR

These are highly specialized racing machines, as sophisticated as the fuel dragsters but sheathed in plastic copies of production-car bodies. Almost any kind of modification of engine and suspension is

Not one, but two parachutes are needed to decelerate this Funny Car, a Dodge Ramcharger in the N.H.R.A. Winternationals at Pomona, Calif.

permitted. Funny cars are highly popular among fans and their numbers are increasing. They burn fuel and perform at speeds in the 200 m.p.h. range. Their designation is AA/FC.

Pro Stock Eliminator

This category consists of production-type American automobiles from the three most recent model years. Engine must be of the same manufacture as the car in which it is being used, but internal modifications are permitted. The original steel body shell must be retained, though lightweight components such as hood, fenders and deck lid may be substituted for original pieces. Designation is PRO.

GROUP II—SPORTS-RACING

Competition Eliminator

This category mixes classes of vehicles, including dragsters (of smaller size and less horsepower than the AA/FD and AA/GD),

Competition Eliminator in the Winternationals at Pomona, Calif.

roadsters and coupes built especially for acceleration. They are super-charged gas burners or nonsupercharged fuel burners. Because of the wide range of classes, handicap starts are necessary. At major National Hot Rod Association events, the final field for this category is determined by winners from 14 classes in earlier heats.

Modified Eliminator

These cars, representing the true hot rodder's art, are a mixed bag taken from winners of no fewer than 30 classes in previous heats. They are extensively modified coupes, roadsters and dragsters, along with modified and semi-modified "streetable" vehicles. All must run on gasoline, and no superchargers are permitted. Handicap starts.

Modified Eliminator in the N.H.R.A. Springnationals at Dallas.

Super Stock Eliminator

One of drag racing's most popular competition categories, this is made up of late-model, high-performance production cars commonly known as "muscle" cars. Some modifications to camshafts, manifolds, suspension and other units are permitted. Sixteen classes are included, eight for standard transmissions and eight for automatic transmissions. Handicap starts used because of the wide range of classes.

Stock Eliminator

These cars are the backbone of drag racing, accounting for a large percentage of the sport's annual competition. The category takes in early-model and late-model stock production vehicles generally known as bread-and-butter cars and is open to approximately 35 classes (the

Dave Boertman in a Chevy Stock Eliminator in the Springnationals.

number varies from year to year), equally divided among automatic transmissions and stick shifts. Again, because of the wide range of classes, handicap starts are necessary.

*   *   *

Most of the organized drag racing in North America is governed by the National Hot Rod Association, based in Los Angeles. There are several smaller groups (sometimes called "outlaws"), but the N.H.R.A. is as pre-eminent in its field as USAC and NASCAR are in theirs. It claims jurisdiction over three-fourths of the drag strips in this country and even a few abroad. Besides sanctioning more than 3,000 drag meets a year, it conducts more than 40 meets on its own with a total paid attendance of more than five million and purse postings of $2 million to $3 million, depending on the amount of manufacturers' awards.

The most important N.H.R.A. events are those in what it calls the Super Season, a schedule of annual meets at various places around the country—the Winternationals, Gatornationals, Summernationals, Nationals, Supernationals and World Finals. (Rival promoters try to imitate these names, but N.H.R.A. distinguishes its meets with one-word spellings of Winternationals, Summernationals, etc.)

In addition, the N.H.R.A. conducts an annual World Championship Series, a schedule of 35 points races—five in each of its seven geographical divisions. Winners work their way up to the World Finals to compete for the sport's world titles. The 1970 World Championship Series featured an over-all purse of $600,000.

CHAPTER 5

Grand Prix, Le Mans and All That

GRAND PRIX" is French for "big prize." In Italian and Spanish it is "Gran Premio," in German "Grosser Preis" and in Dutch "Grote Prijs." These are the names given to a program of races in which a small band of men compete for the world driving championship in brightly colored, low-slung race cars.

The fan who takes racing seriously is occasionally put off by the cheapening of the term "Grand Prix" that has come with the inflation of our language. It is not protected by a copyright or trademark, so any promoter can lay on a race for wheelbarrows or any other kind of equipment, for any kind of drivers and at any place he chooses, and call it, grandiloquently, a Grand Prix.

To the faithful, though, there is only one Grand Prix, a format that began in 1906 at Le Mans, in northwestern France. With evolutionary changes it has come down through the years into the modern era. Today's Grand Prix car is the Formula One, an open-wheel racer with a single seat in an open cockpit. This tiny, fragile rear-engine machine can run 190 miles an hour on the straights; it can snarl around a fast course like Spa at an average speed of better than 150 miles an hour. Today's Formula One is the showpiece of the world's most sophisticated

99

motor competition. The Big Prize at the end of the season is the *Championnat du Monde des Conducteurs,* or World Championship of Drivers.

Thus far the racing we have discussed has been almost exclusively American. Beyond these indigenous races are two classic series that touch the United States—the World Championship of Drivers and the world manufacturers' championship, both of which are F.I.A. world (as opposed to regional) titles.

In a limited sense the Grand Prix drivers are comparable to the American golf professionals who compete on the "tour," a geographic sweep of the United States in the course of a season that lasts nearly a year. But the logistics of the drivers' "circus," as some call it, are more complex. They travel farther, to many parts of the world. They travel with teams of as many as 10 men; fairly often the entourage includes wives of the drivers. The teams have to haul, often by air freight, race cars and back-up units, spart parts, tires, tools, trailers. Drivers occasionally shuttle across the Atlantic four times in a week.

The Grand Prix schedule is conducted on three, occasionally four, continents. The number of races varies slightly from year to year but usually there are 11 to 13. For the 1971 season Grand Prix races are scheduled in 11 countries in this sequence: South Africa, Spain, Monaco, the Netherlands, France, Britain, West Germany, Austria, Italy, Canada, the United States.* These races are great national events, endowed with tradition, held at fixed times of the year. Sometimes the crowds number in the hundreds of thousands and the occasion resembles a gigantic outing or carnival.

The first Grand Prix of the United States was held in 1959 at Sebring, Fla., and the second in 1960 at Riverside, Calif.

---

*It is possible that Argentina will be added to the schedule in 1972. Until 1971 the calendar included a Gran Premio de Mexico. However, after the 1970 race the Commission Sportive Internationale lifted the championship status of the Mexican race because of the promoters' inability to control the crowds. If Formula One races are again run in Mexico, they cannot count toward the title until the C.S.I. restores the championship status.

Since 1961 the Grand Prix has been held on the first Sunday of October at Watkins Glen, a congenial park-like venue overlooking Seneca Lake in the Finger Lakes region of upstate New York. Watkins Glen is the cradle of post-war road racing in the United States. As with the G.P.'s of Europe, the patrons come great distances. Most of them are young, from the colleges of northern New York, New England and Canada. To be on hand for the practice sessions and for the race itself, they camp two or three nights inside and outside the grounds. A few are arrested for drunkenness, disorderly conduct, fighting, burning of latrines and general hell-raising. In fact, a temporary magistrate's court is set up each evening in one of the track buildings and the local rent-a-cops haul off the prisoners in rent-a-trucks.

By Sunday morning they are unkempt and untidy and not quite clear in the eye. But most of them are sincere race fans. They would have to be, to endure those chilly autumn nights on the hills above Watkins Glen.

The Grand Prix at Watkins Glen offers one of the richest purses in road racing anywhere in the world—more than $250,000, a quarter of a million dollars, with a first prize of $50,000.

In the World Championship of Drivers the custom is to have one race in each country. But because the United States is so broad and because the potential purses are so enormous, the United States will have two Grand Prix events beginning with the 1972 season. The Commission Sportive Internationale has approved a second G.P., this one for the road course of the new Ontario Motor Speedway in California. Obviously this is far enough away to avoid a geographical conflict with Watkins Glen. And to avoid a date conflict, the California race will be held in the spring.

*   *   *

One of the identifying characteristics of a Grand Prix is the high-pitched scream of a few Matra, Ferrari and BRM V-12's in counterpoint to the coarse, bellowing tenor of a dozen

Ford-Cosworth V-8's. Nearly all the successful Formula One cars now use the basic Ford-Cosworth engine, so in that respect the machines are rather evenly matched. The deciding factors are driving skill and the way a car handles.

Grand Prix racing is quite possibly the most expensive sport on earth. "Nobody ever talks about expense when they're building a racing car engine," Graham Hill wrote some years ago, "and that's probably why they cost such a lot." The lifeblood of Grand Prix racing comes from large companies, mostly European, in and out of the automotive industry. They pour millions of dollars into their race programs and, of course, derive tremendous benefits in the form of advertising, commercial exploitation, publicity and so on. The tire companies also compete ferociously for advantage, subsidizing cars and drivers with seemingly unlimited cash.

Grand Prix racing has produced some unusual men—Juan Manuel Fangio, an Argentinian who won the world championship five times, the first at the age of 40; Stirling Moss, winner of 16 Grand Prix races,* who could read the fine print of a newspaper across the room; Rudolph Caracciola, who delighted in driving at top speed in torrential rain; the late Jim Clark of Scotland, considered by many to have been the best of them all; Jack Brabham, an Australian, won the world championship three times, in 1959, 1960, and 1966. Eleven years after winning his first championship, Brabham was still a formidable competitor, winning the 1970 Grand Prix of South Africa, placing second in the Monaco G.P. and finishing high up in others. He retired at the end of the 1970 season at the age of 44. Graham Hill, world champion in 1962 and 1968, was still competing after his 40th birthday, though a severe injury in the 1969 United States Grand Prix had blunted his effectiveness.

Another unusual aspect of Grand Prix racing is occasionally overlooked: it stands by itself as a truly *international* sport for individuals. The 1970 winners, to illustrate, consisted

---

*But, as with Sam Snead and the United States Open, he never won the world driving championship.

102

of an Australian, an Austrian, a Scot, a Mexican, a Belgian, a Swiss and a Brazilian.

The most successful Grand Prix driver today is Jackie Stewart, a charming, happy and vivacious Scot who has inherited the mantle of his late countryman, Jim Clark. Stewart was a champion trapshooter before he got into racing. Although of limited formal education, he is one of the most articulate and well-informed men on the circuit and a most astute businessman. He reads a great deal and is cultivated in his tastes. He is witty and handsome and is often called the "Mod Scot" because he has the biggest mop of hair in racing and dresses in the most advanced clothes. On the track, when not driving, he wears a black Dutch boy cap that is a sort of trademark. Jackie and his wife, Helen, live well near Geneva in Switzerland, a haven from British tax problems.

Stewart is a perceptive student of racing. "To the extent that Grand Prix racing is a very big business, perhaps even an industry," he said in an interview some time ago, "it must be conducted like a business, especially by those of us who have been fortunate enough to succeed in it.

"Racing is too serious a thing to be taken lightly. I love the sport, but I know all about the money and the safety. I am safety-minded because I love my family. I also go for safety because I want to be in this game as long as possible.

"I have studied every aspect of safety not because I was afraid, but in order to put all the chances on my side. You can't go through life or racing without taking some risks. But your risks must be calculated. If you don't understand that you are a fool."

*   *   *

Grand Prix racing is regarded by many as the pinnacle of driver achievement and for this reason the Grand Prix "circus" is an exceptionally tight community. In all the world there are no more than 25 men or so who are considered qualified to race Formula One machinery. In a typical season the entire roster consists of about 18 regularly assigned drivers from 10 countries and perhaps six or eight independents who pick up occasional rides.

Drivers accumulate points on the basis of their finishing positions in each race:

Position	Points	Position	Points
First	9	Fourth	3
Second	6	Fifth	2
Third	4	Sixth	1

The World Championship of Drivers was organized in its present form in 1950. From then through the 1970 season only 34 drivers had won championship races. Jim Clark and Juan Manuel Fangio won 25 and 24, respectively, and Stirling Moss 16. After them the list trails off. Any driver is distinguished to have won five or six Grand Prix.

Few Americans compete in the Grand Prix, mostly because they do not find the money big enough. American drivers, being the professionals they are, pragmatically race wherever the money is—they would probably race up a wall if it paid enough.

In the decade 1960–69 only four Americans raced regularly in Grand Prix competition—Phil Hill, the 1961 champion and the only Yank to win the title; Dan Gurney, Richie Ginther and Ronnie Bucknum.* Gurney, who ran his own team in the later years, dropped out for financial reasons in 1968; the others had retired earlier. Lately Mario Andretti, three-time winner of the United States Auto Club driving championship, has entered Grand Prix competition.

Grand Prix events are held on road courses only, over distances of 250 to 325 kilometers (155.3 to 201.8 miles). The longest circuit is the 14.2-mile Nürburgring course in the Eifel Mountains of West Germany, so immense that no driver can memorize all its turns. The shortest course is the 1.9-mile route

*Other Americans who raced intermittently include Jim Hall, Lloyd Ruby, Walter Hansgen, Bob Bondurant and Masten Gregory.

in the Principality of Monaco, where Prince Rainier and Princess Grace reign. The Grand Prix of Monaco runs through the streets—or "round the houses," as the British say—of Monte Carlo on a narrow circuit of many gradients and numerous tight turns that cruelly punish car and driver. The driver needs to change gears about every five seconds. The race is so exhausting that it is kept short: it runs only 156 miles.

If Grand Prix racing is regarded as the pinnacle of driver achievement, it also represents the peak of attainment for car builders or *constructeurs*. A Formula One car must be quick and, though quite fragile, it has to be strong enough to finish the race. These machines are light but powerful. They look simple yet they are deceptively difficult to develop to race-winning pitch. The French call them "nervous."

Clay Regazzoni in a Ferrari Formula One car at Le Circuit Mont Tremblant, St. Jovite, Quebec.

What is a Formula One car? Besides being an open-wheel racer with a single seat in an open cockpit, it is built to conform to a "formula" that has been evolving for more than 60 years. The current formula limits engine size to a displacement of 3 liters (183 cubic inches) or, if the engine is supercharged, to 1.5 liters (91.5 cubic inches). But under the challenge of competitive pressure, talented designers have been able to inspire from 425 to 450 horsepower out of that tiny power plant. The high-performance engine, a superb gear box, enormous "doughnut" tires, jewel-like steering and suspension systems—these together make the Formula One car the world's most advanced racing machine.

The formula under which the cars are built is established by the Federation Internationale de l'Automobile. The present formula became effective in 1966 and is not due to be changed, if it is at all, until after the 1972 season.

The rules require a minimum weight of 530 kilograms (1,166 pounds). The car must be equipped with a self-starter and reverse gear to help the driver move out of difficulty after a spinout and a stalled engine. It must have a dual-circuit brake system in which one circuit serves as a safety back-up for the other. The driver must be able to enter or leave without opening or removing panels or doors (though the steering wheel may be removed for this purpose). The car must have a roll bar and anchoring points for the driver's safety harness. It must run on commercially available gasoline carried in a rupture-resistant bladder-like tank.

Some cars have had a chassis and engine of the same make, like Ferrari, BRM and Matra. But in most cases, until a few years ago, the car was a combination of a chassis by one builder and an engine from a manufacturer with whom he had made a deal. Thus there were the Brabham-Repco, Cooper-Maserati, Cooper-BRM, Lotus-BRM.

Since mid-1967, however, one engine has pre-empted the field: the compact, lightweight V-8 of 425 to 450 horsepower designed for Ford of Britain by Keith Duckworth of Cosworth Engineering ("Cosworth" is derived from the names of its two principals, Frank Costin and Keith Duckworth).

The Ford-Cosworth engine, mounted in a variety of cars, was beaten only twice in 1967; it won 11 of its 12 races in 1968, and in 1969 it swept all 11 of the Grand Prix. It was not until 1970 that Ford was effectively challenged by two makes of 12-cylinder engines, and even then Ford won eight of 13 races. Ferrari won four and BRM one.

The Formula One (or F-1) car is slung so low (as in the

case of the Indianapolis racer) that the driver's line of vision is barely above the huge wheels. The body is designed in the shape of a flattened cigar to present a low profile and thus minimum wind resistance. The rear-mounted engine makes a slope snout possible to further reduce the frontal silhouette. The driver half lies, rather than sits, in the narrow cockpit. The cockpit fits so snugly that the driver seems to *wear* the whole car, like a suit of armor. It happens to be a very dangerous suit because it contains the fuel tanks—one on each side of the driver and one above his legs.

For portions of the 1968 and 1969 seasons many Formula One cars carried "wings" or air foils to induce negative lift— that is, to exert a downthrust to enhance the car's adhesion to the road. The foils extended high into the air, sometimes as much as five feet. Some builders mounted them fore and aft. One set-up that Jack Brabham experimented with was so bizarre that Bruce McLaren asked him if he had filed a flight plan. Some of the wings, flimsily mounted on upright rods, tended to fly off and thus were dangerous both to spectators and drivers. The air foils of two cars did fly off in the Grand Prix of Spain on May 4, 1969. Two weeks later, on the eve of the Grand Prix of Monaco, wings were prohibited by the Commission Sportive Internationale. Now Formula One cars are permitted to have a different form of air foil, but it is secured to the chassis.

The most notable development in recent years has been the trend to wider tires, "doughnut" affairs with treads of 15 or 16 inches. These make a better "footprint" on the road and provide a more effective way of transmitting the engine's power to the ground. They also greatly improve the car's cornering ability.

Cars with four-wheel drive were tried briefly, in 1968 and 1969. The improvement in performance was questionable, not enough to offset the problems of added weight and mechanical complexity.

Among the present makes of car are Lotus, BRM (for British Racing Motors), Brabham, March, McLaren and

Tyrrell from Britain; Ferrari and De Tomaso from Italy, and, most recently, Matra-Simca from France.

*   *   *

So much for the Grand Prix, which is essentially a competition for drivers. Manufacturers, too, have a championship of their own for sports cars, prototype sports cars, and special grand touring cars. This championship is nearly as glamorous as the Grand Prix. There are several reasons. For one, it is a prestige competition among factories. For another, many Grand Prix drivers also work in this series. Lastly, its showcase event is run on perhaps the most famous race course in the world—Le Mans. Other races are held on the same European courses where Grand Prix are run. There is also a magnificent mountain race in Sicily, the Targa Florio, and there are three events in the United States—at Daytona Beach, Fla., Sebring, Fla., and Watkins Glen, N.Y.

In French the name of this series is *Championnat Internationale des Marques.* All F.I.A. literature translates this as International Championship for Makes. "For" sounds awkward, especially when "of" would seem to do better. No matter: what is usually used is a more descriptive title, the world manufacturers' championship or variants of that.

There are several ways in which the manufacturers' championship differs from Grand Prix racing but the two most important are these:

(1) Manufacturers' races are endurance events of at least six hours or 1,000 kilometers (620 miles). Each car must have at least two drivers.

(2) The competition is open to what British fans call a mixed bag—prototype sports cars of Group 6, sports cars of Group 5 and special grand touring cars of Group 4. Within this competition there also is an F.I.A. International Cup for special grand touring cars.

All this will be explained shortly, but first a necessary digression: throughout the 1967 series and especially in the races at Le Mans the big beautiful monster prototypes—the 7-liter Fords and Chaparrals and the 4-liter Ferraris—stole the show. For two consecutive years, 1966 and 1967, factory Fords from the United States won at Le Mans. Then a funny thing happened on the way to the Winner's Circle. The Commission Sportive Internationale, strongly influenced by the French, received a hint from the De Gaulle Government and forthwith outlawed the big foreign prototypes by reducing their engine limit to 3 liters. Ostensibly the C.S.I. acted in the interests of safety—those foreign cars were so-o-o-o big for French courses and so-o-o-o fast for Le Mans—but the fact was that the French Government had spent more than $1.5 million subsidizing the development of a 3-liter racing engine for Matra. Cutting the alien infidels down to size was the best way of protecting the new engine from the embarrassment of defeat.

Ford and Ferrari quit endurance racing because they were outraged by the cavalier treatment they had received from the C.S.I. The effect of the 3-liter limitation was to shift the interest in the manufacturers' championship from the prototypes to the 5-liter sports cars.

Factory Fords from the United States never did come back, although subsequently a few outdated British-made Ford GT-40 sports cars did run and win for other teams. Commendatore Enzo Ferrari, having left in a huff, concentrated in 1968 on formula racing. He refused to go to the expense of manufacturing 50 sports cars, which was then the required minimum production. Since the minimum-production figure was reduced to 25 in 1969 he has reappeared in endurance racing with the 512S and 512M sports cars. Porsche also developed some fine

Porsche 917K sports car, winner of the 1971 manufacturers' races at Buenos Aires and Daytona.

cars, notably the 917 and 917K. Porsche won the manufacturers' championship in 1969 and 1970.

As in the case of Grand Prix scoring, standings in the manufacturers championship are determined by the points won in each race—9, 6, 4, 3, 2 and 1 for first through sixth places. The manufacturer is permitted to count only his best position. To illustrate: If Porsche wins the first three places the manufacturer earns only 9 points for first place, and nothing for second and third places. Even so, there is an advantage in placing more than one car high up at the finish. In the example cited above, Porsche denies its rivals the 6 points for second place and the 4 points for third place. Thus:

1—Porsche	9 points
2—Porsche	0 points
3—Porsche	0 points
4—Ferrari	3 points
5—Ford	2 points
6—Matra	1 point

Porsche earns 9 points for first place; nobody wins the 6 points for second place and the 4 points for third place. Ferrari picks up only 3 points for fourth place, which leaves Porsche in a strong position when these results are added to the results of other races.

The rules for the manufacturers championship do not require lovely, faraway place names, but that's how it works out in Europe—Brands Hatch in England; Monza in northern Italy; Spa-Francorchamps in Belgium; the Nürburgring in West Germany; Le Mans in France, and the Targa Florio in Sicily, last of the heroic open-road races. Then there are the endurance races run in this country—24 hours at Daytona Beach, 12 hours at Sebring and six hours at Watkins Glen.

Outside of the club events of the Sports Car Club of America and the stock car programs of the United States Auto Club, Americans seldom see mixed-class races. Endurance races bring together an amazing conglomeration of vehicles—big Ferraris, Porsches and Camaros rubbing hubs with tiny Fiats

A mixed bag at Sebring. Left to right, special grand touring (Corvette); prototype (Matra 650); prototype (Porsche 908), and special grand touring (Corvette).

and Lancias, open cars, closed cars, fast cars, slow cars. The fields in endurance races are large—up to 70 in this country, 55 at Le Mans,* 80 in the Nürburgring and sometimes more than that in Sicily's Targa Florio. To the inexperienced American eye this massing of categories and subcategories is a mishmash comprehensible to few but the rules makers and manufacturers. The purpose of this mix is to provide something for everybody—particularly the manufacturers, who can exploit a "first-in-class" finish.

Granted there is a certain amount of confusion with races within a race and subclasses within classes. But be brave: there is a way of figuring it out with a sort of scorecard. This is how the field is made up:

Prototypes (Group 6)—Maximum displacement 3 liters (183 cubic inches). Examples, Matra-Simca 650 and 660, Alfa Romeo Tipo 33–3, Porsche 908, Ferrari 312P.

Sports cars (Group 5)—Maximum displacement 5 liters (305 cubic inches). Examples, Ferrari 512S, Porsche 917, Ford GT-40, Lola T70.

*Racing in the Vingt-Quatre Heures du Mans is by invitation, and many invitations are reserved for the little French tiddlers that get in the way of the fast cars. They are one of the reasons Le Mans is unnecessarily dangerous.

Special grand touring cars (*Group 4*)—No limit on displacement. Examples, Porsche 911S, Corvette, Shelby GT-350, Ferrari GTB-4.

We come to the first complication—"over 2 liters" and "under 2 liters" in the prototypes and the sports cars. Under F.I.A. rules "under 2 liters" has no standing: championship points are awarded on an over-all basis regardless of engine size. But to get a lot of cars out there on the course, promoters are permitted to fill out the field by offering prizes and bonuses to cars under two liters. This helps build up all those "in-class" victories; it also explains why you see little Datsuns and Volvos out there with the giants at Daytona Beach and Sebring (though not in most European endurance races). In any event, you have what in Automobilese is called placements "over-all" and "in class." Only one car can finish "first over-all," but behind that one you have many combinations like "first in class, fifth over-all," "first in class, ninth over-all," "second in class, sixth over-all" and so on.

Enter now a second complication, also intended to fill out the field. The organizers of a race are permitted to admit the special touring cars of Group 2, even though they are not eligible for championship points. These are the highly modified four-seat sedans like Mustang, Camaro and Javelin (next chapter) with 5-liter engines. But wait: within Group 2 there also are cars with engines of less than 2 liters, like BMW and Alfa Romeo. Again, the purpose is to "stuff the turkey," to give the spectators a big show. Interestingly, the larger Group 2 cars compete well even though they do not earn points. In 1968 at Daytona a Mustang finished fourth over-all behind the three winning Porsche prototypes. In fact, the Mustang and other cars of its class were running in a *Trans-American race* within a race for the International Championship for Makes. Later that year another Trans-American race was run within the 12-hour manufacturers' endurance event at Sebring, where a Camaro finished third over-all. This kind of combination has not since been repeated.

*   *   *

Above, touring cars of over 2 liters engine displacement, in this case a Mustang (foreground) and a Javelin.

Below, touring car of under 2 liters, an Alfa Romeo.

Below, mixed classes in the Twenty-four Hours of Daytona include a Camaro Trans-Am car (right) and a pair of prototypes—Ferrari 312P (left) and Matra 650.

There are a number of other world-famous races and rallies that do not touch the United States but are included here to round out the subject. A rally in the European sense is rather close to being a race in that the contestants are required to adhere to a schedule requiring high speed and usually under rugged conditions.

The International Rally Championship for Makes is made up of eight events including the Monte Carlo Rally and the East Africa Safari. To my mind the latter, which I have reconnoitered, is the greatest of them all—four days and four nights along the bone-jarring, harsh terrain and nonroads of Kenya and Uganda (and sometimes Tanzania). It is a grueling

East Africa Safari Rally: zebras make way for a Datsun.

3,000 miles through mud, potholes and ruts, over mountains and plains, across dry river beds and overflowing creeks past hundreds of thousands of wild animals. The East Africa Safari demands the best of men and machines. It is dangerous—contestants have drowned in flash floods and crashed in the fog of dust created by the cars. Only autos that are especially prepared (at costs running into the thousands of dollars) can survive this ordeal. The field varies from 90 to 100. About a dozen or less make it to the finish line.

Japan is second only to the United States in the production of motor vehicles, and Japanese children are growing up completely oriented to cars. It is easy to see why Japanese motor racing is developing international stature. The major event is the Japan Grand Prix in October for Group 7 sports-racing cars. Competitors in the Japan Grand Prix come from all over Asia. Another popular format is the "Tasman" race in May for the open-wheel formula cars that run earlier in the year in the Tasman Series of New Zealand and Australia. In addition, Japan has an extensive stock car racing program, with winners being invited, expenses paid, to race at Daytona International Speedway in Florida.

Only mad dogs and Englishmen, in Noel Coward's old song, go out in the midday sun. To bring Coward up to date add the 25 or 30 race drivers who run the Macao Grand Prix in the 95-degree heat of a humid afternoon in November. Macao, a 400-year–old Portuguese trading post, is an incongruous dot on the coast of Communist China, tolerated for reasons known only to Peking.

The Macao Grand Prix attracts entrants (usually wealthy weekend warriors who also come for a spot of gambling) from Hong Kong, Japan, Australia, Malaysia, Singapore, Thailand and Indonesia. It brings together nine or ten classes of automobiles—fendered sedans and sports cars mixed with open-wheel formula machines. Such combinations are unheard of in the United States.

Another remarkable aspect of the Macao Grand Prix is that the course is astonishingly similar to the Monte Carlo circuit where the Grand Prix of Monaco runs. There are seaside straights from which the careless can plunge into the sea. There are hills, hairpin turns, narrow streets and wide streets. Even the names recall Monte Carlo—Fishermen's Bend, Statue Corner, Reservoir Bend, Moorish Hill, Maternity Bend.

It is in keeping with Macao's cloak-and-dagger tradition

that a Lotus Elan that has been running in the Grand Prix there is owned by 15 associates of the United States Central Intelligence Agency. The shareholders, most of whom are based in Taiwan, are employes of Air America, a C.I.A. airline.

Below China, in Southern Asia, is Thailand. To its usual impassable roads and nonroads add bandits, Communist terrorists, land mines, armed contestants, piles of vegetables by the roadside, impenetrable dust, water buffalo and a prince or two for a touch of class. Now you have some of the components of the 'Round Thailand Rally, a rugged workout of 1,460 miles and 37 hours that may soon rate an international listing. The 'Round Thailand, new in 1969, offers a course that is not so formidable as, say, the East Africa Safari. But in what other rally might you get into a fire-fight with bandits or be ambushed by terrorists?

No more than 40 per cent of the route is hard-surfaced. About half is of laterite, a composition of red earth and ground stone that is mucky after rain and dusty in dry weather. Perhaps 10 per cent of the route follows no road at all and consists of lava flow, dry river beds, bush and the like. Some nonroads appear on maps as highways. But then, as they say, that's Asia.

The Tasman Series, named after the sea that separates New Zealand and Australia, is a miniature Grand Prix circuit modeled on the European classic. In years past the organizers used to pay enormous appearance fees to lustrous drivers like Jackie Stewart, Chris Amon, Graham Hill, the late Bruce McLaren and the late Jim Clark. Recently, however, the Tasman has decided to drop the expensive star system for a more straightforward competition between New Zealand and Australian drivers. A few Americans are invited but hardly subsidized: they receive a minimum guarantee, enough to cover travel expenses, and from there on they are expected to earn their money by winning it. The cars used are Formula 5000, nearly identical with those we call Formula A in this country.*

*The main difference is that Formula A cars are permitted to use fuel injection. Abroad, in Formula 5000, carburetors are required.

Races of the Tasman Series in New Zealand and Australia could not get off to a proper start without appropriate fanfare. Here, the pre-race ceremonies at Mount Maunganui, New Zealand.

The Tasman, which has always enjoyed a glamorous perch in motor racing, consists of seven races—four in New Zealand and three in Australia, each with a purse of about $18,000, which for Australia and New Zealand racing is good.

In the face of India's desperate economic condition, motor sports there have a low priority. But despite the obstacles, Indian enthusiasts have set up a strenuous cross-country rally of, they hope, international standards. The All-India Rally, running 1,375 miles through 12 of India's 14 states, uses narrow and poorly surfaced roads that probably are the world's most crowded—not only with trucks, buses and bicycles but with thousands of sheep, goats, cattle, ox carts, dogs and pedestrians, none of whom are willing to relinquish the right of way.

A few years ago I covered a Grand Prix, so called, in a park in Belgrade, Yugoslavia, where there is, surprisingly, a great deal of interest in motor racing. The competition was for small sedans—the European Touring Car Championship for Group 2 cars—and the drivers came from all over Western Europe. They, too, traveled in a "circus" like the Grand Prix drivers, moving from one country to another for their scheduled races.

117

The organization of the Belgrade event would have chilled American promoters: no crowd control to speak of, with spectators lining the edges of the unguarded roadway, free to dash across or to straighten hay bales when needed. At the end of the race, as soon as the checkered flag was given to the leading two or three cars, the crowd broke ranks—this with 15 vehicles still on the way in.

American fans are spoiled, relatively speaking, with programs, car identifications, background data, driver biographies, lap-speed conversion tables, seats—all that pampering. None of that in Belgrade. The fans are content to watch the cars whiz by, with no information provided on the progress of the race and never mind who's leading. After all, there's no admission charge.

As for concessions, every right-thinking, red-blooded American promoter counts on making a buck or even $1.10 from his straw-filled hamburgers. In Belgrade some little entrepreneur has a friend drive him to the race course with a few cases of super-sweet Yugoslav pop. At about 6 or 7 cents a bottle, the supply sells out within an hour, and the profit is his alone. That would make them shudder at Indianapolis or Daytona.

The Grand Prix of Belgrade, for small Group 2 sedans, is run in a public park. Admission is free.

CHAPTER 6

An early road race, this one in 1950, at Watkins Glen. George Weaver's Grand Prix Maserati R-1, known as "Poison Lil," leads a Bugatti 50 aloft and over the tracks.

"Ben Hur
With Gear Changes"—
Professional Road Racing
and the S.C.C.A.

T HE LATE Wilbur Shaw, a great race driver who turned to promotion in his later years, attended the first road race in 1948 at Watkins Glen, N.Y. What he saw appalled his oval-track mind. "All those people," he said, "and no admission charge. It's murder!"

You can be sure things have changed since then. Road racing in the United States commands an intensely enthusiastic following happy to buy tickets. It is a sophisticated crowd, affluent and well educated. These people are rather cosmopolitan and they have a certain breadth of view that you won't find at, say, a USAC or NASCAR event (no white socks, either).

Road racing is the specialty of the Sports Car Club of America, and its members are considered relatively European in outlook. As Chris Economaki, the resident sage of the American racing press, puts it, "They're leery of anything west of Brest." The European orientation is understandable. For one thing, most sports cars are manufactured in Europe. The specifications are in European terms—engine displacement, for example, is measured in cubic centimeters. Most of the tradition of road racing is European. Its over-all ambience is European. Drivers from Europe campaign in S.C.C.A. professional events.

The club is the only voice of American sports car racing in international councils. Finally, its rules originated with the type of regulations employed by the F.I.A. (really Royal Automobile Club), although the S.C.C.A. has Americanized them.

Women participate in road racing, something that is unthinkable in USAC and NASCAR—at nearly all the tracks of those organizations, with minor exceptions, women are not even permitted to enter the pit areas. In S.C.C.A. racing some women are drivers and a few are qualified mechanics. Many wives and girl friends of drivers work in the pits, keeping lap times or lap charts or just looking decorative. Others help out in the scoring shack and do signal work on the course.

Aside from the participants, road racing seems to attract more women spectators than any other racing format. And indisputably the participants and spectators are the most beautiful birds in the world of motor sports, dressed imaginatively and often audaciously. In contrast, the women spectators at USAC and NASCAR events seem to be wearing burlap.

The fans of road racing find it exciting, colorful, even romantic. It has the oldest tradition in motor competition. It recalls names like Nuvolari, Fangio, Moss, Clark. It conjures up associations with Le Mans, the Targa Florio, the Nürburgring. The venues of road racing in this country are more congenial than oval tracks—park-like settings such as Road

120

America in Wisconsin, Lime Rock in Connecticut and Watkins Glen in upstate New York, the deserts of Riverside and Laguna Seca in California, the seaside dunes of Bridgehampton (so much like the Zandvoort course in the Netherlands) and the lake country around Donnybrooke in Minnesota. And across the border in Canada there is Le Circuit Mont Tremblant with its Laurentian Mountains backdrop.

Road racing, which has been characterized as "Ben Hur with gear changes," is, to repeat, the special domain of the Sports Car Club of America. More than 90 percent of this country's road racing, professional as well as amateur, is held under S.C.C.A. sanction. The club, a nonprofit organization of more than 18,000 members (the number varies from year to year), describes itself as "the only national American racing organization that concentrates on the type of automobile competition traditional elsewhere in the world."

The club asserts that it conducts more races than any other single racing organization on earth—each year about 300 weekends of racing throughout the country, with a weekend program including six to 20 races. Most of these are "amateur" programs where the attendance is sparse or where, to save money on insurance costs, spectators are not admitted at all. The professional races, however, boast a respectable total attendance of more than one million.

Much S.C.C.A. literature emphasizes that the club is a member-oriented organization dedicated to the "needs and pleasures" of its membership. The connotation is one of amateurism, of surgeons and housewives and engineers racing Alfas, Porches and Triumphs on Saturday afternoons at Lime Rock or rallying over the weekend through the California countryside or running a gymkhana Sunday morning at the A. & P. parking lot. All quite true, but the larger fact is that most of the nationwide attention the S.C.C.A. attracts is based on the *professional* competition it has been sanctioning since 1962. In effect the club is schizoid. One side consists of the dues-paying members. The other side is a highly sophisticated department, built up over a fair bit of member resistance, that is up to its velocity stacks in a multimillion-dollar professional racing business. If the Sports Car Club of America had not staked out professional road racing as its own turf, some other organization would have moved in and probably not managed it so competently. The S.C.C.A. is justifiably proud of its program of professional racing, worked out under the leadership of James E. Kaser (he left the club in 1970 to form his own racing-related company). It is based on a schedule of 35 or so races that pay out close to $2 million a year in purses and prizes. The club sanctions three series of professional races, each consisting of 10 to 14 events held throughout the United States and Canada.* Those series are:

THE CANADIAN-AMERICAN CHALLENGE CUP, better known as the Can-Am, which ranks with the fastest road racing in the world. The Can-Am, begun in 1966, has been enormously successful in attendance, purses and prestige. The machines that run in the Can-Am are designated Group 7 sports-racing cars, two-seaters with no limitations on engine size and few restrictions on anything else. They are beautifully sculptured, raucous monsters that generate adrenalin among race fans. They also represent the best of show biz in motor racing.

The Can-Am is a competition for drivers, with purses, prizes and accessory awards totaling nearly $1 million a season. Seven of the races are usually run in the United States and three in Canada. They range from 150 to 200 miles in length.

THE TRANS-AMERICAN CHAMPIONSHIP, known as the Trans-Am, for the sports sedans or "pony cars" such as Mustang, Camaro, Javelin, Barracuda, Challenger and Firebird, with engines of up to 5 liters displacement. There is a separate class open to smaller sedans, mostly European, with engines of under 2.5 liters (abbreviated U-2.5 to distinguish them from the larger Trans-Am cars). The Trans-American Championship

*The Sports Car Club of America maintains a close relationship with its opposite number to the north, the Canadian Automobile Sport Clubs. When races that are part of S.C.C.A. series are run in Canada, the sanction there is issued by the Canadian Automobile Sport Clubs. The leadership of this alliance, though, is entirely American. For all practical purposes the S.C.C.A. writes the rules and negotiates the deals.

is a competition for manufacturers rather than drivers. Although the cash awards are secondary to the promotional advantages of winning, a Trans-Am race does carry a minimum purse of $25,000 ($20,000 for the sports sedans and $5,000 for the small sedans), and this is supplemented by several thousand dollars' worth of accessory prizes. Of the 11 Trans-Am races in the 1970 season, 10 were conducted in the United States and one in Canada. The duration of Trans-Am races ranges from $1\frac{3}{4}$ hours to $2\frac{1}{2}$ hours for the larger cars; for the small sedans the usual length is one hour.

THE CONTINENTAL CHAMPIONSHIP, open to single-seat, open-wheel cars known as Formulas A, B and C, with major attention on Formula A (also known as Formula A/5000). This relatively new competition for drivers has quickly caught on in popularity. At the start of the 1971 season the series was renamed the L&M Championship after its sponsor, a cigarette manufacturer.

The rules tend to equalize the capabilities of the cars and thus place the premium on driving skill. When victories in 13 races are spread among seven drivers, when four cars finish within 60 seconds of the winner, then you have the kind of competition the fans like. As my colleague Pete Lyons says, "Good racing is when you don't know who'll win."

For the 1970 season purses and awards of the Continental totaled close to $400,000. Ten of the races were run in the United States, three in Canada. Races for the Formula A cars are usually 90 to 100 miles long. The smaller B's and C's, which race together, run about half that distance.

The S.C.C.A. also represents ACCUS in the two world-championship series that visit this country. This involves sanctioning four races—the Grand Prix of the United States and three of the endurance races that make up the world manufacturers championship. The Grand Prix is the most important, partly because it is one of the units of the World Championship of Drivers and partly because of its enormous purse—$250,000. This race is run on the first Sunday of October at Watkins Glen. (The Commission Sportive Internationale has approved, beginning in 1972, another Grand Prix in this country, at Ontario Motor Speedway in California.) The endurance races are the Twenty-four Hours of Daytona, the Twelve Hours of Sebring and the Six Hours of Watkins Glen.

*   *   *

From the late 1890's to the 1920's American racing was run on both road courses and oval tracks. But road racing disappeared soon after World War I because of the danger to drivers and spectators, because the public resented the temporary closing of roads and because there was no practicable way of charging admission. Racing moved almost completely to fairgrounds horse tracks, usually a half-mile or a mile in length. The stars of the day included Barney Oldfield and Eddie Rickenbacker.

At the fairgrounds spectators could be charged admission and could see the whole race from a grandstand. With promoters pushing oval tracks, a generation or more of Americans grew up with the impression that a car could only turn left and had only one gear.

Road racing was revived after World War II with races on the streets of Watkins Glen and Bridgehampton, N.Y., and around Pebble Beach, Calif. Again it ran into the formidable problem of safety. In 1952–54 the Strategic Air Command of the United States Air Force gave road racing a considerable boost by making available SAC bases on which road circuits could be laid out with rubber pylons and hay bales. Such improvised courses were far from perfect, but one body of opinion believes that the airport courses saved road racing from interruption and possibly extinction. The races are reported to have been major promotions with creditable attendance even by today's standards.

More important, those years provided enough time to start construction of real road courses. A few courses still exist on nongovernment airports but they are now outclassed by nearly 40 enclosed and permanent circuits built explicitly for road

124

racing. The specially built courses simulate country roads with turns and grades but without the trees and utility poles. They are privately owned and represent real estate investments in the tens of millions of dollars. A road course can be any length the designer wishes; most American courses are 1.5 to 4 miles long.

The appeal of road racing is its challenge and variety, the demand it makes on a driver's skill and intelligence. Road courses are like golf courses: no two are alike and each has its own personality.

Road courses provide left *and* right turns, ranging from shallow arcs and "esses" to 180-degree buttonhooks. Courses also climb and dip with the terrain, and some elevation changes can be abrupt and hairy. At the Nürburgring in West Germany there are perhaps 20 crests where a Formula One car completely leaves the ground. At Bridgehampton the front straight ends in a drop-off that suggests a take-off from an aircraft carrier.

In a road race each driver works out his own "groove" or "line," the path through the circuit that is the fastest possible one for him and his car. In doing this he approaches as closely as he can the theoretically ideal path for a given car under given conditions, such as weather, condition of the road surface and so on.

In racing language turns are called "corners." Speeds through the corners can vary anywhere from 20 to 120 miles an hour—each corner has a theoretical maximum speed at which a given type of car can go through it. Almost always the driver takes the corners in a power slide or drift, a delicately controlled maneuver in which the car seems to be moving slightly crabwise, within inches ("the racer's edge") of losing adhesion with the road.

"In slow, out fast" is the general rule, The driver has to keep in mind his position and speed, the condition of his car and the surrounding traffic as he exits a corner so that he is properly "set up" or "in shape" for the next turn. And he does this lap after lap after lap, never daring to let his concentration falter. Changing gears more than 20 times each lap is not unusual. Courses that are long and twisty require even more gear changes.

Drivers race one another, to be sure, but they also race against the course, working to shave off a tenth of a second here and another tenth there for better lap time—and a lead on the opposition.

To drive well requires the greatest of skill but it also demands a special kind of car. The machine has to be very responsive, with tremendous acceleration and braking power. Tires and suspension are designed to give it great road-holding ability. It must have a gear box that enables the engine to operate at maximum efficiency for every speed demanded by the course. Of the specific cars used in road racing, those that run in the professional series of the S.C.C.A. rank with the most important:

CAN-AM

The Canadian-American Challenge Cup is open to two-seat racing cars designated Group 7 in Appendix J of the International Sporting Code of the Federation Internationale de l'Automobile. The Can-Am represents exquisite refinement of the Group 7 car. It is the fastest road-racing machine in existence, with no limitations on engine size, body contours, over-all dimensions, size of tires and wheels, drive-train specifications or total weight. For convenience a Group 7 machine is usually called a sports-racing car, with a hyphen or slash (/), to distinguish it from the F.I.A.'s Group 5 sports car (Appendix B).

Because of Group 7's freedom from restrictions, designers are not encumbered by established conceptual axioms; they work in a realm beyond the ultimate reaches of previous formulas and each design represents an individual way of thinking. It is this latitude that has attracted the best brains in race car design—men such as Robin Herd (March and earlier McLarens), the late Bruce McLaren* (McLaren), Jim Hall (Chap-

* Bruce McLaren, a brilliant car builder and driver, was killed June 2, 1970, while testing one of his Can-Am cars at Goodwood, England. McLaren, a New Zealander, was 32 years old.

126

Denis Hulme in the McLaren-Chevrolet in which he won his second Canadian-American Challenge Cup championship.

arral), Eric Broadley (Lola), Len Terry (Eagle) and the anonymous geniuses in the Porsche and Ferrari works. These men and others have produced the most sophisticated designs ever seen in road racing, exotically sculptured art forms that streak along the straights in a blur of color and sound at 200 miles an hour. Without much exertion these cars can accelerate from a standing stop to 100 miles an hour and return to a complete stop *within 10 seconds*. At 7,000 r.p.m. the McLaren-modified Chevrolet engine pushes the McLaren M8D up to 110 miles an hour in low gear, 140 in second, 175 in third and more than 200 in top.

The Chevrolet V-8 is the dominant engine. A few favored teams like McLaren and Chaparral receive the most advanced designs of aluminum-block power plants of 465 cubic inches and more, to which they add fuel injection and other improvements. For public-relations purposes and possibly to avoid antitrust and other difficulties with the Government, General Motors professes to have nothing to do with racing—this despite the prevalence in the Can-Am cars of those extraordinary V-8's (you cannot buy them from your friendly neighborhood dealer). General Motors' ambiguous position in racing is a standing joke in the racing community. "I'd like to thank General Motors for making all this possible," Bruce McLaren once said at an awards dinner, "but they'd only say they didn't know what I was talking about."

Although the McLaren, Chaparral, Lola, Eagle, Ferrari, March and Porsche cars differ in their details, they do have some common characteristics. To begin with, the chassis is made of aluminum-magnesium alloy or other metals that are exceptionally light, like titanium. The body shell is of light-weight fiberglass. The chassis has great torsional rigidity to increase road holding. There is independent suspension all around.

The cars usually have ventilated disc brakes and four-speed or five-speed Hewland gear boxes, manufactured in England. (Hall has used a modified automatic transmission.) The "dough-nut" tires may run 18 to 20 inches wide at the rear. The cars weigh about 1,500 pounds. When they are pushed by engines of 700 horsepower that works out to about one horsepower for each two pounds.

Each car has a low-slung body of aerodynamic contour, with a ground clearance of three to five inches.

The best Group 7 cars—McLaren, Lola, Ferrari and modi-fied Porsches—are manufactured in Europe but seldom run there in road races (though there are excellent Group 7 cars that compete in European hill climbs). The formula was written for the F.I.A. by the Sports Car Club of America.

In this fiercely competitive field a designer may come out with one element, one component, that makes the rest of the field obsolete—or forces it to follow suit. Jim Hall developed the air foil for the Can-Am, which caused a revolution (it is now restricted for safety reasons). Hall is a pioneer in many other phases of race-car aerodynamics, including spoilers, div-ing planes, air exits and body shapes. He is the only race-car builder to use automatic transmission successfully and he was among the first to build fiberglass bodies.

In 1970 Hall introduced his "vacuum cleaner" car—the Chaparral 2J, a so-called ground-effect vehicle that holds to the road more securely than a car equipped simply with an air foil. The rear of the car is a box-like enclosure; two auxiliary fans (powered by a separate snowmobile engine) draw air from the enclosure. This action creates a partial vacuum within the box.

128

Jim Hall's innovative Chaparral 2J, the "Vacuum Cleaner," in its first Can-Am race at Watkins Glen. The driver is Jackie Stewart, 1969 world champion.

The atmospheric pressure outside the car, being greater than the pressure inside the car, exerts a "downforce" on the car. Hall found this downforce gave the car great stability, enhancing its handling in the corners and increasing its braking capability. By the end of 1970 the Chaparral 2J had become academic. Responding to protests by Hall's competitors—especially the McLaren racing team—the Commission Sportive Internationale declared the car illegal because it violated the rules governing movable aerodynamic devices.*

Bruce McLaren's team swept the Can-Am championships of 1967, 1968, 1969 and 1970 many months before each of those seasons began: his planning was that flawless. Also, being so well financed by Goodyear, Gulf, Chevrolet and Reynolds Aluminum, McLaren was able to test when his competitors were still scrambling to build their cars.

TRANS-AM

The cars that run the Trans-American Championship for manufacturers are small sedans with a maximum wheelbase of 116 inches and an engine displacement of no more than 305 cubic inches (5,000 cc).

The cars are divided into two classes, "over 2.5 liters" and

---

*At its annual meeting in January, 1971, the United States Auto Club also rejected the ground-effect vehicle. In this case, though, the ruling was against a proposal on paper rather than against a car already built at great expense.

Trans-Am race at Mid-Ohio Sports Car Course. The lead car, No. 16, is a Mustang driven by George Follmer. Others are a Javelin, with Mark Donohue driving, and Swede Savage's Barracuda.

"under 2.5 liters." The larger cars include Camaro (Chevrolet), Mustang (Ford), Javelin (American Motors), Barracuda (Plymouth), Challenger (Dodge) and Firebird (Pontiac). The small sedans include Alfa Romeo, BMW, Renault, English Ford and Fiat from Europe, Datsun and Toyota from Japan, and the Chevrolet Vega 2300 and Ford Pinto from the United States.

The production rule of this series was designed in the hope that the public would consider these machines not pure race cars but vehicles available for general sale. Therefore the manufacturer is required to produce 2,500 units within a 12-month period or a quantity equivalent to 1/250th of the production in the preceding year, whichever is greater. In practice this means American Motors needs to produce only 2,500 Javelins to be eligible. Chevrolet, a much larger manufacturer, is required to produce 8,200 Camaros.

Despite the production rule, the Trans-Am Javelin that Mark Donohue races is not really available at the corner store.

What is available is the *basic* car that the team starts with and converts into an all-out race car. The governing word is "preparation." By the time the team manager finishes "preparing" the car and a specialty shop finishes "preparing" the engine, you are a long way from the showroom model.

To "prepare" means to transform an automobile from its original "stock" design into a race car. The pioneering technology in car preparation was developed by NASCAR competitors. Their methods have been taken over by technicians in S.C.C.A. competition with certain modifications and refinements. The preparation of the over-2.5-liter Trans-American sedans is very much the same as the work done on the NASCAR machines discussed in Chapter 3.

It takes about three months to prepare a unit to be a racer and the cost comes to $20,000 to $25,000. This does not include the couple of spare engines the team must keep on hand, which cost approximately $5,000 to $6,000 apiece.

Start with the engine. Its factory-made skeleton—that is, the block and some basic components—is usually sent to a specialty shop for a process called "blueprinting." In this process the mechanics take the manufacturers' specifications and then produce an engine far superior to any that the manufacturer can turn out on the assembly line.

Almost every part is the "same," yet different. That is, pistons, valves, cams and crankshafts are of the same dimensions but of infinitely better finished quality.

Actually there is so much latitude in practice that the mechanics go beyond blueprinting—beyond the manufacturers' original specs. It is necessary to follow only the general configuration and valve layout of the original design. From there on the mechanics can modify the cylinder heads and install special manifolds, cams, valve gear, pistons, crankshafts, beefed-up pushrods and the like. And not only are there engine specialists in this business; there are specialists *within* engine specialization, such as camshaft men and crankshaft men. When all these experts are through with an engine, it puts out more than twice the horsepower.

Why doesn't the S.C.C.A. require *genuine* production engines in Trans-Am racing? The answer is that stock passenger car engines would break up at racing speed. Racers need those forged crankshafts and pistons, special oiling systems and so on just to keep the engine in one piece.

While the engine is being converted into a racing power plant, the preparation of the body and chassis is proceeding. The basic Detroit body-and-chassis unit is rebuilt for two reasons: to make the car safe for racing and to make certain it goes where the driver steers it.

The separation between a conventional passenger vehicle and a racer begins in the factory, where a car body is pulled at random from the assembly line.

At this point the car is known as a "body in white"—it is not even painted yet but is in its natural metal color. It is essentially just a body on a chassis—it has no engine, no wheels, no suspension parts and not much of anything else. The interior is utterly bare.

The body in white is sent to the racing shop for special preparation. Often enough the preparation begins with a sly bit of cheating: the body is dipped in an acid bath or subjected to some similar process to thin the metal and thus reduce the weight. Another trick is to substitute thin glass in the windshield.

As for the legal work, the biggest job is installation of the roll cage, a sort of frame within a frame that surrounds the driver. It is made of 0.090-inch seamless steel tubing and is welded to the frame, padded with foam rubber.

The roll cage is a life saver. In a wreck the sheet metal of a car may break up and fly apart but the cage holds together. A safety harness anchors the driver to the cage, so that even if the car flips, his body does not hit the steering wheel, gearshift lever or anything else inside the vehicle. It is the roll cage that prevents the car from being mashed into a ball.

A Trans-Am sedan is at least 10 times safer than a production car. Every structural member is beefed up, rewelded, reinforced—torsion bar, sway bar, shock absorbers, suspension parts, spindles, wheels, tie rods, linkage and so on. The team mechanics install the suspension parts, racing wheels and tires, a bucket seat, interior panels and other items that make the car operable and competitive. They also reshape the stock fenders to provide clearance for the racing tires. They add an oil cooler and certain engine accessories.

A car that bounces at high speed cannot be controlled. The entire suspension system is reworked to keep the car level and stiff to offset centrifugal forces encountered on high-speed turns. The system must also withstand the pounding and stresses of a race. To stay on the ground a race car needs rear springs of four to ten leaves (depending on track conditions) in place of the standard seven-leaf spring. Up front, heavy-duty coil springs—different ones for each course—will be installed to vary the spring rate. Shock absorbers are used in various light, medium and heavy combinations, again in relation to track conditions.

Wheels are replaced by sturdier ones with 8-inch rims, mounted with racing tires nearly a foot wide. Heavy-duty disc brakes are installed. The standard axle is replaced by a "full floating" axle. The main advantage is safety: the half-shafts cannot pull out in the event a wheel comes off or comes loose.

Racing-quality gauges are installed and so is an automatic fire extinguisher. The precautions against fire include a safety fuel cell, whose design prevents gasoline from sloshing or spilling and retains the fuel in case of an accident. Even if the car flips over on its back, a ball-shape check valve prevents gasoline from spewing out. A metal bulkhead between the cockpit and the rear gas tank protects the driver against injury from a fire; the bulkhead also adds to body strength.

Batteries are moved to the trunk for better weight distribution. Doors are bolted shut. Safety clips are installed on the windshield, rear window, hood and trunk. Hub caps and headlights are removed. A few finishing touches—a plastic jar and tube are installed so that the driver can sip water, iced tea or fruit juice during the heat of the race. And now, with a big numeral, some gaudy paint work and an acre of advertising decals, the Trans-Am "stock" car is ready to go racing.

There are not many differences in the preparation of a Trans-Am machine and a NASCAR Grand National car, and those differences are minor. In NASCAR preparation a sturdy bar is installed under the length of the car to provide a solid anchor for the driver's specially contoured seat and harness. In addition, wheels have rims of $9\frac{1}{2}$ rather than 8 inches. In Trans-Am cars standard glass is retained. In NASCAR's Grand National cars extra-strong shatterproof glass goes into the windshield and rear window and the side windows are removed altogether and replaced with heavy fabric screens.

Grand National and Trans-Am cars can mount a small spoiler beneath the front end even though the commercially sold counterpart is not equipped with one. The bucket seat of a Grand National has an accessory not seen in the Trans-Am. This is a head rest on the right side. The reason is that in NASCAR races on oval tracks all the turns are left turns and centrifugal force tends to push the driver's head to the right side. Since his head is already weighted with a heavy helmet it takes strong muscular effort to keep it where it should be, and the head rest helps. Also, bucket seats in Grand Nationals are braced on the right side, again to help the driver withstand centrifugal force. But for all practical purposes the way a Grand National car is created is nearly identical with the preparation of an S.C.C.A. Trans-Am machine.

CONTINENTAL

The Continental is open to "formula" cars. These are machines built to S.C.C.A. specifications—or formula—for the class in which they will compete. The largest are the Formula A's, the smaller ones are Formulas B and C. The A's race by themselves. The B's and C's race together as a combined category that produces its own driving champion.

The big A's attract the major share of attention because they make good sense as a sports spectacle and a financial investment. They are dramatic, noisy and fast. And since they

Continental Formula A/5000 cars at St. Jovite. George Follmer in a Lotus 70-Ford leads Gregg Young in a McLaren M10B-Chevrolet.

use stock-block engines and are limited to a small gasoline tank capacity, the lid is kept on costs. Occasionally these cars are called Formula A/5000 in recognition of the limit on engine size, 5,000 cubic centimeters (305 cubic inches).

In appearance the Formula A car is a hybrid of the classic Formula One car of the international Grand Prix and the "Indy" car of the Indianapolis 500. It has open wheels*—that is, no fenders—and it has a single seat in an open cockpit. The most distinctive characteristic of the Formula A car is its air foil, a wing mounted at the rear. The purpose of the air foil is to exert negative lift and thus increase a car's adhesion to the road surface.

One particular power plant, almost universally used, exemplifies American thinking—the big-bore engine manufactured in mass numbers. Certain restrictions are imposed to keep down costs. The engine must be produced in quantities of at least 1,000 a year. It must be "stock block," which means its valves are actuated by conventional pushrods rather than overhead cams. The block and cylinder heads must be retained, the camshaft may not be relocated, the number of main bearings may not be altered, and supercharging is prohibited. How-

---

* Open-wheel racing is comparatively dangerous because there is always the possibility that wheels of adjacent cars will come into contact. When that happens the overtaking car may vault over the other machine or either car may lose a wheel, spin out, roll over and so on.

135

ever, the entrant may substitute his choice of pistons, connecting rods, valve gear, crankshaft, clutch, flywheel, induction system (usually fuel injection) and exhaust system. With such modifications the Chevrolet engines that dominate the Continental series produce approximately 500 horsepower.

The car must weigh at least 1,350 pounds. Fuel capacity is limited to 30 gallons and the fuel must be commercial pump gasoline. The car must have an on-board starter and a dual-brake system and is limited to two-wheel drive. Virtually all the A's use English-made Hewland gear boxes.

In addition to the 5,000 cc. stock-block engine from the approved list that is used by most of the field, two types of "unrestricted" engines are eligible. Both are exactly from Formula One. The first is the standard Grand Prix, an all-out racing engine (overhead cams and so on) with a displacement of up to 3000 cc. (3 liters). The second is permitted to have a supercharger provided the piston displacement is 1,500 cc. (1.5 liters) or less—again, just as in Formula One. Cars powered by these unrestricted engines must weigh at least 1,105 pounds. Their fuel-tank capacity is limited to 26 gallons.

Formulas B and C cars are similar in appearance to the A's but smaller. The B car must weigh at least 848 pounds and permissible engine displacement ranges from 1,101 to 1,600 cc. To keep out highly sophisticated and expensive power plants, the S.C.C.A. has a limited list of Formula B engines that it will approve. The 1971 list consisted of Lotus-Ford 1600 twin-cam, Alfa Romeo 1600 twin-cam (including the GTA), Porsche pushrod 1582, Datsun 1600 SOHC, BMW 1600 DOHC, Ford 1500 pushrod, Ford 1600 pushrod, Fiat 124 DOHC.

Formula C cars, weighing a minimum of 750 pounds, use engines of up to 1,100 cc. displacement.

Formulas B and C prohibit supercharging.

CHAPTER 7

When Is an Amateur?

T IME WAS when it was valid to define an amateur as an athlete who did not accept his prizes in money—or, as it was expressed from a less charitable viewpoint, who did not accept checks. There were variations from one sport to another, but in general there was a true relationship between the unpaid athlete and the root of the word "amateur"—to love. The athlete who loved a sport for its own sake, who competed for no more than fun and a trophy—this was an amateur.

Now the meaning is considerably blurred in many sports, in motor racing as much as any other. The American Road Race of Champions, conducted each November by the Sports Car Club of America, is conventionally regarded as an "amateur" show, a national run-off bringing together more than 400

137

points leaders who have qualified in 60 "national" races in the seven geographic divisions of the S.C.C.A.

There are no purses in the American Road Race of Champions. "No purses" implies amateur. But are they really all amateurs, these stockbrokers, artists, lawyers, lab technicians, secretaries and businessmen? Not really. Some are factory-team drivers who are paid a fee, salary or retainer to compete in the run-off and the preceding national races because the manufacturers of sports cars and small sedans want very much to come out with winners that they can exploit in their advertising.

If you happen to be driving independently an Alfa Romeo, MG, Triumph, Datsun, Formula Ford or Volkswagen Formula Vee or Super Vee, you may also win a "support" prize from one of those manufacturers. There are thousands of dollars' worth of "contingency" prizes—that is, the manufacturer of a lubricant, additive, spark plug or whatever will pay you a prize if you win while using his product. (That's what those funny decals are all about.)

But no one earns much money from contingency or support prizes, either at the American Road Race of Champions or at any of the 60 national races leading up to it. What every "amateur" driver hopes for is to win a few dollars here and there to help defray his costs in this forbiddingly expensive hobby.

The S.C.C.A. gave up trying to enforce "rules" of amateurism in 1962. As things stand now, any "nonprofessional" or "semi-pro" who is qualified on the basis of ability is free to enter purely professional races like those of the Canadian-American Challenge Cup, where the purses and prizes are large enough to attract the world's best full-time race drivers. Thus the S.C.C.A. no longer distinguishes between professional and amateur drivers. It does distinguish between professional and amateur events.

At the other extreme there is nothing to prevent such professional drivers as Mark Donohue, Sam Posey, Peter Revson or George Follmer from competing in a weekend S.C.C.A. national race where no purse is offered.

A semantic problem has plagued the S.C.C.A. In 1968 the club, in a major reorganization, set up a department of "professional racing"—no problem there in characterizing the Can-Am, say, or the Trans-American Championship. But what of the S.C.C.A.'s nonprofessional department? The S.C.C.A. settled for the phrase "club racing." Those "club" races are not simon-pure—there are those contingency prizes and that support money. But then the club races are not professional, either, on the scale of a Can-Am. Club events range from the lower-keyed races for club members to the highly commercialized American Road Race of Champions.

The phrase "club racing" doesn't solve all the difficulties of definition but it has helped solve a problem. There was noticeable box office resistance when spectators were asked to pay to watch "amateur" racing. Calling this competition "club racing" has made a substantial difference.

*　　*　　*

The Lord loved amateurs—He made so many of them. And however they may be defined we shall always have them with us. Although the growth of professionalism in the Sports Car Club of America has imposed some strains, the organization continues to affirm that it is a member-oriented association whose basic policy is to "emphasize, sanction and conduct national and regional automotive sports events to satisfy the needs and pleasures of its members." About 5,500 of those 18,000 members hold special competition licenses issued by the club under expert and rigid supervision.

Some disenchanted members have argued in club meetings and in motor-sports publications that they are being neglected by the S.C.C.A. for the sake of the club's professional program. But the fact is that the S.C.C.A., with the help and supervision of member-volunteers, conducts 300 weekends of racing throughout the year at 90 sites all over the country. Since a weekend consists of six to 20 races, the total number of events is well over 2,000.

In addition, the club and its 105 regional units conduct 70 or so schools for race drivers, considered the best training program in the racing world. They also conduct rallies big and small, including a national championship; field trials; auto shows, *concours d'élégance,* hill climbs, gymkhanas, tours and "other activities centered around the automobile."

This extraordinary schedule is carried out by unpaid volunteers who are experts in technical inspection, timing, scoring, officiating, signal work and communications, even medicine. They can lay on anything from a modest parking-lot autocross to the Grand Prix of the United States. They work club races and they work all those professional road races that happen to run in their geographical region.

The weekend club races are divided into two types—approximately 130 "regionals" for drivers of limited competitive experience and a series of 60 "national" races in which more advanced drivers compete for points. Good racing and spirited competition can be seen in the national races. Leading drivers in the nationals qualify for the run-off in November, the American Road Race of Champions. Altogether those 400 points leaders drive 22 classes of cars. The American Road Race of Champions has alternated between Riverside, Calif., and Daytona Beach, Fla., but the S.C.C.A. now plans to run it consistently on the Road Atlanta course in Georgia.

*   *   *

How does a beginning driver acquire and sharpen his ability for this kind of competition? The program of driver training and club racing offers an opportunity to acquire experience. An aspiring driver must be 21 years old, must be in top physical condition and must be a member of the S.C.C.A. (It also helps if he has a car.)

He is required to attend at least two of the 70 or so S.C.C.A.-conducted drivers' schools, logging at least six hours of on-track instruction from qualified senior drivers. If he passes the stringent examination, he receives a novice permit that

140

allows him to compete in local races under observation. If he shows proficiency, he may then earn a regional license, and eventually a national license for higher levels of competition.

What about the cars used in S.C.C.A. racing? The variety is extraordinary, close to 200 models and types. Nearly 40 manufacturers are represented in the production-sports-car category alone. Nearly all sports cars are imported, so that owner-drivers are at least 2,500 miles away from the manufacturers. These are conditions that impose problems unknown in European racing and they are dealt with in a complex manner designed to provide the maximum competition in a sport carried on for fun while protecting the owners' investments.

The most active categories of competition are production sports cars and sports-racing cars. Altogether, the General Competition Rules of the S.C.C.A. set up seven categories:

An instructor explains the signal flags at a drivers' school at Bridgehampton (N.Y.) Race Circuit.

1. PRODUCTION

These are the conventional familiar sports cars seen on the streets and adaptable to racing—Sprite, Corvette, Triumph, Porsche, Jaguar, Datsun and so on, plus a few limited-production cars like Lotus and Cobra. The rules allow certain modifications and optional equipment that improve performance; but in permitting modification the major emphasis is on changes that enhance safety, reliability and handling.

The S.C.C.A. has a system by which, in fairness to competitors, it grades production sports cars not by engine size but on the basis of their lap-speed potential. This system of performance rating makes racing more equitable because it recognizes the fact that two cars of equal engine size—say a 3-liter Austin-Healey and a 3-liter Ferrari—do not have the same potential. The premium is placed on driver ability rather than on the ability to buy the newest and most expensive machinery. Cars are not handicapped because of obsolescence. They simply move from one class to another as they age or are succeeded by faster models of the same make. As a result, it is not unusual for cars that have been out of production for 10 years to continue to be highly competitive. This performance-rating system is unique; it makes "S.C.C.A. Production" the greatest used-car racing category in the world.

The club's ratings are revised toward the end of the year in light of the season's experience. Currently there are 180 models in eight classes designated A through H. Cars are conspicuously marked for a race with two letters and a number. In 15 BP, for example, the 15 identifies the entrant on the program and the BP means a class B Production car.

Classes are usually mixed to offer a more interesting program and save time. With D Production, E Production and F Production mingled on the same circuit, the cars are competing for class victories. Think of it this way: you have a race in which there are horses (D Production), greyhounds (E Production) and cheetahs (F Production). The horses race one another for victory in their class; similarly, the greyhounds are racing for

A pack of F Production cars bunches up in a turn during an S.C.C.A. regional race at San Luis Obispo, Calif.

a greyhound prize and the cheetahs are racing for a win in the cheetah class. So now you have three races running simultaneously on the same course.

But there is one more race going on. This one is for the "over-all" victory—that is, one of those beasts will win not only in his class but will beat all the others for an "over-all" victory. An animal running sixth over-all may be leading its class; a faster animal running fourth over-all may be only fourth in *its* class. Thus this hypothetical finish:

1—Cheetah	first in class	first over-all
2—Cheetah	second in class	second over-all
3—Cheetah	third in class	third over-all
4—Cheetah	fourth in class	fourth over-all
5—Horse	first in class	fifth over-all
6—Greyhound	first in class	sixth over-all
7—Horse	second in class	seventh over-all
8—Greyhound	second in class	eighth over-all
9—Greyhound	third in class	ninth over-all
10—Horse	third in class	tenth over-all
11—Greyhound	fourth in class	eleventh over-all
12—Horse	fourth in class	twelfth over-all

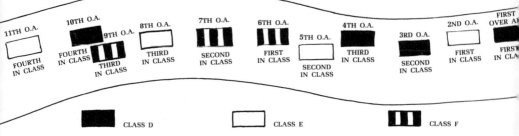

CLASS D	CLASS E	CLASS F

Another way of illustrating three races within a race.

Ordinarily the over-all victory is no big deal. On form and on the averages of previous performances, it is logical to expect one class to beat the others. It becomes impressive if one of the lesser competitors surprises everyone by winning first over-all—if, in the example preceding, one of the greyhounds beats all the cheetahs and horses.

2. SPORTS-RACING

These are the glamour cars of club racing. Although their thin disguise includes such conventional components as passenger seats, doors and fenders, they are intended for nothing but racing. The fastest can reach 200 miles an hour on a 3,000-foot straight. Sports-racing cars fall into the Group 7 category of the F.I.A.'s Appendix J. They are similar to the cars that run the Canadian-American Challenge Cup series, though in club racing there is a broader range based on engine size. Class A is unrestricted, just like the Can-Am car. The engine-size limits of the other classes are: Class B, 2,000 cc.; Class C, 1,300 cc.; Class D. 850 cc.

Most of the larger sports-racing cars use American V-8 engines in chassis built by specialty companies abroad (McLaren, Lola) or in the United States (Chaparral, Genie, McKee). Ferrari provides its own engines. Some of the larger cars are hand-me-downs, bought at bargain prices after a season or two in the Can-Am. Many of the smaller ones are backyard specials.

144

3. SEDAN

These are mass-produced cars similar to F.I.A. Group 2 (see Appendix B at the back of the book). In some cases they are the same as the sedans that run the professional Trans-American Championship Series, though the breakdown by engine size is more refined:

Class A—2,501–5,000 cc.   Class C—1,001–1,300 cc.
Class B—1,301–2,500 cc.   Class D—Below 1,000 cc.

The larger cars include Camaro, Mustang, Cougar, Dart, Barracuda, Javelin. The smaller ones include Alfa Romeo GTA, Lotus-Cortina-Ford, BMW, Volvo, NSU, Renault, Mini-Cooper, Abarth.

4. FORMULA S.C.C.A.

These cars are the same as those that run in the professional Continental Series (preceding chapter), outright open-wheel racers with a single seat in an open cockpit. Formulas A, B and C resemble the international Formulas One, Two and Three with one notable addition. Besides the 3-liter Formula One engine of unrestricted design, Formula A also includes cars with the 5-liter stock-block engine. In fact, the 5-liter engines predominate.

5. FORMULA VEE

These are the sprightly single-seat, open-wheel cars based on the components and 1,192 cc. engines of the Volkswagen. Modifications are limited, most of them relating to safety and durability. Minimum weight 825 pounds; wheelbase 81.5–83.5 inches.

Formula Vee cars, an American invention, constitute the largest racing class extant. They are popular among amateurs because they are inexpensive to buy and prepare. With so few modifications permitted, the pay-off is on driver skill and car preparation. Another reason for their popularity is that they give novice drivers an opportunity to learn racing before going on to bigger engines.

The only trouble is that Volkswagen stopped selling the 1,192 cc. engine here in 1965. This means second-hand engines normally used in racers have all but disappeared from the market, even from the junkyards. Since 1969 VW has been producing engines of 1,600 cc. for sale in the United States. In recognition of these facts of life the S.C.C.A. created in 1969 the Formula Super Vee, which began racing in 1970.

6. FORMULA SUPER VEE

This new formula takes advantage of the fact that thousands of 1,600 cc. VW engines are available. Super Vee rules are more liberal than the Vee regulations, which means better performance. The existing Formula Vee class is left unchanged by the adoption of the Super Vee class, and support programs for both classes are provided by Volkswagen of America.

7. FORMULA F

Here is another new S.C.C.A. class—it began in 1969—for open-wheel racers with a single seat in an open cockpit. It is based on the internationally successful Formula Ford, using an English Ford Cortina 1,600 cc. engine under strict engine-preparation rules. Chassis construction is relatively unrestricted.

A Kaimann Super Vee, built in Austria by one of the pioneer Formula Vee constructors. Powered by a 1,600cc. Volkswagen engine, it has a top speed in the 140 m.p.h. range.

CHAPTER 8

Fun and Games

A Corvair Bandito, classified as a two-wheel-drive buggy, running the Baja 500.

*T*HE ROADS of Baja California, the remote peninsula region of northwestern Mexico, "are still as they were in the Year One after the creation of the world." That is what a Jesuit missionary reported more than 200 years ago and there has been little perceptible improvement since then. The twisted, rutted path of what is wistfully called "the main route" virtually disappears into soft sand or rocky foothills. Of the roughly 1,000 miles between Ensenada, a resort near the United States border, and La Paz, at the southern end, about 670 are among the most forbidding in North America—sandy stream beds, volcanic rock, chuck holes, stones, torrid desert with grades as steep as 40 degrees. This wretched route, beyond insult, denies passage to all but the strongest vehicles—and men.

So here is this bone-jarring, car-crunching trail where 15

miles an hour in some stretches is reckless speed, and what do you suppose they do with it? They run a race on it. Not just a sociable scramble among a half-dozen friends but an exercise in mass masochism—more than 250 teams of two men, each team willing to pay a $250 entry fee. The entries are not necessarily "cars" but "vehicles"—motorcycles, buggies, four-wheel-drive machines, light trucks and even specially prepared passenger automobiles, all competing over the inhospitable terrain.

This is called off-road racing, a relatively new enterprise that is part sport and mostly business. Manufacturers of buggies, motorcycles, tires and other automotive products are in off-road racing to cash in on the popularity of off-road vehicles. While amateurs compete for adventure and fun, professionals race to publicize the companies with which they are affiliated.

The major organization in this field in the National Off Road Racing Association, known as NORRA and based at Woodland Hills, Calif. NORRA is not a sanctioning body in the conventional sense; rather, it promotes races. Its big race, usually run in October or November, is called the Mexican 1000, though the distance from Ensenada to La Paz may vary. Competitors are free to choose their own routes (even beaches), provided they check in at eight combination control points and fuel stops. Beginning at 6 A.M. on the first day, the vehicles take off at one-minute intervals from Ensenada. The winners are the contestants who cover the distance in the lowest elapsed time. Elapsed times range from 21 to 30 hours or more, depending on the type of vehicle.

Anything can happen in a Mexican 1000 and usually does. In one race a Volvo-powered Burro, having lost its left front wheel in an accident, was driven the final 60 miles on three wheels. The transmission of a Volkswagen buggy, jarred out of position, was recoupled to the engine with a chain. One contestant, exhausted after 24 hours of pounding, fell asleep in the co-driver's seat without having his seat belt fastened. What woke him was finding himself rolling in the gravel—he had been thrown from his buggy at 50 miles an hour.

148

There is almost no habitation and there are no road signs, so getting lost is an occupational hazard, which is why the drivers wear wrist compasses. The uniform for the occasion is a sheath of dust, a day's growth of beard and bloodshot eyes. From a reconnaissance plane it is easy to spot a racer, be it a buggy, motorcycle or production car. Who else would be down there in that impossible terrain?

NORRA runs a companion race in the spring, the Baja 500, which starts and finishes at Ensenada. The reason that victory in the Mexican 1000 and Baja 500 is so important is not the paltry cash purses but the promotional advantages. There are eight classes of competition: (1) stock cars, (2) light trucks, (3) production buggies, (4) experimental two-wheel-drive vehicles, (5) production four-wheel-drive vehicles, (6) experimental four-wheel-drive vehicles, (7) motorcycles with engines of less than 250 cc. and (8) motorcycles with engines of more than 250 cc.

Each of the class winners can advertise that his entry "won" the Mexican 1000 or Baja 500. This arrangement is convenient for manufacturers of buggies and other vehicles and the hundreds of "four-wheel-drive" shops capitalizing on the popularity of off-road vehicles in the Western United States.

Off-road racing for fun began in the early 1960's and serious professional racing about 1966. To the outside world the most prevalent off-road racer is known as the "dune" buggy, usually based on the shortened chassis of a standard Volkswagen. Within off-road racing, however, the word "dune" is dropped as too restrictive. The homemade bucket of bolts still exists but is outgunned by sophisticated and expensive all-out racing machines.

The professionals treat off-road racing as a serious business. More than 100 light aircraft following the action in the Mexican 1000 are there to support the factory teams on the ground. They carry spare parts and mechanics for service at any of the eight airstrips used as checkpoints.

The high stakes involved in promotional advantages make the competition quite strenuous, and the attrition rate is ex-

Motorcycles are comfortably at home in off-road racing. This one is running the Mint 400 in the Nevada desert near Las Vegas.

ceptionally severe. Less than one-half the starters make it to La Paz within the 50 hours required to qualify as finishers.

Motorcycles find the race a piece of cake. They are swift and agile. Because motorcycles have been in the off-road business for generations, racing know-how is an inheritance of the bike riders. A motorcycle frequently is the over-all winner.

Aside from the Mexican 1000 and the Baja 500, shorter races are run in the deserts of California, Nevada and Utah by other racing organizations, which are developing programs of short-course spectator events. The most successful is the Mint 400, in the area around Las Vegas. Again, as in the long-distance races, these events are highly commercial, with manu-facturers competing vigorously for promotional advantage. This is why big-name drivers and show-biz personalities are so often part of the package.

*   *   *

From one extreme to another—desert runs to ice racing. When it snows in a big city like New York the authorities urge people not to drive. In Canada and New England and other regions of the northern United States where snow is a way of life, enthusiasts race on ice. In Canada, championship ice races are feature attractions of the annual carnivals that brighten the winter months. One ice race I covered in Quebec attracted more than 25,000 spectators (admission was free). Purses are either modest of nonexistent. Why, then, would anyone go out of his way to compete on ice? The answer is that it is exhilarating. Why would a spectator risk frostbite? To see a live demonstration of skill and split-second timing in retaining control on a glassy surface.

Most ice races are organized by car clubs as amateur events and are comparable to the summertime club racing programs. The best racing is with tires embedded with hundreds of sharp metal studs one-fourth of an inch in diameter and protruding five-sixteenths of an inch. With studded tires, cars can approach 100 miles an hour on a straight. Races are also run, of course, for cars with nonstudded tires.

Ice races are not so dangerous as they might seem. For

Ice races are one of the more popular features of the winter carnivals in Canada. This race is being run on the Plains of Abraham, a municipal park in Quebec City.

one thing, they are usually run on frozen lakes and rivers or on the frozen surface of a field where there are no trees, utility poles and fences to strike. Whatever contact there is between the cars is usually a glancing blow because the vehicles slide away from the impact.

The route of an ice race can be delineated with bulldozed snowbanks or rubber pylons. An ice course is laid out much the same as a road course in ordinary racing—shallow turns to encourage speed and acute ones to slow the cars to 10 or 15 miles an hour. Would you believe straightaway speeds of more than 90 miles an hour and lap speeds of better than 60 miles an hour—a mile a minute—on ice?

A race is especially good when cars run in closely packed bunches. A cluster in a tight corner looks like a slow-motion ballet as the drivers weave and bob from side to side in search of traction. They provide plenty of action as they fight to get clear of the pack and out in front.

The cars that do well in ice racing are those with engines and drive at the same end—for example, a Volkswagen with its rear engine and rear drive or a Mini Cooper S, a tiny British car with all its works at the front end. The Saab, a Swedish car with front engine and front-wheel drive, is in a class by itself. Cars are not so elaborately prepared as they are in other kinds of racing. It is feasible to run one's everyday car in an ice race and even without studded tires.

Skillful driving is more important than good machinery. On the ice direction control is maintained with steering wheel and throttle, with a minimum of braking. You aim the car into a corner, correcting the skid with opposite lock on the steering wheel and a slight backing off on the throttle. If you feel you can handle a bit more slide, you apply more throttle.

Motorcycles also race on ice, and on oval tracks as well as road layouts. Like the automobiles, they use studded tires. The surprising thing is that lap times on an iced-over dirt track can be a second or so quicker than they are on the same oval in the summertime. On the straight of a half-mile oval the bikes can do 80 or 85 miles an hour.

Each rider uses his well-shod left foot as an outrigger to keep from tipping over. Even so, it is hard to see what prevents the machine, on the icy surface, from sliding out from under him. Visibility is also difficult because the leading cycles churn up snow that forms a wall of haze in front of the following machines.

Motorcycle races use a fair amount of the drafting and slingshot techniques familiar in stock-car racing. The bike races are short, seldom more than five laps. The idea is to keep the field from spreading out too much. Also, it's c-c-c-c-cold out there.

*   *   *

Here is the rippling Batten Kill River, still unsullied, one of the most gracious brown-trout streams in the Northeast. Herds of Holsteins graze in rolling pastures. An occasional mountain meadow relieves the solidity of slopes covered with millions of sugar maples. Here is one of Vermont's summer-torpid villages, Manchester, with white houses of classic New England design and sidewalk passages of marble. Above all this towers Mount Equinox, at 3,835 feet one of the highest mountains in southern New England, providing unhindered panoramas of the Green Mountains of Vermont, the White Mountains of New Hampshire, the Berkshires of Massachusetts, the Adirondacks of New York. In this bucolic serenity one weekend a year . . .

Vroom, vroom, VAR-O-O-O-O-M!

The alien presence is the annual hill climb, a motor-sports format that deserves more popularity than it now enjoys. Nearly 50 cars, ranging from Sprites to a couple of throaty Group 7 Lola-Chevrolet sports-racing cars, charge up the two-lane macadam road of Mount Equinox at two-minute intervals, racing against the clock. The course runs for 5.2 of the trickiest miles in any type of racing, with 41 turns, nine switchbacks (hairpins) and an elevation increase of 3,140 feet. To one making a reconnaissance run in a race car with an expert driver much of the course seems a blur of greenery and scenery, a screech of tires clawing sideways, a constantly changing engine whine as the revs climb and drop with each change of gears, a stench of oil and burning rubber. And the driver is constantly aware of places with a 1,500-foot drop into oblivion. The helmet is only token protection.

Variety? There is one straight, a gently graded plateau called The Saddle, where the big cars do 120 miles an hour. The steeper switchbacks call for low gear at no more than 15 to 20 miles an hour. The calculator cranks out an awesome figure. The record average speed for Mount Equinox is 75.241 miles an hour, set by John V. N. Meyer, a wealthy Long Island real estate man who has been running in club races for more than 20 years. He seems to win the Equinox Hill Climb about once every two years, which explains why he is called Mr. Equinox. If the phrase didn't sound so awkward, Jack Meyer might also be called Mr. Giant's Despair, for he is also a five-time winner of that hill climb at Wilkes-Barre, Pa.

The main thing in hill climbing is to know the course. "You could bring Denny Hulme in his McLaren," says Meyer, "and in the first two runs I could beat him. But after he's learned the course, he could easily clobber me."

Learning a hill is not as simple as learning, say, the road course at Lime Rock. On a road course the driver has a few hours' practice. Not so on a hill, where practice is limited because the cars run one at a time against the clock. The best competitors are those who have run the same hill 10 years, 15 years.

Virtually all the contestants have competition-prepared cars that they run in conventional road races. Good tires, made of a sticky compound for maximum adhesion, are a must. Hill-climb drivers use the stickiest compounds they can buy, even though they don't last long. The driver shifts gears as little as possible to save fractions of seconds. The car best suited to a hill climb is rear-engined. This configuration places weight over the drive wheels and lightens the front end, making steering easier.

Hill climbs are a major organized sport in Europe, highly

154

professional.* The sport is popular in the United States but has not kept pace with road racing. Equinox and Giant's Despair are two of the better known venues for hill climbs sanctioned by the Sports Car Club of America. There are dozens of others, from coast to coast. Important hill climbs are listed in the competition calendar of the S.C.C.A.'s monthly magazine, Sports Car.

* * *

Rallying in the United States is a sort of tour requiring precise navigation based on unfamiliar written clues given contestants only a few minutes before the start of the event. Its enthusiasts describe it as "over the river and through the woods to Grandmother's house when you don't know the way and you don't know when you're expected, but you must be there on time."

A rally uses public roads and highways. Under no circumstances do the rally instructions ever require contestants to violate speed limits.† A rally can be a simple, low-key affair for a few hours on a Sunday afternoon, like 75 miles from the shopping-center parking lot and back, or it can be an intense 500-mile competition of championship caliber, run for two days. Some serious rallies also include night portions. One of the most rugged rallies on the S.C.C.A. calendar is the annual Press On Regardless, which runs four *nights* over 1,200 miles of logging trails and other nonroads in the Lower Peninsula of Michigan. It is scheduled in the late fall, when the weather brings rain, snow and fog. This is the one American rally that comes close to the European style—that is, a high-speed test of car durability and driver skill.

Rallying requires a two-member team or crew, which often consists of a married couple. One member drives, the other navigates. Beginners run "unequipped," or "by the seat of the

---

* In the United States there is only one professional hill climb of any consequence—Pikes Peak, a USAC event usually held on or close to Independence Day.
† European rallying is quite different—it is more like a race, requiring high speeds in navigating from one check point to another. It is highly commercial, with factory teams dominating the competition.

A well equipped rally car carries precise odometers and time pieces and special lights. Many also carry computers.

pants." The more earnest rallyists invest hundreds of dollars, possibly thousands, on such equipment as computers, calculators, precise odometers that measure distance to the hundredths of a mile, special radios for minute-by-minute time signals.

Off the road the rally is folksy. Most contestants know one another from previous rallies. For a two-day event the host club may even provide baby sitters for competitors who bring their children. Very often rallyists take along their pet dogs and cats.

There are two objectives in a rally: to stay on course (usually the driver's job) and to maintain a specified schedule (the navigator's job). What makes the schedule so difficult to maintain is holding the average speeds stipulated from one point to another. They change in the instructions with disconcerting frequency.

The rallyists run legs of varying length from one control point to the next. The function of the control points, anywhere from five to 35 of them, is to record the rallyists' time on each leg. Their positions are rarely divulged in advance. You come around a bend on a country road and there you find three or four control-point workers (they're always volunteers) sitting

156

at a bridge table in the shade of a tree. You must reach this unannounced check point at exactly the "official" time specified for the leg. You are penalized one point for each hundredth of a minute you are early or late, or 100 points a minute up to a maximum time specified by the rallymaster, which may be as much as five minutes (500 points). Assume the maximum permitted is five minutes; if you are early or late by more than $1\frac{1}{2}$ times that maximum—in this case seven and one-half minutes—you are considered to have missed the checkpoint altogether. In that event you are penalized 750 points. If you get hopelessly lost and never do find the checkpoint at all, the penalty still is 750 points. In a good rally against expert competition, missing a control is enough to knock you out of contention.

The stylized route instructions are terse and depend on understood abbreviations. In quoting from a road sign the rallymaster may use "RIP" for "reading in part." "CAST 27" means "change average speed to 27 miles an hour." Clues for turns and speed changes may be landmarks, buildings, cemeteries, fountains; more often they come from signs beside or near the road. The signs may be high or low, left or right, but they must be sufficiently large and reasonably positioned to be read from a moving car. The signs may be road markers, warnings, street names, distance markers, trade names on barns, advertisements, signs for real estate developments, signs in front of houses (Beware the Dog or Philip's Folly), signs for pizza palaces—anything.

Usually the rallymaster extracts a significant word or two from a sign and capitalizes the selection. For example, from "Fresh Eggs Sold Here" he may write in the instructions: "Turn right at EGGS."

Rallying is based on decimal measurements. Miles are divided into hundredths. Minutes are divided not into seconds but into hundredths. Thus, "20 hun" means 20/100 of a minute. Rallyists' clocks are calibrated in hundredths. In one championship rally, right after the lunch stop on a hot Saturday afternoon, the rallymaster had slipped in "pause .50 hun at

CANAAN 6." No fewer than 48 of the 64 teams competing were caught napping. They erroneously read the instruction as 50/100 of a minute, or 30 seconds, and that was how long they paused at that distance marker six miles from New Canaan. What they overlooked was the decimal point: it actually made the pause 50/100 of 1/100 of a minute. That worked out to 1/200 of a minute, or less than ¼ of a second. To the teams who recognized the trap, the "pause" was insignificant, and they kept moving. But the 48 teams who sat there for 30 seconds built up a penalty of 50 points (at the rate of 100 points a minute).

Another exercise is counting correctly, as in this sequence of instructions: "(27) CAST 50 at the first PASS; (28) CAST 42 at the second PASS."

Simple? Not really. You must remember that no instruction, unless explicitly excepted, carries over into the next one. In effect, once you complete an instruction you must obliterate it from your mind and take up the next instruction as an entity in itself. The inattentive rallyist changes average speed to 50 miles an hour at a sign that says "Do Not Pass." And at the next such sign he slows down to 42.

Wrong! He must complete Instruction 27, which is a change of speed. Then he must consider Instruction 28 as *another* instruction, a self-contained unit having nothing to do with Instruction 27. What Instruction 28 tells him to do is to look for *two* signs that contain the word "pass" and to change average speed at the *second of those two signs*. So, although Instruction 28 refers to the "second" PASS, the car must have gone by *three* such signs (one in Instruction 27 and two in Instruction 28) for the rallyist to be correct. An error here, of course, throws off the average speed and the car reaches the control point late.

Occasionally words are used to trap a contestant, as in "CAST 44 at the second MAIN ROAD." An unwary team goes looking for two main roads. But that's not what the instruction says. It tells the crew to change average speed not at a certain main road but at *the second of two signs* containing the words "main road." In this case these signs happened to be arrow signs several miles from the main road, so naturally an error affected the average speed of the leg.

And then there are percentage changes. The route instructions have you toddling along at, say, 34 miles an hour. At the twin mail boxes you are told to "increase speed by 10%." That increase is 3.4 miles an hour, raising the average speed to 37.4 miles an hour.

Farther along the road, after an intervening distraction or two, you pass a cemetery gate where you are instructed to "decrease speed by 10%." The instinct is to drop back to the previous 34 miles an hour. But no: the requirement is 10 per cent less than the 37.4 miles an hour, which works out to a new speed of 33.66.

One of the most important persons involved in a rally is the rallymaster, a member of the host club. If the event is to be of championship caliber—that is, one counting for points toward the S.C.C.A.'s national rallying championship—the rallymaster and a few of his friends may spend all their weekends for six months or so reconnoitering thousands of miles of road, selecting likely stretches, compiling notes on them (signs, turns, landmarks, surface) and measuring distances over and over with accurate odometers. If the rallymaster surveys a given stretch in late winter, he must remember that it will look quite different at rally time in July. Almost always the roads chosen are back roads—both for esthetic reasons and to avoid traffic-laden highways where average speeds could be fouled up. The rallymaster has to be dead certain his information is valid for the day of the rally—it would be a small disaster if a "For Sale" sign were removed a day or two before the event—and so he surveys it right up to the last morning.

He has to be absolutely certain of his distance measurements, for otherwise he surely will catch hell from some very sharp competitors. All average speeds must be computed so that no speed limits need be exceeded. And finally the rallymaster must write instructions that make it possible to follow the course. You follow the course with words, not road maps. In fact, road maps are useless on rallies because they do not show the minute detail that rally instructions cover.

The philosophy of a good rallymaster is to run a contest among the entrants, not a battle of wits between himself and the rallyists. Clues may be laconic or cryptic. They contain traps for the unwary because that's what rallying is all about. But the good rallymaster writes instructions that are fair. "Route instructions are not intended to be ambiguous, confusing or misleading," said the general instructions of a Berkshire rally that I recall, but are "intended to keep you on the official rally course, if adhered to exactly." There's the rub: "if adhered to exactly." In a way the rallyist has to brainwash himself of preconceptions and do only what the instructions say—nothing more, nothing less.

During the running of a championship rally the rally-master, who has spent all those months setting it up, hangs around at one of the check points or at the lunch stop, haggard from loss of sleep, unshaven and wearing a worried look. He wins no money or trophies for his efforts. His only reward is praise from the teams who have competed in his rally. If he has done a good job—instructions that are challenging but fair, interesting back roads, beautiful countryside—the competitors compliment him the way dinner guests congratulate their host: "Great rally, Nick . . . Very smooth . . . Just perfect! Neat exercise . . . You're a fink, Nick, but we love you."

*　　*　　*

There are no crowds, no banners, no armbands. The cars that the participants whip through the event are in most cases the same ones they drive every day except for a set of racing tires that is needed for these weekend meets.

This is a gymkhana, also known in various parts of the country as an autocross or slalom. It is a contest in which automobiles are maneuvered through a short course of turns and gates delineated by rubber traffic pylons. Runs are timed to the thousandth of a second, which is why this sport demands precision more than speed. A car well driven suggests the per-

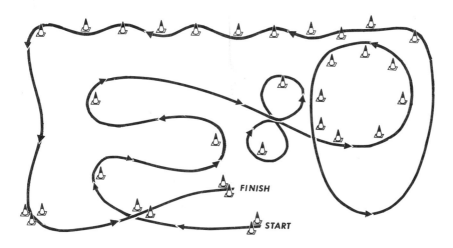

FINISH

START

formance of a perfectly schooled riding horse. When a driver is very good, in exquisite control, his run may be considered artistic.

But the important thing is that everyone has fun. Of course there are serious gymkhanas counting toward championship of various sorts. But most of the Sunday afternoon meets on the supermarket parking lot are modest affairs conducted by local car clubs with lots of camaraderie, swapping of driving tips, kibitzing the timekeepers, chucking the chins of one another's babies and dogs—that sort of thing.

A typical course, about 3,000 feet long, is illustrated above. It is relatively "open" to facilitate quick times. The course includes a figure 8, a 1,000-foot slalom, a 160-foot circle and an extremely tight corner with two gates.

The figure 8 is a spectacular maneuver. The driver bears down on the pylon rather fast, usually in second gear. He brakes hard, downshifts, locks the steering wheel to the left. The idea is to pivot around the cone with the front end of the car, controlling the slide of the rear end by delicate use of the throttle. Having spun the first pylon, the driver circles the next cone with a right turn and then dashes out toward the next test.

The slalom is very much like the slalom of skiing—a row of pylons set in a straight line. The slalom illustrated here is fast because the cones are set comparatively far apart. The

161

slalom can also be made "slow" by placing the cones closer together. In either case the expert drivers clear them by about two inches as they weave in and out between them.

When the pylons of a slalom are evenly spaced, the driver establishes a rhythm. But some gymkhana chairmen like to cross up the driver by setting the pylons at diminishing, increasing or even irregular intervals.

There is a penalty for clouting pylons: for each one tipped over, three to five seconds are added to the driver's elapsed time. And if the contestant strays off course, his run is disqualified.

The nomenclature of the sport is a trifle confusing. As previously stated, in some regions a gymkhana may be called an autocross or slalom. Some clubs make a distinction based on speed: an autocross is "open," with generous straights and easy turns; a gymkhana is "tighter," emphasizing maneuverability rather than speed. And slalom, as we have seen, can have two meanings: the name of this kind of meet or a straight row of pylons in it.

A gymkhana course is rarely more than a mile long. It can be laid out however the organizers like—tricky or straightforward. Most clubs have long since abandoned gimmicks like reversing and garaging.

A gymkhana is not much of a spectator sport. It is being inside the car that provides an exhilarating experience. For a passenger taking a practice run with an expert the sensation is one of screeching tires, violent side-to-side tossing and abrupt

A Porsche 911 completes a hard right hander and attacks the next gate of pylons.

changes of direction. A malodorous, eye-smarting dust comes from the powdered rubber of burning tires. To the newcomer the startling thing is that the cars can take such punishment. They pitch and tilt and there is extraordinary stress on suspension and steering. Engines operate at full range of power, from top r.p.m. to idling speed. (These abrupt changes do occasionally cause a car to come unglued.)

Gymkhana is safer than racing and it satisfies the desire of many car enthusiasts for competition. Women compete successfully because this sport requires skill more than brawn. Although it is not as expensive as racing, car owners can spend a fortune, if they want to, on engine preparation (polished cylinder heads, special cams for low-end torque, balanced crankshafts, suspension tuning and high-performance parts). The more serious competitors have cars exclusively for gymkhanas; there are even shops that specialize in preparing cars for this type of competition. Nearly everyone uses racing tires and pressures are kept high—35 or 40 pounds—to induce sideways slides.

For safety, tech inspections are a required prelude. Among other things, the stewards examine brakes, steering and throttle linkage (there must be at least two dependable return springs to close the throttle). Hub caps and all loose objects in the car must be removed. Most clubs require the drivers to wear safety helmets.

As a rule the machines best suited to gymkhanas are imports. They are either sports cars or small passenger cars with firm suspension, first-class brakes and impeccable steering. Most American cars are at a disadvantage because of their cumbersome weight, wheelbase and width. Even the comparatively small American "pony" sedans are a handful to manage in a gymkhana. "You don't use finesse," says the owner of a Mustang. "You simply throw the car at the pylons."

Automatic transmission is always outperformed by manual gear changing. There is no way for automatics to match what a skillful driver can do with his first and second gears, constantly and swiftly changed.

163

CHAPTER 9
Money, Money, Money-
or It Takes Cubic Dollars

IT TAKES great bunches of money to go racing. Professionals in Motion, a company that develops marketing and promotional programs built around the sport, estimates that $500 million a year is spent in racing by automobile and accessory manufacturers, sponsors, promoters and car owners. Add the weight of 50 million paid admissions, add the money the fans spend on automotive products, add the effects of television advertising in connection with racing events—add these and other factors and you have a "float" in the neighborhood of $1 billion.

A race track isn't just a li'l ol' race track anymore: it is thought of as the pivot point of a "marketing area." Racing has the appurtenances of a gigantic marketplace in which manufacturers and the whole distribution apparatus show their

164

merchandise. Everything about racing is expensive—hence the phrase "big numbers."

Racing is a dangerous sport with exciting competition and superstars whose income frequently tops the income of the big-ticket golf pros and baseball and football players. It is show biz, offering entertainment for the millions replete with thrills, drama, comedy, corn and, sometimes, death.

Its arenas are among the largest in sports. One of them, Ontario Motor Speedway, was financed by a bond issue of $25.5 million. Crowds of 100,000 to upward of a quarter-million are not uncommon at the big arenas. Speculators and conservative investors build new tracks in the hope of tapping new markets or of crowding out, by the superiority of their facilities, the obsolete slum-like layouts that have endured too long.

Racing has its major leagues and minor leagues, its fortunes and bankruptcies, its big spending and penny-pinching. It has been described as a cruel sport but it is also a rough business, with disaster awaiting the incompetent and the unfortunate. Yet there are thousands of investors who take the plunge directly in racing ventures or through stock and bond issues.

One of the most important aspects of racing is the tax picture. Tax considerations are extremely significant sustainers of race operations—for car owners, drivers, sponsors and many others.

Andy Granatelli, himself a great gambler, calls racing "the last of America's pure, unpasteurized, two-fisted enterprises." He should know.

Racing is backed by a loyal following—fans who pay up to $50 a seat. It is fashionable these days to characterize racing as "The Sport of the Seventies." Psychologists speculate interminably about the reasons for all the interest in racing. One theory is based on the human instinct to compete. I suspect another part of the answer lies in our perpetual love affair with the automobile, often our most expensive possession (the automotive boom that followed World War II in Western Europe and Japan shows this is not exclusively an American phenomenon). Hardly anyone who attends a baseball game is interested in buying a catcher's mitt; scarcely anyone who goes to a football game is planning to buy a pair of shin guards. But just about everyone who pays to see an auto race or a drag meet owns a car and lusts to buy a better one; he is a lifetime prospect for the automobile industry.

In fact, racing has created a miniature business within itself, one that is sure to grow. We now have entrepreneurs who evaluate, develop and institute marketing and promotional programs that exploit the charisma and commercial potential of racing.

Of course, many of the companies that use racing as a sales tool are in some phase of the automobile industry. But it is significant that many organizations that sell their products through racing have nothing at all to do with automobiles. Their products include soft drinks, alcoholic beverages, toys, cigarettes, clothing, home-heating systems, variety-store items —anything.

One of the most successful of the new marketing firms is the aforementioned Professionals in Motion, based in Cleveland and headed by Fred Marik, which can put together any kind of package a client needs, even a complete race team if necessary. Its clients include Sun Oil Company; Sears, Roebuck; Dow Chemical, and American Motors, all of which use racing as a selling device.

An Indianapolis advertising agency, Ruben, Montgomery and Associates, has a division devoted entirely to marketing on the basis of racing. David Blackmer, the agency vice president who runs the division, is an experienced hand at assembling a package of advertising, sales promotion and public relations. He builds up goodwill among the advertiser's dealers and customers by taking them to races and introducing them to racing personalities. He distributes TV film clips, newsletters and race information to newspapers and radio stations and he runs a speakers bureau. His best known client is STP, one of the truly outstanding promotionally minded organizations in this country.

Jim Cook of Los Angeles engineered one of the most spectacularly successful sponsorships of recent years, Topper Toys' backing Al Unser. In its first year of racing, Topper's entry, the Johnny Lightning Special, won the Indianapolis 500 and nine other USAC races, making the name Al Unser a household word among the child population of the United States. And did Topper sell toys!

Cook's other clients include Firestone Tire and Rubber Company, Samsonite, Quickick and car owners on the USAC circuit. Like Marik and Blackmer, Cook regards auto racing as a big business that must have efficient management in terms of both sponsors' objectives and racing teams' operations. After bringing teams and sponsors together, he works with both. "Many good companies have been lost to racing," he says, "because they were treated badly in their first attempts at this business."

Another influential company is Motorsports Merchandising in Madison, Wis., which serves du Pont, Coca-Cola and others. The principals are John Cooper, an alumnus of the advertising business and of Chrysler marketing, and Chris Economaki, editor of National Speed Sport News and the sport's best-known broadcaster.

The economic organization of the racing business can be compared to a spider web, complex but with every filament somehow affected by what happens to every other filament. Many transactions often involve not just two parties but four, five or more—drivers, car owners, promoters, sponsors, mechanics, factories, suppliers, team managers, agents, television stations, advertisers—even the full-breasted chick working as a hostess in the hospitality lounge.

*   *   *

Racing is probably the most expensive sport in the world and for some of its participants the most lucrative. In 1969 Mario Andretti, who had come here as a teen-age refugee from Trieste, earned more than a million dollars. After winning the world driving championship in 1969, Jackie Stewart stood to earn at least $500,000 from racing, his race-related business enterprises, endorsements, appearances and other sources.

In just one race, the Indianapolis 500 of 1970, Al Unser won $271,698; in the same great season he grossed approximately half a million dollars in prize, accessory and lap money. Under the customary arrangement for the division of winnings, Unser kept about half, the other half going to the team and to the car owners, Parnelli Jones and Vel Miletich. Any driver who wins the 500 is assured of an income of well over a quarter-million dollars in the year of his Indy triumph. Near the end of the 1970 season, Unser was sporting on his helmet case a sticker that said, "I gave to the I.R.S."* Andretti, whose best year had been 1969, saw the sticker and told Unser, "I gave last year."

A. J. Foyt, the biggest money winner ever in racing, won over $3 million in about 10 years. And his income from other sources has exceeded his winnings. Foyt earns money from his race-related businesses (for example, he sells Ford racing engines), from the race teams he owns, from franchise deals using his name, from advertising endorsements and so on. His contract with Goodyear is probably the most formidable in the business. One man more than any other is credited with having raised the money standards for race drivers: that is A. J. Foyt. Drivers owe him the same kind of debt that the golf pros owe Arnold Palmer.

Stock car drivers like Richard Petty, Lee Roy Yarbrough and David Pearson have won more than $200,000 in successful years. Denis Hulme and the late Bruce McLaren each won more than $160,000 in Can-Am seasons alone—in addition to their earnings from other sources.

Cale Yarborough, who was cultivating tobacco and cotton at the age of 14, earns well over $100,000 a year from racing. Others in the vicinity of that figure are Bobby Unser, Parnelli Jones, Dan Gurney (who retired at the end of the 1970 season), Art Pollard, Bobby and Donnie Allison, Charlie Glotzbach,

*Internal Revenue Service.

Buddy Baker, Mark Donohue, Peter Hamilton, Jim McElreath and Roger McCluskey. In drag racing, superstars like Don (Big Daddy) Garlits, Don Prudhomme, Ronnie Sox, Dick Landy, Leroy Goldstein and Leonard Hughes are easily good for more than $100,000 a year each.

Mark Donohue, the boyish-looking "Captain Nice" who is one of the most versatile of American drivers, once said in an interview: "I thought long and hard before I decided to become a professional driver. This is a risky business. But I'll tell you one thing: I don't want to be poor again. I don't think I could go back to being a $10,000-a-year engineer."

"Anyone who gets in a race car takes chances," Cale Yarborough has said. "But it's a good life. Racing has been good to me, and I don't know how I could make this much money outside the sport."

Naturally, these men are distinguished standouts. But it is safe to estimate there are at least 75 American drivers whose income runs between $50,000 and $75,000, and there are a good deal more in the $25,000–$50,000 bracket.

Many race drivers earn substantial income from outside sources, including businesses and investments. Until a few years ago several American drivers would spend some time racing in Europe. They do not do it any more because there isn't enough money in European racing to make it worth their while. In fact, most successful American drivers now say, "I can't afford to race in Europe."

Race drivers are a sophisticated breed these days, as knowledgeable in their financial dealings as the high-income stars of other sports and show business. The wealthier ones have contracts with professional management firms that render a variety of services. These services include negotiating contracts, investing the clients' money, overseeing their business activities, setting up television and personal appearances, arranging ghost-written books. A few of these "total management" firms, notably Sports Headliners and Mark MacCormack, also represent high-income stars from other sports.

Many successful drivers endorse products and lend their

names to business enterprises such as service stations, car washes, car-rental companies, dry-cleaning chains and franchise operations. With tax problems being what they are, drivers engage the best accountants to advise them on dealing with the Internal Revenue Service.

*   *   *

In the working relationships between drivers and car owners there is a standard pattern, but there also are many nonstandard arrangements. As a general rule, though, a driver keeps 40 to 50 percent of the purses and contingency awards he wins, with the rest going to the car owner and the team. The driver keeps all the personal loot, such as cars, clothes, watches, jewelry and trophies (and a weekend with the race queen, if and when that is ever offered). The car owner, from his share, pays team expenses, such as mechanics' wages and the costs of constant travel. If the driver owns his race car, then of course he keeps all his winnings.

In the minor leagues there are a fair number of drivers who own their own cars. In big-time racing, where costs are astronomical and finances more complicated, there are fewer owner-drivers—A. J. Foyt, Jack Brabham, the late Bruce McLaren, Gordon Johncock, Jerry Grant and Mel Kenyon have been the most notable ones in recent years. Dan Gurney dipped into and dropped out of owner-driving a few times. Mario Andretti managed well enough when he had a $100,000 sponsorship from Overseas National Airways and additional help from Firestone. But when Firestone retrenched and was forced to cut off his subsidy, Andretti could not balance his budget on the O.N.A. sponsorship alone. He sold his whole operation to Andy Granatelli and signed up as a hired foot for Granatelli at a $50,000 salary plus 40 per cent of the winnings and bonuses of $25,000 each if he won the Indianapolis 500 and the USAC driving championship. He won both in 1969, his biggest year.

Occasionally it happens that a driver is hired for just one race, like the Indianapolis 500, or a few races of a series like the Canadian-American Challenge Cup. In such cases he may be paid a substantial fee. Its size depends on the strength of his bargaining position, but payments of $10,000 are not unusual.

In major races where the purses are relatively small, drivers work primarily on salary. This is especially true in such factory competition as the world manufacturers' championship or the Trans-American Championship. On the NASCAR circuit a big-name driver under contract to a manufacturer may receive a salary plus a share of his winnings.*

The traditional European system of payoff is strange to American race fans and to some even a trifle distasteful. The purses in Europe are so small that they are scarcely worth competing for. So promoters pay drivers and teams "appearance money" or "start money" based on each driver's popularity with the fans, his bargaining ability, his standing in the points competition and a number of other considerations. Whatever the drivers win in a race is velvet. The Europeans justify this arrangement on the ground that a car might not last the whole distance, finishing out of the money; result, a lot of expense and risk for no return.

In the American tradition we prefer to have our drivers "race for their money." One noteworthy result is that a promoter can put all the money he intends to pay the drivers into a large purse, which can be exploited for its publicity value (in contrast with appearance money, which is never even mentioned.) The American custom is to spread the purse money far down through the finishing order, so that drivers way back in the field can earn at least a little something for their effort.

The United States Grand Prix, held in October at Watkins Glen, puts up an extraordinary purse—for the 1970 event, $250,-000, with a first prize of $50,000. This is the biggest purse in Grand Prix anywhere in the world. Also significant, the Watkins Glen purse is graduated down through the full field, which

*The race teams as a whole—mechanics, owners, co-drivers, helpers also share in the winnings.

varies from 20 to 24 positions,* with even the last-place car earning $6,000. This is a highly satisfactory substitute for European-type appearance money, which for some drivers might be even less than $6,000.

Within North America there is an interesting anomaly: both the Canadian and United States Grand Prix operate on the premise that the big purse money is enough to pay traveling expenses, but the Mexican Grand Prix works on the old European system of small purse and secondary inducements.† In late September, for the Canadian Grand Prix, the "circus" charters one plane for all the race cars, and the teams fly over from Europe on commercial airlines—all this at their own expense. After the Canadian race the troupe moves by surface to Watkins Glen for the United States Grand Prix—again at their own expense.

After the United States Grand Prix the show moves on to Mexico—the cars by truck and most of the personnel by air. This time, though, the travel expenses are paid by the organizers of the Mexican Grand Prix. The Mexicans also pay for the return transportation to New York. From there the troupe pays its own way back to Europe.

The European appearance-money system caused something of a flap early in the Canadian-American Challenge Cup series, which began in 1966. Several European stars demanded appearance money. The Can-Am purses, however, were tremendous by European standards. Officials of the Sports Car Club of America, which sanctions the Can-Am, had coaxed the promoters into putting up these big purses and were convinced that the American public would respond to a whole series of races that feature big, above-the-table purses. Eventually the S.C.C.A. people persuaded the promoters to insist that the drivers "race for their money" because there was so much money to be had. A few Europeans were obstinate indeed,

---

*The same thing is done in the Indianapolis 500, where purse money is spread through all 33 positions.

†At this writing there is some question whether Grand Prix races will continue in Mexico.

but the S.C.C.A. successfully stood its ground.

With the S.C.C.A. this is a philosophic principle, sold by persuasion rather than enforced by a formal prohibition. In fact, the club has long had its General Competition Rule 3.4.1, which permits drivers to accept start money and organizers to offer it "as they may wish." This is not so much a contradiction as it is a recognition of reality: the club is reluctant to prohibit something it cannot control anyway.

The Can-Am policy has been severely buffeted, forcing the S.C.C.A. to reconsider its position. The greatest weakness of the Can-Am series has been its dearth of competition as the McLaren team easily won the title year after year. European teams have refused to send cars, drivers and mechanics to this continent because of the high cost and great risks—for any of a hundred reasons a car may fail to complete a race and thus finish out of the money. In the hope of attracting more competitive cars, especially from abroad, the S.C.C.A. changed the Can-Am's prize structure at the start of the 1971 season, with each of the 10 races carrying a minimum purse of $75,000. The practice now will be to distribute $55,000 in purse money all the way down to 20th finishing position. The remaining $20,000 is to be divided among the 10 fastest qualifiers—$2,500 for the pole position and $17,500 divided among the next nine fastest qualifiers. The qualifying fund is unique in racing. The purpose of all this is to assure the teams of at least some cash to cover some expenses.

None of this means that American promoters do not pay start money. But there is less of it than there was some years ago, and there is less of it here than in Europe. The defending champions of USAC and NASCAR are entitled, by the regulations of those clubs, to an appearance fee each time they compete. The roving European factory teams that race for the world manufacturers' championship receive substantial start money in the American endurance races at Daytona, Sebring and Watkins Glen. In these cases it is the teams, not the individual drivers, doing the negotiating. If a team knows a promoter is hard up for entries, the price goes up. The Watkins

Glen six-hour endurance race, to illustrate, is held in July, by which time the manufacturers' championship may have been won. The factory teams are still obligated to race because their sponsorship deals are for a season or a series. Once the title is decided, however, the pressure to race with a fully staffed, all-out effort is no longer so strenuous. Still, the factory teams can be persuaded with money.

The promoter of a comparatively unimportant race, anxious to get some name drivers into his field, will bargain with them to insure their entering. "How much deal money did you get?" is a common phrase.

In drag racing the American Hot Rod Association, a rival to the ACCUS-affiliated National Hot Rod Association, encourages "booking in" drivers, which means paying them an appearance fee. A "seated" driver in the A.H.R.A. professional series can collect $600 to $1,500 for a three-day show, depending on his popularity and the frequency with which he competes. Sometimes the appearance money is handled as a minimum guarantee against whatever purses the driver can win—that is, the appearance money is part of his winnings. In most cases, though, the appearance money is paid *in addition to* his winnings.

The rationale is that booking assures better fields for weekly and local events. Advocates of booking say they can put on a really good show with the stars they are able to attract.

Booking is less prevalent in the major national shows. The superstars *must* enter and remain competitive in the major events if they are to maintain their reputation and drawing power for the smaller meets.

The National Hot Rod Association says it would not book a driver into a major show any more than Indianapolis Motor Speedway would think of trying to lure A. J. Foyt into the 500 with start money. But, significantly, the N.H.R.A. says individual drag-strip operators are free to book in drivers if they want to. This is comparable to the S.C.C.A.'s General Competition Rule 3.4.1.

"Tow money" superficially resembles appearance money but is not the same. Tow money is usually paid at smaller tracks where there are weekly shows. Tow money is modest and goes not to stars but to their opposites—the little guys who are struggling to stay alive. It is expensive to travel from one track to another, carrying one's race car on a trailer or in a van and hauling all the necessities such as spare parts, tires and tools. So the promoter helps the driver who needs it with tow money. It may be $50 or $75, or something per mile—at least something to reimburse him for his expenses. This also is sound public relations. When some of the little guys become stars they may remember promoters who helped them when the going was tough.

*   *   *

In big-league racing many "name" drivers are signed up with one of the major tire companies—Goodyear or Firestone in conventional racing, M. & H. in drag racing. The most prestigious drivers receive substantial monthly or race-by-race retainers.

From a distance it is easy to identify a driver's tire affiliation. Racing coveralls are usually provided by the tire companies and the lettering and ornamentation are loud and clear—blue and gold for Goodyear, red for Firestone. Among the most notable Goodyear names are A. J. Foyt, Dan Gurney, Mark Donohue, John Cannon, Roger McCluskey, Denis Hulme, Richard Petty, Lee Roy Yarbrough. Among the Firestone names are Mario Andretti, Al Unser, Parnelli Jones, Lloyd Ruby, George Follmer.

Occasionally the tire companies set up their drivers or car owners in a sideline tire business such as a retail store or regional distributorship. Distinguished drivers also receive tire-testing assignments.

Tire testing is one of the most important aspects of racing. Goodyear and Firestone produce thousands of specially designed racing tires. Many compounds of rubber and chemicals are formulated for a specific race at a specific track, for specific cars and for a specific time of year, taking into consideration such factors as banking of the turns, make-up and temperature of the track surface, weight and aerodynamics of the car and so on. The drivers spend many hours at empty tracks, going 'round and 'round, experimenting with and observing the efficacy of many different compounds and types of construction.

Payment for tire testing averages about $10 a mile. It is easy to accumulate 500 miles in a week of testing. At the end of the year, depending on the mileage rate paid, the testing may have been worth at least $100,000 to the driver and his team.

Drivers, moreover, have advertising commitments to other products—lubricants, additives, fuels, spark plugs and the like. Occasionally a driver may be unable to accept a ride because his own sponsor deals conflict with those of the car owner— different tires, different fuels and so on. Dan Gurney, for example, had to give up a great McLaren ride in the Can-Am series because he was receiving support from Castrol while the McLaren team had Gulf Oil as one of its principal sponsors.

The United States Auto Club, the National Association for Stock Car Auto Racing and two of the three professional series of the Sports Car Club of America maintain point funds, which are sort of kitties or pools divided among the leading drivers at the end of a season. Shares are awarded on the basis of points won during the season's races—so many points for first place, so many for fourth, and so on.

One purpose of a point fund is to put pressure on drivers to run as many scheduled races as possible each season—the more races they run, the more points they accumulate and hence the more money. Indeed, NASCAR's formula awards points for each of the races run regardless of finishing position.

A point fund is made up of assessments against the promoters of the season's individual races and against the sponsor of the series if there is a sponsor.

*   *   *

Like everything else in racing, the business of owning a race car is complicated. Even the nomenclature is misleading: in big-league racing most car owners do not "own" their cars at all. They are simply the nominal owners acting for the real owners, the backers who for one reason or another do not publicize their relationship to the car.

In NASCAR's Grand National racing and the S.C.C.A.'s Trans-American Championship, certain car "owners" are essentially contractors commissioned by the manufacturer to operate a race team. Here the "owner's" primary responsibility is the preparation of the car. On the NASCAR circuit the best known owners have been Holman & Moody for Ford, Petty Engineering for Plymouth, Cotton Owens for Dodge. In the Trans-Am Bud Moore won the championship for Ford's Mustang. Roger Penske won two Trans-Am titles for Chevrolet's Camaro before he got a better financial deal with American Motors' Javelin. Penske's multi-million-dollar contract with American Motors is augmented by a fine sponsorship from Sun Oil Company (Sunoco). Now Penske and his star driver, Mark Donohue, fly to the races in style, in a Lear jet.

In some ways the car owner, especially on the USAC championship circuit, is like the Broadway theatrical producer—he operates the team effort without putting up any money of his own, though he does retain a good share of the profit. Profit, some owners will ask, *what* profit? Only a few owners make any money in racing, they say. Some use their losses to offset tax liabilities incurred in their primary businesses or charge the losses to advertising and publicity. Others just lose money, period.

In minor-league racing the owners keep coming back year after year. These men are a dedicated lot, genuinely devoted to racing; often they are the ones who give the Andrettis, the Unsers and the Joneses their starts in midgets or in jalopy stock cars.

The owner of a car that wins a purse pays his driver the agreed-upon percentage. He pays his mechanics' wages and other bills. But he is usually not obliged to divide his share of the winnings with the backers—they put up the money for publicity or commercial benefits and generally that's all they expect.

So the car owner keeps his share. But winnings alone are never enough to finance a racing operation. In the USAC championship division, which includes the Indianapolis 500, it costs well over $200,000 to field the most modest team. The expenses only begin with the basic car and a back-up car, spare engines, driver, chief mechanic, pit crew, travel and living costs and who knows what else.

It is a fact of life that the owner of the winning car in the Indianapolis 500 is lucky to break even.* A case in point is the 1970 race, in which Al Unser won $271,698 in a car owned by Parnelli Jones and Vel Miletich (and heavily sponsored by Topper Toys). In that same season Unser won nine smaller USAC races. Yet the season winnings of approximately $500,000 were not a guarantee of profit. It is estimated that Jones and Miletich invested upward of $500,000 on equipment—the team had four cars for Unser and another team driver, Joe Leonard, and maintained shops in California and Indianapolis. Travel expenses are enormous, especially with a 24-race schedule that requires long trips. Salaries for first-class mechanics like George Bignotti and top drivers like Unser and Leonard keep the budget high. Some chief mechanics can earn more than $100,000 in winning years—in fact, there was an *assistant* mechanic who earned more than $75,000 one year. It takes a formidable subsidy like the Topper Toys sponsorship to keep the Jones-Miletich team going.

Despite these formidable realities, as many as 90 hopeful entries show up at the Speedway at the beginning of May to compete for the 33 positions in the starting line-up.

Any serious NASCAR Grand National effort is in the $100,000-a-year class—the car alone costs at least $20,000. The Group 7 cars of S.C.C.A.'s Can-Am series are out-of-sight expen-

---

* This is reminiscent of the horse player's prayer: "Lord, let me break even today—I need the money."

sive because so many of their components are nonstock and hand-made. To design, develop and prepare a Can-Am car from scratch takes really "big numbers"—Jim Hall's Chaparral 2J, Don Nichols's AVS Shadow and Peter Bryant's two Ti-22's are estimated to have cost more than $100,000 each and perhaps close to $300,000. Of course, heavy subsidies were involved.

Even if cars are "series produced" to meet F.I.A. requirements, they still are expensive—Porsche built 25 identical 917's in one season and they sold for $35,000 each. Except for an occasional Croesus, Grand Prix racing is impossible without substantial sponsorship deals.

A competitive sprint car costs between $7,000 and $12,000, a midget around $10,000. Modified stock cars that run in the weekly shows in the small towns can be bought for $3,000 to $5,000. In drag racing it costs $30,000 to field an AA/fuel dragster or funny car, and sometimes the cost rises to $50,000. And these are only the purchase prices—all the extras start from there.

Obviously, since winnings alone cannot keep a team going, a car owner needs outside financing. So he goes out looking for sponsors, offering them a deal: we campaign this car, you get the exposure and promotional value. For a stipulated amount of money, to take a typical example, the sponsor has the name of his company or product painted on the car and the owner agrees that it will be entered in a certain number of races during the season, thus insuring its exposure to thousands of spectators. Such a sponsorship may run to approximately $75,000, but some deals go well over $100,000. A good-size budget is around $150,000.

Occasionally a sponsorship will involve only one race, such as the Indianapolis 500, the California 500 or the Daytona 500.

On the USAC championship circuit it is common for a car to have some implausible name like the Lucius D. Poindexter Air Conditioning and Home Heating Special or the Mother Jones Nutmeg Deep Fried Premium Bacon Rind Special. The trade name is so assiduously promoted that sometimes it is difficult to find out, even in the program, what the car *really*

179

is—an Eagle-Offenhauser, a P. J. Colt-Ford, or whatever. The sponsor's product may be anything at all—toys, orange juice, a resort, a chain of variety stores, household heating equipment, a broadcasting network, prefabricated houses, stationery and the whole spectrum of automotive merchandise. The net effect is to make the race car a rolling billboard, and since racing has always been blatantly commercial no one objects. The practice of naming a car after a sponsor is followed to a lesser extent in NASCAR and the S.C.C.A. than in USAC but is growing.

Perhaps the most important aspect of the car-owning business is to work a deal with one of the tire companies. Most often a tire company is the major "stockholder" of a race car. Sometimes the nominal owner does not know whom he will hire as a driver until the tire company tells him. Car builders produce race cars without knowing who will use them—the tire companies take care of that.

For a long time Goodyear and Firestone have subsidized individual racing teams, in many cases providing the money to build and develop the car, pay the driver and crew and keep the operation going during the season. The pay-off is in promotional advantage—the opportunity to run four-color ads, big billboard ads and television commercials drawing a connection between a tire and the winning of a race. In recent years the tire companies—and the oil companies as well—have trimmed their racing expenditures somewhat, but they still are in there.

Even a basic sponsorship is not enough to pay all the bills, so the car owner also brings the accessory companies into the picture—spark plugs, fuels, lubricants, shock absorbers. Their support may not be so great as that of the tire companies, but they do pay the car owners to use their products in his car. That's what those seemingly silly little decals* are all about— they are worth anywhere for $100 to $10,000 each. Occasionally the decals are used in exchange for unlimited amounts of products—clothes, instruments, motorcycles.

* Decals are limited in size, generally to about 12 square inches, while the car is racing. But at picture-taking time owners of winning cars may substitute larger decals—after all, "exposure" is what the advertiser is buying.

Those bright decals on a winning car also qualify the owner for manufacturers' contingency awards—that is, the team wins prizes from Brand X lubricants, Brand Y spark plugs and Brand Z shock absorbers if the car is using those products. The contingency awards are usually solicited by the race-sanctioning organizations.

What is true in USAC and NASCAR is likewise applicable to the N.H.R.A. and S.C.C.A. professional series. Bruce McLaren, whose team swept the Can-Am championship four consecutive years, could never have built those magnificent papaya-color cars without enormous sponsor and subsidy deals from Goodyear, Chevrolet, Gulf Oil, Reynolds Aluminum and Bosch spark plugs.

*   *   *

We come now to the promoter (or "organizer" if he's a Europe-oriented snob). To acquire a date of any consequence he first has to pay a sanction fee to the appropriate club. Taking NASCAR as an illustration, sanction fees range from $100 for a weekly show to $12,500 for a 500-mile Grand National. In the Sports Car Club of America the sanction fee can be as high as $7,500 for a Canadian-American Challenge Cup race,* which happens to be what Indianapolis Motor Speedway pays the United States Auto Club for the Indianapolis 500 sanction.

Having bought the sanction, the promoter is required to "post" a purse by depositing it with the sanctioning body or in a controlled bank account (this is how a purse is "guaranteed,"† meaning it is protected against the promoter's changing his mind or skipping town or against any other hanky-panky). Purses may vary according to the requirements of the sanctioning body, the length of the race and other considerations.

---

* In S.C.C.A. racing the promoter's contract also requires him to pay a "race organization fee," ranging from $1,000 to $5,000, to the local S.C.C.A. region, which provides the volunteer manpower needed to staff a race—stewards, corner workers, communications people, etc. The promoter is also required to make his track available to the S.C.C.A. region for club racing.

† "Guaranteed" also means the minimum amount of prize money that is guaranteed to be paid. This does not include contingency awards.

The largest purse anywhere in the world is paid by the Indianapolis 500, which now tops $1 million, including accessory awards. The Daytona 500 payout is over $200,000; the World 600 at Charlotte pays $160,000 to $170,000. NASCAR purses start with a base of $7,500 for a 100-mile event and beyond that they are subject to negotiation. The weekly shows for modified stockers pay from $1,500 to $6,000.

The Sports Car Club of America scale requires a minimum purse of $75,000 for a Can-Am race. The minimum purse for a Trans-American program is $20,000 for the over-2.5-liter cars and $5,000 for those under 2.5 liters. For a Continental Championship program the purse is $19,000 from the promoter and about $6,000 from the series sponsor if there is one.

Drag racing also has its big numbers. The N.H.R.A. Nationals have a total payout of $350,000, and the club's World Championship Series offers more than $625,000 for the 35 meets.

Some United States Auto Club championship races are run for a stipulated purse. Others are run for a minimum guarantee against 40 per cent of the gate receipts,* whichever is larger. The minimum may be $25,000 for a 150-mile race and more, of course, for longer races. Purses are bound to increase in the next few years as teams struggle, under the pressures of inflation, to keep up with their ever-rising costs.

Below the championship level, hundreds of races are run for smaller purses. Those of USAC sprint-car races may range from $6,500 to $15,000 against 40 per cent of the gate; for midget races the purse may be $2,000 to $6,000, also against 40 per cent of the gate.

The independently sanctioned midget races pay from $1,000 to $3,000. Many drivers make a circuit of three tracks over a weekend—Friday night, Saturday night and Sunday night. And they work hard for their money, because they have

---

* The 40 per cent provision has a long tradition, dating to the era when races were run on publicly supported fairgrounds and rented horse-race tracks and the promoter did not need to pay for overhead, year-round payroll, plant improvement and maintenance, taxes, promotion and other fixed expenses. But the 40 per cent cut is impracticable for the larger permanent tracks, which represent huge investments and which do have those year-long costs.

to survive the elimination heats just to make the feature or "the main," which will pay $750 or so for first place.

*   *   *

Quite often a promoter receives help from a sponsor in putting up the purse. This is true more in road racing than in the oval formats, but the practice is growing there as well. Sponsorships explain the designation of races with particular names, such as Marlboro Trans-Am, Schaefer Trans-Am, Players Grand Prix (in Canada), Inver House Continental, Castrol Can-Am, Los Angeles Times Grand Prix (the Can-Am at Riverside, Calif.), the Motor Trend 500, the Falstaff 400, the Miller High Life 500, Questor Grand Prix.*

The idea is to get all or part of a purse from a sponsor who wants the publicity value of having his name attached to a big race. Cigarette companies, compelled by Federal law to withdraw from television advertising, have diverted some of their ad budgets into racing. Tobacco companies have been active in European and Canadian racing for many years, but such promotion is comparatively new in the United States. (Cigarette manufacturers, incidentally, are prohibited from exploiting personalities in their American advertising—no "So-and-so smokes Brand X.")

To a purse a promoter or sanctioning club adds the awards offered by manufacturers of various accessories. When you win a race you win not only the purse but also certain accessory prizes. These prizes are called "contingency" money—you win them contingent upon your having used the donor's product on or in your car. There may be dozens of such accessory awards—for tires, fuel, spark plugs, shock absorbers, additives, coolants, lubricants, etc.

Contingency money helps a promoter because it inflates the size of the payout for publicity purposes. It is common practice for his press releases to harp on, say, "posted awards"

---

*Sponsors may also support an entire series of races, such as Marlboro and USAC's championship division, Johnson Wax and the S.C.C.A.'s Canadian-American Challenge Cup, and L&M cigarettes and the S.C.C.A.'s Continental series.

of $60,000. Perhaps $45,000 comes from the promoter—that is called the purse—and the remainder from contingency awards.

However, not all "posted" money is paid out. To illustrate, Goodyear and Firestone may each offer a $1,000 prize to the winner. But only one company will need to pay out the $1,000 because a driver is not permitted to use the products of competing advertisers—he may use only one or the other. And so it goes with all the rest of the contingency awards—Champion vs. Autolite in spark plugs, Monroe vs. Koni in shock absorbers, STP vs. Wynn's in additives. The result is that a good deal more money is "posted" than is paid out.

It is traditional at Indianapolis for the winner to pose drinking a slug of milk, for which a milk foundation pays him $800. It is interesting to speculate what might happen some day if the winner's sponsor is a soft-drink manufacturer or brewer.

*   *   *

We know the promoter has to pay a sanction fee and put up a purse. Also, he has the same kind of expenses that other businessmen have—payroll, insurance (which can be brutally costly), advertising and publicity, taxes, security, entertainment of VIP's and the like. The cost of producing a Can-Am show is between $125,000 and $150,000; for other road races the "nut" is somewhat less.

Aside from a sponsorship deal, if he has one, where does the promoter get the money to pay for it all?

First and foremost, from gate receipts, with ticket prices running anywhere from a few dollars to $50 for the choicest locations. Relying on his business experience and intuition, the promoter must determine how high to peg his ticket price without charging so much that the customers will be frightened away. This calls for fine judgment: sell for $5, and you may not make expenses; sell for $8, and again you may not make expenses.

Beyond the ticket sales, many promoters charge a couple of dollars for parking. They also collect extra fees, sometimes as high as $12 above the price of the general admission, for an afternoon in the "privileged" areas—the paddock in road racing and the infield at some oval tracks. Promoters of road races earn a nice buck from special seating: traditionally the fans roam from one vantage point to another, either sitting on the ground or standing; but for the spectators who want to sit on benches, the promoters have erected bleachers at the most interesting corners and straights—at an extra $2 to $5 on top of the general admission ticket. Somehow it seems a bit much.

If a race is televised as part of an over-all season contract between the sanctioning body and the broadcasting company, the promoter receives a share of the television payment. In the United States Auto Club a typical $40,000 deal breaks down this way:

Added to purse	45%	$18,000
Promoter's share	45%	$18,000
USAC share	10%	$ 4,000

Indianapolis and Ontario retain the right to make their own television (and radio) deals without going through sanctioning organizations.

In the National Association for Stock Car Auto Racing the drivers' share is smaller, and this is a major source of contention between the drivers and the promoters. The drivers believe they are entitled to a major share of the TV proceeds, since it is on the basis of their performance that a race is telecast at all.

Telecasts can be live, delayed, closed-circuit and, in the near future, on cable TV. The biggest races, such as the 500's at Indianapolis, Ontario and Daytona, are on closed-circuit TV—that is, the signal is carried only to theaters around the country, where admission of $5 or $7.50 is charged. In closed-circuit deals the track is in a strong negotiating position vis-à-vis the television people. Thus far Sports Car Club of America events have had almost no TV exposure. The tight money market, the technical difficulties involved in making a road race interesting on the TV tube, the fragmented and sometimes lackadaisical selling effort—all have had a harsh effect on S.C.C.A. aspirations.

The prospect of television loot has the racing industry drooling—*this* is where the money is, *this* is what will save us all. But auto-racing TV is still in its infancy. In esthetic terms the quality of telecasts has been poor; present techniques are so crude that they actually make a USAC championship race or a NASCAR event look slow and dull. In financial terms racing receives peanuts in comparison with what pro football, golf and other sports get for TV rights.

Back to the track itself: promoters take a cut from the refreshment stands and other concessions. It's lovely for the track if the spectators can be induced to spend an average of $1 apiece on refreshments and souvenirs. Soft-drink companies are delighted to pay for exclusive rights on the premises. You will notice, of course, that prices inside the track are higher than they are outside. Moreover, though in some states it is illegal to require concessionaires to sell only one brand of beer, you learn from experience that almost every track is a one-beer track—that's the way it is, baby.

On the NASCAR stock car circuit a fair number of promoters have a deal with Union 76 for exclusive advertising and exploitation of its gasoline and lubricants on the premises. In return, Union 76 provides free gas to all the competitors and helps the track promote the show on local radio and television stations and in the local press. In the other club circuits promoters also make deals with gasoline companies.

Advertisers pay to hang banners or run their ads on pit walls and billboards, on clocks, on scoreboards, on traffic pylons. Some have bridges over the track named after their products. But the most offensive form of advertising, the most reprehensible, is the huckstering blared over the public address system. Funny thing: you can rarely hear the announcer's report of who is leading, but somehow he always finds a quiet moment to make a pitch for a product. It is one thing for the track announcer to thank the local ambulance corps, cops and volunteer firemen, or even to con you into visiting the concession stand to buy one of those ptomaine 75-cent hot dogs, but it is quite another to assault a captive audience with commercials for all kinds of merchandise. If the audience were there free of charge, there might be an excuse for the commercials. But *assault* an audience that has *paid* to get in? When commercials on television or radio become excessively obnoxious you can always switch to another station; in newspapers and magazines you can ignore the ads if you want to and flip to the next page; but when you are part of a captive audience no such escape is possible (which is why many states prohibit radio advertising in buses). Some day some fan may start an interesting lawsuit against a promoter and/or advertiser.

Frequently the promoter makes a deal for the pace cars—or, in the case of drag racing, the courtesy cars. These gaudy white convertibles with all the advertising on them are valuable promotion for their manufacturer. He gets the opportunity to drum their name into the consciousness of a responsive audience at a big race. Perhaps a dozen convertibles of the manufacturer's make may be conspicuously bustling about the grounds, having been lent to club officials, track staff, VIP's and others.

The pace-car deal can be profitable for the promoter, depending on just how he swings it with the manufacturer. It is also possible to work out a pace-car agreement with the local dealer of a particular make.

On the stock car circuit many promoters participate in the "NASCAR Plan," in which NASCAR, with its great bargaining ability, buys from one of the Detroit manufacturers a whole fleet of pace cars at huge discounts. In this way NASCAR publicizes one make of car all season long at most tracks on the circuit. The pace cars are distributed among promoters, who get the free use of one or two cars for a year. At the end of the year NASCAR sells the pace cars.

For the manufacturer, a pace-car deal can be quite expensive, especially at the Indianapolis 500. There the cost runs to $200,000 or more. The manufacturer must provide dozens of "official cars," give parties and maintain a hard-hitting tie-in promotion, including national ad campaigns. But these pace-car arrangements do pay off in sales.

The promoter of a substantial race can realize a tidy profit from the advertising revenue and sales of a souvenir race program. Smaller NASCAR tracks that do not have the staff or facilities to produce a good souvenir program or solicit ads for it can buy one from NASCAR. It comes with an insert of two or four pages pegged to the local scene and the race of the day. The promoter receives a cut from the sales of this book to the fans.

A promoter can pick up some money from the rental of garage space in the paddock area to the race teams (only the larger tracks have garages). He can earn money by renting the track out for the testing of cars and tires. Finally, he can rent the track to advertising agencies for the taping of television commercials, to producers of racing films and to auto manufacturers for the introduction of new models to the press and other media.

Promotional and other problems vary from one place to another, and no one formula can be effective for every track. Some of the small tracks that put on weekly shows are immensely profitable. Others have found that frequent races are costly in terms of payroll, advertising, insurance and taxes. Among these there is a growing tendency to follow the concept of the big tracks—that is, a maximum of two or three major races a year.

The risks in auto racing are enormous. A promoter can lose his crowd to some other event in the area—a football game, a baseball game, even a TV broadcast of some important athletic contest. His promotion may go sour or he may waste money on ineffective advertising, with the result that the crowds stay away in hordes.

More than most sports, auto racing is at the mercy of the weather. A rainy day can destroy a race, with losses running into thousands of dollars. All oval racing is stopped or canceled when it rains. It is not easy to postpone a race because a "rain date" is not always available. And even if a rain date can be scheduled, all the money spent to attract a crowd to today's race is wasted, all the wages paid to employes who reported for work today is lost—and the promotion campaign has to be cranked up all over again.

There was a race at Beltsville, Md., in which the promoters kept the NASCAR Grand American drivers in town, paying the teams' expenses through four days of rain until they could get their race running on Thursday night. The promoter's reasoning was that they could make at least some money if they ran their race, even on a weekday evening, but that they would lose heavily if they canceled.

In road racing the event goes on in any kind of weather, but the fans are under no obligation to attend. It's one thing if it starts to rain during a race—at least you've got your spectators inside the park. But it is disastrous if the weather is rainy or even cloudy on the *morning* of a road race: in that event the fans simply do not stir from home and the promoter has to run his race, complete with purse and prizes, to a nearly empty house.

Unlike the owners of baseball and football teams, the promoters of auto races are always highly visible. It is not unusual for some fan to corner Sam Nunis and complain about his seat or to chide Irvin Fried about the parking space. All the fans know Les Richter, who was famous as a pro football star before he entered racing, and they seek him out to talk with him. They all know Mal Currie, Clif Tufte, Jim Haynes, Bill France Sr. and Bill France Jr. Tony Hulman stands there in the view of a quarter-million patrons. All the track owners are out there among the customers.

And it is easy to spot the promoter as he scurries from one crisis to another. He is the man who has the most worried look on the premises.

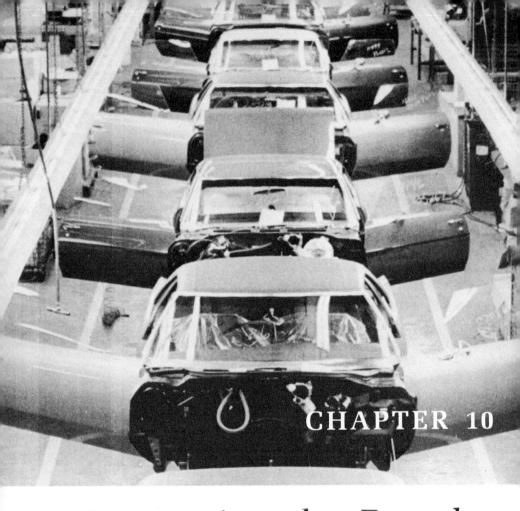

CHAPTER 10

Improving the Breed,

or Win Sunday, Sell Monday

FROM THE LITANY of American automotive trivia one of the most frequently cited verses is that the first Indianapolis 500, run in 1911, gave us the rear-view mirror. The fact is that as far back as Dec. 1, 1906, The Automotive Trade Journal carried an advertisement for a rear-view mirror. And aside from

190

its inaccuracy, the mirror myth does a disservice to the really significant contributions of auto racing to passenger cars. To racing add sports cars, backyard mechanics, motor enthusiasts, youth and what Detroit calls "real automobile men"—all have had an influence on today's *total* car. Contemporary automobiles handle better, last longer, are safer, perform more efficiently and look more credible than the waddling, multicolor, finned ludicrosities of the 1950's.

Competition serves as the proving ground for the cars sold at your friendly neighborhood dealer's. A race car must do everything that a conventional car does on the street—accelerate, brake, shift gears, turn—but it does so under murderous conditions that expose flaws in design, construction and materials. From the racing cars of the late 19th century to today's precision-engineered machines, the demands of the sport have accelerated the evolution of automobiles.

Lightweight alloy pistons, thin-wall engine blocks, sure-fire spark plugs and ignition systems, refined fuel-injection methods and highly sophisticated carburetor systems—the development of all these improvements has been hastened by the pressure of race competition.

Cylinder blocks, camshafts and valves have been strengthened in production cars on the basis of analyses of racing engines that broke down under the stress of high speed for long periods. There are better drive trains nowadays that waste a minimum of energy. The fretful little inefficiencies of accessories have been eliminated. The difficulties discovered as a result of high-speed racing might not have shown up in normally operated cars for several years.

Racing engineers, like their cars, work best at full throttle. Under competitive pressure they have improvised brilliant ways of making their machines run quicker, even of holding them together. Some of these battle-born innovations eventually reach the conventional production cars. Contributions come from every type of racing—stock cars, sports cars, dragsters, Indianapolis, Formula One. Five hundred miles of continuous racing at an average speed of 150 to 155 miles an hour, for example, is considered the rough equivalent of 100,000 miles of consumer use.

Components can be subjected to very severe tests under simulated conditions of thousands of miles. But there are no stresses like the stresses of racing. The vital consideration here is that racing increases and enhances the reliability and safety of today's mass-produced cars.

Racing shortens test time and saves money. Engineers can learn in a day what would otherwise take months of normal use to expose. Laboratory and proving-ground experiments cannot always determine whether a new system, component or material is ready to be approved for production. Some working conditions are too complex and involve too many variables to be simulated. But a single long-distance road race can quickly prove out a theory or a part.

Factory-backed racers are completely torn down after a race and studied for fatigue, wear and stress. From these studies come significant changes and refinements in components, materials and systems. These in turn lead to smaller, lighter and more efficient engines that combine high performance, fuel economy and relatively cleaner emissions.

And then there is safety. Here, too, racing has made notable contributions—faster-stopping disc brakes, dual-brake systems, wide-tread low-profile tires that enhance stability and put a more effective "footprint" on the road, precise steering geometry, rigid frames and underbody structures, steel beams inside the doors to withstand broadside collisions, hydraulic shock absorbers, body-restraining harness. Sway bars and carefully balanced suspension systems mean a more solid ride and quicker response to steering. Some sports cars are now sold with rollover bars.

Besides such palpable improvements as these attributable to racing, there is something that Jacque H. Passino, formerly one of Ford's racing impresarios, calls a "bank of knowledge." By this he means the constant exchange of information between the race engineer and the production man "out there in the weeds who has a problem to solve, like a breaking piston pin."

At the post-race examination of an engine in the shops, says Passino, "a passenger car guy comes by and learns something."

*　　*　　*

The relationship between racing cars and the production cars sold to the public works the other way around, too. Not only do manufacturers incorporate race-tested ideas into their commercially sold vehicles, but consumers demand some of these improvements *before* the manufacturers offer them.

Today's customers are sharper, more knowledgeable than those of a generation ago. James E. Kaser, former director of professional racing for the Sports Car Club of America, recalls that in the 1950's the American public was satisfied with any bechromed dreamboat that could move. But tastes have changed with the times, he observes, and the popularity of sports cars has had a pronounced effect.

"We've made a lot of people aware of automobiles," he says, "aware of the safety aspects, aware of the handling qualities cars should have. This has been reflected positively in the kinds of cars you can buy today."

In the area of improved quality Kaser cites metallurgy and forgings; power-to-weight ratios; the extraction of more power from an engine; new tire compounds and technology; efficient cylinder heads. He acknowledges that automobiles would have improved without racing but emphasizes that what racing has done is to intensify the process of progress.

The drivers of sports cars are another source of consumer demand for quality. Because a good sports car—Porsche, Ferrari, Alfa Romeo, Jaguar, Aston-Martin, Corvette—is designed to meet the high-performance standards of competition, it has a healthy built-in margin of performance and safety for everyday street use. When sports car drivers go shopping for quality, Detroit is most attentive.

John Bishop, an industrial designer and president of the International Motor Sports Association, says the so-called "sporty" cars like Mustang, Camaro, Javelin, Barracuda, Chal-

193

lenger and Firebird owe much to racing and the influence of the youth market. "A dozen or so years ago," Bishop asks, "did we imagine that Detroit would provide four-speed gear boxes, disc brakes and limited-slip differentials as commonplace options? It wasn't so long ago that we had to look to Europe for these performance, safety and fun items."

Jacque Passino also has credited young car enthusiasts with many of today's developments, including styling improvements. Sheet metal or chrome junctions of lines have been replaced by the molded, sculptured look, a flowing contour derived from the functional, aerodynamic lines of the race car. And much of the garishness of multicolors has been ridiculed off the road. The lightweight magnesium or even the imitation "mag" wheel comes from the race car and it does not flaunt a giant hub cap.

Many young people are involved in the hot-rod movement. They are the reason why speed-equipment shops are prospering all over the country. These shops sell performance items developed not by car manufacturers but by specialized companies that cater to hot-rod enthusiasts and the sports car crowd. They sell hot cams, racing carburetors, limited-slip axles and all kinds of other devices for extracting more power, speed and durability from "stock" engines and cars. And Detroit keeps a vigilant eye on these shops and their clientele.

*   *   *

Motor racing is big business. There is an old saying in the auto world: Win Sunday, sell Monday. Racing keeps on growing because of its tie with one of the largest industries in America. And that industry depends largely on the enthusiasm generated at the race track when it comes to increasing sales— not only of automobiles but of hundreds of related accessories and supplies. When Semon ("Bunky") Knudsen was president of Ford Motor Company, he said: "We sell racing and we create excitement and interest in our products through racing." That philosophy can be traced all the way back to the founder of the company, Henry Ford. After racing his "999" at the turn of the century, he realized a pioneer increase of from zero units to more than a million units in 15 years.

Dealer showrooms are decorated with posters depicting victories on road courses, oval tracks and at drag meets. Even the names of car models suggest strength and swiftness— Charger, Cougar, Mustang, Cyclone, Torino, Barracuda, Dart, Grand Prix, Le Mans, Firebird, Javelin and so on.

Until the start of the 1971 season Ford was probably the most active manufacturer openly participating in racing ("probably" because the companies never discuss their racing budgets). Ford's most conspicuous effort has been with sedans in the races sanctioned by the National Association for Stock Car Auto Racing (NASCAR). Stock car racing provides a ready showcase to stimulate the interest of the car-buying public.

In addition, Ford engines have broken the long-time supremacy of the Offenhausers at Indianapolis. In the world manufacturers' championship series a giant Ford power plant won so overwhelmingly at Le Mans that the French-influenced Commission Sportive Internationale legislated that engine out of competition. In the last few years the Cosworth-Ford engine has been dominant on the Formula One, or Grand Prix, circuit. Mass-produced Ford V-8's power some of the Formula A racers that compete for the Continental Championship of the Sports Car Club of America. Ford's Mustang won the S.C.C.A.'s Trans-American Championship three times. And on top of all this Ford is strongly engaged in drag racing.

Chrysler comes close to Ford, particularly with Dodges and Plymouths on the NASCAR circuit. Chrysler engines have powered more successful dragsters than any other power plant. Plymouth's Barracuda has performed creditably in Trans-American competition and so has Dodge's Challenger.

American Motors Company has also got into the act. For many years shackled by an "elderly" image, it suddenly developed an aggressive attitude that changed the picture overnight and its Javelin shook up the Trans-American Championship series.

Because of General Motors' corporate policy, the Chevrolet Division cannot flagrantly participate in racing. But its presence is unmistakable. Chevrolet's success in road racing has been spectacular. Its Camaros won the Trans-American Championship two consecutive years. Specially built aluminum-block racing engines power the bright orange sports-racing cars of the McLaren teams that have so long dominated the Canadian-American Challenge Cup. Moreover, Chevy racing engines are installed in most of the other cars in the Can-Am races, and Chevrolet's mass-produced V-8's are predominant among the Formula A cars running for the S.C.C.A.'s Continental Championship.

*   *   *

Of course, what is good for the domestic manufacturers is equally good for the foreign ones. Datsun of Japan is one of the largest of those supporting motor racing in this country. But unlike the American manufacturers, Datsun gives its primary support to club racing rather than all-out professional competition. Its reasoning is that the Sunday club events sanctioned by the S.C.C.A. are where it can compete with its marketing rivals to show what its cars can do.

Datsun's factory backing consists of the maintenance of two teams (east and west) to run in S.C.C.A. club events and, of course, the annual national run-off, the American Road Race of Champions. Its support, aside from salaries to its regular drivers, includes cash prizes and other assistance to competitors placing well in Datsuns. In national S.C.C.A. competition Datsun usually wins at least 40 first places a season.

Like the American manufacturers, Datsun and the other major Japanese producer, Toyota, derive technical benefits from racing. Such items as disc brakes, independent rear suspension and overhead-camshaft engines are a few of the performance features that are standard on Japanese sports cars and sedans.

Volkswagen of West Germany is also heavily committed

196

to racing—and under conditions that are nearly ideal: VW does not have to race against other makes. The reason is that the S.C.C.A. maintains two racing classes that consist entirely of Formula Vees and Formula Super Vees, which are open-cockpit racers based on Volkswagen components. Formula Vee cars compete only among themselves; Super Vees likewise compete only among themselves. Formula Vee, as previously noted, is the largest class in auto racing (nearly all of it in "club" events).

Volkswagen subsidizes most of the expenses of the big Vee and Super Vee championship races at Daytona Beach and elsewhere in the United States. It gives cash prizes to winners of smaller Vee and Super Vee races. It also pays the expenses of six or more leaders of American VW competition to run Vee races in Germany.

Ford of England is responsible for the creation of another open-wheel, open-cockpit racing class akin to Volkswagen's Super Vee. This is the Formula Ford, with a 1,600cc. engine based on the Ford Cortina. Formula Fords run in club races of the Sports Car Club of America and the all-out professional races of the International Motor Sports Association.

Other foreign manufacturers committed to racing in varying degrees include Ferrari, Porsche, Peugeot, Matra-Simca, Alfa Romeo, MG, BMW, Triumph, Saab and Volvo.

And, of course, the industries related to automobile manufacturing are engaged in one way or another in racing. The most important are the tire companies. Goodyear and Firestone have invested millions of dollars in developing safer and more durable tires for racing and, by extension, for passenger cars. Wide treads, low profiles, belt construction, radial ply—these and other developments come from racing. As for the other companies, the list is long—petroleum, lubricants, additives, coolants, spark plugs, shock absorbers, brakes, carburetors, electrical equipment, suppliers of metals and plastics and so on. Most of them invest in development programs, in sponsorship of races and race cars. And, as in the case of the car manufacturers, the results eventually appear in the commercial market.

Win Sunday, sell Monday.

Pit popsy.

CHAPTER 11

The Things You Hear!

IT IS CUSTOMARY in motor-sports books to append glossaries. Invariably they include the standard words like *monocoque* and *dry sump* and, to show the author has class, a few Briticisms like *shunt* and *dicing*. Many phrases are long established and immutable. To avoid violating a hoary tradition, this book also includes a glossary. I must say that many of the definitions in it, being my own, are pretty good. (*Quel chutzpah!*)

The trouble with a glossary, though, is that it is only a bloodless list of words and phrases. It cannot convey much of the feel, the sense, the imagery of motor racing's speech. Setting aside those phrases that are purely technical, there still is a fair amount of language that is indigenous to racing. Some of it is borrowed from the slang of American youth, some from regionalisms. Some phrases are simply economic. Only the

198

keenest etymologist would dare say this phrase or that comes exclusively from motor racing. Yet, taken altogether, racing does have something of a language.

One of the phrases most frequently heard in the racing community is "no way." There is no law that limits these common words to racing, yet it seems to be an ingrained part of the sport. It means futile, impossible. Could Unser have caught Leonard? *No way.* Will your car be ready for Milwaukee? *No way.* Let's see if we can get this mutha to go faster. *No way.* Do you love me? *No way!* I wanted to buy it, but there was *no way.* The unusual thing about these ordinary words is that they are normally rendered in a sing-song manner. For emphasis or in mock exuberance, they will be verbalized rather loudly: "N O W A Y !"

Richard Petty gave the phrase a more positive twist after winning the 1971 Daytona 500. He said, "There's no way of being more pleased."

"The way to go" is something good, praiseworthy, enviable, something recommended. Thus when four-wheel drive was still legal in USAC, Mario Andretti looked over Al Unser's four-wheel-drive race car and said, "This is *the way to go.*" When USAC promoters decided to run two short heats instead of one long race, they said, "We think this is *the way to go.*" If, in preparing dinner for guests, you put more clams in the clam chowder, that's *the way to go.* If, in running a restaurant, you stint on the clams to raise your profit, that's *the way to go.*

A promoter reports that the expenses of a recent race were high and the gate disappointing. He "took a bath," which is to say he lost money, or, occasionally, he "took a sponge bath."

Speaking of money, you sometimes have to deal with a major force possessed of economic clout, like television, a star driver who can demand his price, a well-financed promoter who will not be denied—a force with exceptional bargaining leverage. This is the 800-pound gorilla.

Q. Where does an 800-pound gorilla sleep?

A. Anywhere he damn pleases.

If an 800-pound gorilla walks into your home and demands a seven-course dinner, would you be likely to refuse him? If the television people say they want your race to start at 4:30 P.M. instead of 2 o'clock, if they want every ninth lap run backward, you'll do it. You're dealing with an 800-pound gorilla.

If you agree with something that has just been said, the appropriately courteous response is "You better believe it." Not "you had better" or "you'd better," but "you better."

"This salami stinks."

"You better believe it."

The word "right" is used in agreement, too, but I have the impression it is rather inattentive, as though the party of the second part is impatiently waiting for his turn to speak.

"I'm eating this salami sandwich when this broad—"

"Yeah, right!"

"Right" may also be used as an interrogatory attention getter, when the party of the second part is not completely focusing on you:

"I'm eating this salami sandwich, right?"

"Yeah, right."

Another attention getter is the question "OK?" The speaker wants to be certain his listener understands and is ready to follow the train of thought:

"I'm eating this salami sandwich, OK?"

"Yeah, right."

Sometimes it suggests the speaker is taking his audience along one careful step at a time:

"It was a sunny day, OK? Tri-X was all I had, OK? So I stopped down to f.22, OK?"

"OK" may also be used as the acknowledgement of a question:

Q. Where did you find this bird?

A. OK. I was snooping around. . . .

English racing people use the adjective "quick" in the sense that Americans use "fast." This is a *quick* car, he drove a few *quick* laps, he was *quick* at Edmonton, how *quick* were you this morning? The interesting thing is that this Briticism has caught on in the United States. American race drivers and mechanics who are seldom exposed to foreigners and who have not gone beyond high school use "quick" with comfortable assurance.

Englishmen also say "sort out," meaning they have to find out what's wrong with a balky car; they are shaking down a new car; they have work to do. We are still *sorting out* the engine, we've got some *sorting out* to do, I won't know till I've *sorted it out*. The phrase also has something to do with thinking things through and solving problems: I simply said it was in violation of the contract and left it to Teddy to *sort out*.

The English also speak of a "mixed bag," a well-organized program of races in which many types of cars are acceptable. The American equivalent is "race what you bring" or "run what you bring."

"Bad-mouth" is a verb of Southern origin that means to derogate. Why do they *bad-mouth* the Can-Am? Or I heard you been *bad-mouthing* me.

There are some usages you are not likely to find in Webster or Fowler. But if the purpose of language is to communicate a mental picture, you cannot improve on "he got sideways." Any driver hearing a description of an accident knows what is meant by "*he got sideways* coming out of No. 2." Similarly, "he got out of shape" is immensely expressive when a mishap is being discussed. This can be extended beyond racing, as in "The business was getting *out of shape*." Another expressive word is "T-bone." It means being struck broadside. He got sideways and before he could straighten out, David *T-boned* him.

The racing community uses "win" as a noun: It was Donohue's third win of the season, we worked hard for the win, nothing pays off like a win.

"Scrutineer" would probably be classified by Fowler as a barbarism, but it is well established and understood in road racing. A scrutineer is the tech inspector who goes over every nut and bolt in your car to determine whether it conforms with the regulations and is safe for racing. A scrutineer may report after an inspection that an approved car is "sanitary." Also, a race steward may warn drivers against rough stuff or cheating: "I want a nice, *sanitary* race."

201

A "ride" is a job or assignment driving a race car. Gurney lost his ride with the McLaren team, Joe is looking for a USAC ride, or his ride with Banjo was the best he'd ever had.

Parts and components are spoken of as "pieces." A crate of pieces arrived this morning. We don't get any money help from the factory, only know-how and pieces.

Sports car events attract the most beautiful women in the world of racing. In England and Canada they are called "birds." In the United States they are referred to as "chicks," "dolls" and "broads." And then there is that beloved appellation indigenous to American road racing: "pit popsies."

Anything marvelous, wonderful or really unusual is "outtasight," one word. There was that Friday afternoon when mechanics and drivers from other crews pitched in to help repair a car damaged in practice. In describing their contributions afterward, the driver of the damaged car said, "Everyone was *outtasight.*"

A superbly prepared car attracts considerable attention in the paddock. Says a fan, "This car's *outtasight.*" The first few outsiders who were privileged to see—or "eyeball"—Jim Hall's extraordinary Chaparral 2J reported it was *outtasight.*

"Wentaway," also one word, means destroyed, ruined, blown up. So does "lunch."

Q. Why didn't you finish?

A. I lunched the engine and the gear box wentaway.

When the actor Steve McQueen drove in the 1970 endurance race at Sebring, skeptics thought it was a publicity stunt for a movie he was making, particularly in view of the fact that his left foot was in a cast as the result of an earlier injury. But his co-driver Peter Revson and others admired McQueen's driving. "He has balls," they said. It means courage. A driver who has *big balls* is very brave indeed. Conversely, a coward—in racing and in other professions—*has no balls.*

A driver who races *balls out* is driving at the absolute maximum, the limit, ten-tenths, extending every effort and heedless of danger. It sometimes happens in such instances that the driver's bravery outruns his intelligence.

202

In drag racing "history" means defeat. Once you have been eliminated from the drag meet, "you are now history."

"Brain fade" is adapted from a mechanical malfunction called brake fade, and it means the lapse of one's normal intelligence, a misjudgment, forgetfulness, plain stupidity. His crash was a case of *brain fade.*

A car that is wrecked is "totaled."

To "hack it" means to barely succeed or barely make out. He couldn't *hack it* with the first three cars. Without tire money these drivers would have a tough time *hacking it.*

"Back off" means to ease off the throttle when going into a turn—or, by extension, to cool it, not go too far, to retrieve oneself from what may be an untenable situation. I started to buy his car but decided to *back off.* He didn't want to risk a law suit, so he *backed off.*

Of course, a driver who backs off too soon and too often does not win many races. Or perhaps through ineptitude or inexperience he cannot hack it in this league. When a driver is unsatisfactory, his car owner may complain of having "cockpit trouble":

Q. How you doin', Chris?

A. Car's OK, but we're having cockpit trouble.

In practice sessions before a stock-car race, everyone is looking for some exotic little secret to give him a margin over the others. Often it is something trivial, but drivers and mechanics take it seriously until it is tried and discarded. This is called "the tip." Sometimes gullible drivers may be psyched by the leaders into using a phoney tip, a hint thrown out to cross them up. Today's tip is to run on overinflated tires; or underinflated tires; or right-side tires on the left side. Often it involves uncritical imitation: if a driver turns some very hot laps and the opposition spots something unusual on his car—say a chrome exhaust—they rush to copy it.

Some years ago at Daytona the roof of Richard Petty's Plymouth was painted black, textured to look like vinyl. His father, Lee Petty, himself a retired driving star, let it be known that the rough texture altered the flow of air over the roof, adding one or two miles an hour speed. That was the tip. One year at Rockingham Freddie Lorenzen won the pole while using the same type of tire compound that everyone else was using. But instead of having white code dots on the sidewalls, Lorenzen's tires had red dots. Actually, he had repainted them red. And in view of Lorenzen's speed, red dots were the tip that weekend. Everyone wanted tires with red dots.

The same sort of frantic searching for advantage goes on in USAC and sports-car racing, where the tip is known as "the hot set-up."

In racing you don't just accelerate: You "get on it." The phrase implies returning quickly to the throttle after having been off it for a moment, as in a turn or mishap. Be sure to *get on it* coming out of the turn. The phrase also implies applying throttle with great force. So does "put your foot in it," which evokes an image of stomping the accelerator so hard that your foot goes right into the innards of the engine.

"On your head" suggests an accident. Take that line through the turn and you'll go *on your head*. He went *on his head* at Daytona but he came out OK.

Anyone who is extending every effort, who is surpassing his usual capacity, is "letting it all hang out." A driver who is running an especially inspired race with great audacity and the utmost skill is *letting it all hang out*. He really gave it everything he had that day, *letting it all hang out*. In addition, it is used in a more limited context: "He was trying so hard to pass when he came through that turn that he *let it all hang out*." It also means shoot the works, go for broke, take great risks, total commitment. "I figured it was then or never, so I *let it all hang out*."

At a United States Grand Prix a few years ago a magnificent pit popsy was wearing a magnificent bikini. The bra was only a sliver away from the ultimate, which prompted an admirer to ask, "Why not let it all hang out?"

But that's a different story.

APPENDIX A

Glossary

A

ACCUS. Automobile Competition Committee for the United States-F.I.A.

A.H.R.A. American Hot Rod Association.

altered. One of the classes in drag racing. As long as the competitor starts with some kind of automobile body, he can modify it nearly any way that suits his needs. Usually these cars do not have fenders or glass.

anchors. In drag racing, brakes.

A.R.R.C. American Road Race of Champions, a run-off to determine national champions of the Sports Car Club of America.

autocross. A competition in which drivers maneuver their cars through a twisting course, usually defined by rubber pylons. Drivers run solo against the clock. Also called gymkhana, slalom.

axle. A spindle or pin on which a wheel revolves, or which revolves with a wheel.

B

back marker (British). A car on the last few rows of the starting grid.

back off. To let up on the throttle; slow down a bit.

bad scene. An unpleasant situation.

bank, banking. 1. Degree of inclination on a turn. 2. A turn that is banked.

bend. 1. A turn, generally shallow. 2. To damage a race car.

big banger. Large engine, usually over 305 cubic inches displacement. Also, big bore.

black flag. A signal by which race officials order a driver to come into the pits his next time around. The purpose may be to inspect damage, to discipline him (by the delay) for infraction of rules, or to withdraw him from the race because his car is too slow or is dangerous to others in the race (for example, it may be throwing oil or a loose piece of metal may be on the point of falling off the car).

blend. Mixture of methanol and nitromethane used in USAC championship cars, dragsters and certain other machines.

blip. To rev or race an engine in short bursts. A dab at the throttle.

block. The cylinder block, the basic structure of an internal-combustion engine.

blown engine. 1. An engine that has broken down under stress. 2. An engine that is supercharged.

blueprint. To tear down completely and rebuild an engine to a degree of precision not possible in usual factory assembly.

body in white. A metal car body just off the production line. It is empty and bare, still in its natural metal color.

bore. Diameter of a cylinder of an internal-combustion engine. The size of an engine can be increased by reboring—that is, making the diameter larger.

boss. Perfect, outstanding. Also, Ford has a car named the Boss Mustang 302.

box. Gear box, transmission.

brain fade. A mental lapse, usually attributable to forgetfulness and occasionally to plain stupidity.

brake fade. When brakes overheat because of constant use they lose their effectiveness. This is called brake fade.

brake horsepower (usually abbreviated b.h.p.) A measure of an engine's horsepower. Incidentally, the brake in this instance is not the conventional brake of an automobile, but a measuring instrument.

BRM. British Racing Motors, a race-car manufacturer.

bubble. Last position in qualifying line-up while the line-up is still being determined. A driver is *on the bubble* when he is in danger of being displaced by a faster driver.

bucket seat. An individual seat, usually one of a pair in the front section of a car. A true bucket seat is severely contoured to provide lateral support.

bull ring. A short oval track, half a mile or less. Because the space is so confining, traffic is always congested. Even the leaders get caught in the traffic because they have to work their way through it as they lap the field.

buy the farm, buy it. To be killed in an accident, in racing or in other circumstances. The expression seems to be used by men in high-risk activities, such as race drivers, to avoid direct reference to accidental death from any cause. It is derived from the retirement cliché of the military services—throughout their careers old sergeants and chiefs speak of *buying a farm.*

C

caliper. A sort of clamp that grips the disc in a disc-brake system.

cam. An off-center (eccentric) formation on a shaft, used to transmit motion.

camshaft. A rotating shaft driven by a gear, belt or chain that carries eccentric formations called cams. This mechanism indirectly actuates the valves in the cylinders.

carburetor, carb. A unit that combines gasoline and air into a vapor for combustion in the cylinders.

C.A.S.C. Canadian Automobile Sport Clubs.

cc. (usually lower case). Cubic centimeters. 1,000cc. = 1 liter = approx. 61 cubic inches.

chassis. The basic understructure or frame of a racer without body-work, wheels, brakes, suspension and steering gear—these components are added.

checkered flag. A flag of black and white squares that signals the end of a race.

chicane. A man-made corner, or turn, placed at a point where the race authorities want to reduce the speed of the cars.

chief steward. He heads the staff of officials at a race and runs the race.

Christmas Tree. The count-down system of lights, mounted on a vertical pole, used to start a drag race.

chute. 1. A straight portion of a race track, also called straightaway, straight. 2. Parachute used to slow down a drag racer after its run is completed.

c.i.d. (usually lower case). Cubic inches displacement.

club racing. Nonprofessional events.

coil, coil springs. Units or members of the suspension system.

come-in signal. Usually an arrow held by member of the pit crew instructing the driver to come into the pit on his next lap.

comingman (British, one word). A new, young driver with excellent potential.

compound. In tire building, a mixture of natural and/or synthetic rubbers together with carbon black, resin, bonding agents and an infinite variety of other additives and chemicals. A compound can be "hard," "soft," "sticky," etc., depending on what is needed in the race and on the track for which the tire is being designed. Compounding is the "black magic" of tire building and because the business is so competitive a compound is one of the most rigidly kept secrets.

con rod. Connecting rod that transmits movement from the piston to the crankshaft.

crankcase. A pan installed beneath the engine to hold lubricating oil.

crankshaft. The shaft that is rotated by the action of the pistons. It transmits power to the drive train and eventually to the wheels.

crash box. Nonsynchronized transmission.

C.S.I. Commission Sportive Internationale, the competition arm of the Federation Internationale de l'Automobile.

cubes. Cubic inches of displacement.

D

dice (British). As a noun, a dice is close racing among two or more cars, with frequent changes of position. As a verb, to dice means to engage in close racing.

differential. This unit, which is near the end of the drive-train system, distributes engine power to the drive wheels.

disc. A fundamental part of the brakes used on race cars, sports cars and better passenger cars. On conventional passenger cars the customary braking system is the drum type rather than the disc type.

displacement (piston displacement and engine displacement are the same). The size of an engine, expressed in cubic inches, cubic centimeters or liters (1 liter = 1,000 cc.).

D.O.H.C. Double overhead camshaft.

downshift. A gear change from a higher gear to a lower one. It is essential in road racing that this technique be mastered so that only the engine speed changes and the car never jerks. The opposite is *upshift*.

drafting. Following closely behind another car, letting the lead car do the work of breaking through the air.

drift. A cornering technique in which all four wheels slide as the car is accelerated through a turn. The drift is intentional and can be controlled by the driver. For example, by applying more throttle he can exaggerate the drift; by backing off the throttle he can reduce it.

drive shaft. The part of the drive train that transmits power from the engine to the driving wheels.

drive train. The entire system that works to carry power from the engine to the driving wheels.

driver. When racing people say "driver" they mean "race driver."

dry sump. Type of design that omits conventional crankcase oil reservoir. Oil is stored in a cooling radiator and is pumped to and taken from engine by separate pumps.

dynamometer. An engine-testing and output-measuring machine, usually installed in soundproof chambers in a factory, workshop or garage.

E

eliminated. Defeated in a drag race.

équipe. French for stable and, by extension, race team. In Italian, *scuderia*.

esses. Continuous series of left and right turns, usually shallow.

e.t. (usually lower case). Elapsed time.

E-Z. A pit signal to the driver that means take it easy. Usually given to the leader or any other driver who is in no danger of being overtaken.

F

F.I.A. Federation Internationale de l'Automobile, the world governing body of motor racing.

fiberglass. A plastic material, very tough, used in race cars—generally molded to form the body.

fishtail. Exactly what it suggests. The rear end of the car weaves from side to side.

flat-out. Top speed.

flying start, rolling start. The formation of race cars is in motion when it takes the green flag at the starting line. In a flying start the cars are moving at high speed; in a rolling start they move at a comparatively low speed.

footprint. A figure of speech describing the area of contact between a tire and the ground.

formula. A detailed set of specifications, usually for a class of open-wheel race car with a single seat in an open cockpit.

formula libre. Anything goes.

four-wheel drive (abbreviated 4-w-d). A system in which engine power is transmitted to four wheels rather than the conventional two.

fuel injection. A system of metering devices that feeds fuel directly into the cylinders rather than through a carburetor. Indirect fuel injection pulses fuel into the manifold just before the cylinders.

full bore. Maximum speed or effort; fully extended. Also, flat-out (U.S.) and full chat (British).

full chat (British). Top speed.

G

gasser. A type of drag racer.

gear box. Transmission.

get sideways. A spin or slide in which the car moves at an angle to the direction of traffic.

go into the country. To leave the circuit—unintentionally, of course.

Grand Prix. For purists, a race counting for points toward the World Championship of Drivers, but loosely used to promote any kind of race.

grid. In road racing, the starting line-up. Also called the *starting grid.*

groove. The most efficient route around a race circuit, taking into account the shape of the circuit, the sharpness of the turns, the centrifugal forces in the turns, the degree of banking, the inclination of the straightaways, individual driving styles and individual car characteristics. Some tracks have such narrow racing areas, particularly on the turns, that the drivers call them "one-groove tracks"; passing is difficult on a one-groove track. *Groove* usually is applied to oval tracks. On road courses, occasionally, the synonym *line* is used: *Andretti's line is different from Donohue's.*

ground clearance. Space between the ground and the bottom of a car.

GT. 1. Grand touring, from the Italian *gran turismo* and the French *grand tourisme.* A sedan of either two or four seats designed for rapid, comfortable travel and with emphasis on good handling and performance. Built in limited quantities. 2. A group of such cars certified as having been built in required volume and to the specifications of Appendix J of the F.I.A.'s International Sporting Code.

gymkhana. A competition in which drivers maneuver their cars through a twisting course defined by rubber pylons. Drivers run solo against the clock. Also called *autocross, slalom.*

H

hairpin. Just what it implies—an extremely sharp turn that suggests the bend of a hairpin. It may also be called a *switchback.*

hairy. Dangerous, wild, frightening, exciting.

half-shaft. Axle shaft.

have a go at it (British). To try something, usually said with optimism.

header(s). A section of the exhaust system attached to the cylinder heads to carry off burned gases from the engine.

heel and toe. Operation of both the accelerator and brake pedals with only the right foot—usually heel on the accelerator and toe on the brake. An essential technique for drivers to master.

hemi. Slang term for an engine with hemispherical combustion chambers.

hill climb. Up a hill from a start line to a finish line, one car at a time, running against the clock.

hobby. A type of stock car racer used by novices.

homologation. The procedure in which a manufacturer, in submitting a car for approval in a given racing class, certifies to the sanctioning body that he is producing the car in the volume required (for example, 1,000 identical units in 12 consecutive months). *The manufacturer homologates his car.*

hot dog, hot shoe. An especially good race driver.

I

infield. Area enclosed by an oval track or by a road course. Can be used for pits, garages, parking, camping and, of course, watching the race. In road racing the counterpart is *paddock* (which see).

IMSA. International Motor Sports Association.

K

knock-offs. Type of single wing nut, easily removed and replaced, for fastening a wheel to its hub. It is not turned with a wrench, but struck (*knocked off*) with a mallet.

Koni. Trade name of a shock absorber widely used in race cars and sports cars.

L

lap (n). A complete circuit of the course.

lap (v). When a driver is running exceptionally fast, he increases the gap between himself and a slower driver. Eventually the distance may become so great that the fast driver has completed one lap more than the slower one. At the moment he passes the slower driver, he *laps* him. The term is also applied to a pack of fast cars that *lap* the slower cars. Incidentally, when a driver who has been *lapped* manages to pass the driver who *lapped* him, he is said to *unlap* himself.

lay it on. To go fast, really fast.

line. In road racing, the most efficient route around a circuit. Equivalent to the *groove* of oval-track racing. Also can apply to the route a driver takes through a particular turn.

liter. Anglicized spelling of litre, a metric unit of measure slightly larger than the American quart. One liter equals 1,000 cubic centimeters. It is equivalent, in the American scale, to approximately 61 cubic inches.

lose it. To lose control of the car.

loud pedal. Accelerator.

M

mag. Magneto.

mag wheels. Wheels cast of magnesium, a light metal.

manifold. A sort of chamber that distributes or collects. The intake manifold distributes the fuel-air mixture from the carburetor to the cylinders. The exhaust manifold collects the gases from the cylinders and carries them to the exhaust pipes.

mark. One of a series. For example, Mark 3 (or Mark III) is the third of a line of a car or other product. Can be abbreviated, as in Mk 3 or M3. Not to be confused with *marque* (which see).

marque. French for make, as in make of car. Not to be confused with *mark* (which see).

marshal. In road racing, a flagman or communications worker, a pit marshal, a grid marshal, etc. Almost always an unpaid volunteer.

methanol. An alcohol that is part of the fuel blend used in USAC championship cars and certain drag racers.

212

Mickey Mouse. A race course that has an excessive number of turns, or anything else that is small, trivial, inept; not to be taken very seriously.

mod (short for modification). "His car has the latest *mods*" describes a really up-to-date car.

monocoque. A chassis designed without a frame. The metal skin (sometimes called "stressed skin") is strong enough to be a structural member. A cardboard cartoon is a monocoque design: the cardboard is rigid enough to do its job without depending on an internal frame or skeleton.

mule. A practice car. To spare his racer, a driver uses a *mule* to learn the course of a road race. Sometimes the mule is lent to other teams.

N

NASCAR. National Association for Stock Car Auto Racing.

nerf. To tap or brush another race car.

nerfing bar. A sort of bumper to prevent wheels from touching.

N.H.R.A. National Hot Rod Association.

nitro. Nitromethane, part of the fuel blend used in USAC championship cars and certain drag racers.

Nomex. Trade name of one flame-resistant fabric used in race drivers' clothing—coveralls, face masks, gloves, socks, underwear.

normally aspirated. An engine that breathes without the help of a supercharger or turbocharger is said to be normally aspirated.

NORRA. National Off Road Racing Association.

O

Offy. Diminutive for Offenhauser, a well-known racing engine.

O.H.C. Overhead camshaft. (D.O.H.C. is a double overhead camshaft.)

oil radiator, oil cooler. Works just like a water radiator—that is, it cools the oil by holding it in a system of tubes, coils or honeycombs exposed to an airstream.

out of shape. Any disturbance of a driver's smooth line of movement. It may be a matter of fishtailing, loss of control or a spin from which he winds up pointed in the wrong direction. It may also be a momentary bobble or a break in the driver's rhythm.

oversteer. In its simplest terms, the back of the car tries to overtake the front—much like the tail wagging the dog.

P

pace car. A car that runs in front of the pack just before the beginning of a race to set the pace. Usually it is a flashy convertible donated by the manufacturer for publicity and promotional value.

pace lap. In oval racing, a brisk circuit of the course leading to a flying start. The cars are in formation and are working up speed so that when they reach the starting line they will be close to maximum. The early pace is usually set by a pace car (above) driven by an official or celebrity who has raced. It pulls off the track at a point short of the starting line; after that the pace, which rapidly builds up to the maximum, is set by the driver in the *pole position* (which see).

paddock. In road racing, a combination work and parking area for the race cars when they are not in action; also used by participants as a parking area for their trailers, tow trucks and everyday cars. Track owners differ in their designation of paddocks, but in general they are next to or close to the pits. In road racing it is traditional to let the public have a close-up look at the race cars and to mingle with the race personnel—and most tracks charge extra admission for the privilege. At some oval tracks the equivalent of the paddock is the *infield* (which see).

parade lap. A ceremonial circuit of the course with the cars in formation and moving slowly so that the spectators can get a good look at them. It precedes the pace lap (which see).

P.D.A. Professional Drivers Association, a quasi union that primarily represents Grand National drivers in NASCAR.

pieces. Components or parts, usually of an engine.

pit, pits. A long strip beside the track, usually on the front straight, where cars are serviced during a race. Usually restricted to participants and officials. Also called the *working pits.* Not to be confused with the adjacent *paddock* (which see).

pit road, pit lane. Road leading into and past the pit area from the · course and from the pits back to the course.

pit stop. Leaving the race course for a stop at the car's assigned position in the pits. The purpose can be refueling, change of tires, repairs, etc.

planing (aquaplaning, hydroplaning). On a rain-soaked surface, when the tires provide little traction, the race cars float on a film of water. This phenomenon is called planing.

pole, pole position. The No. 1 position in the starting line-up, earned by the driver with the fastest lap in the qualifying sessions. In the line-up (or "grid" in road racing) the cars are usually arranged in two

214

long files parallel with the roadway. The two fastest cars make up the first row, the next two constitute the second row, and so on through the field. The driver with the best qualifying time is said to "sit on the pole," so-called because this position gives him the lead going into the first turn. In an oval race or in a road race where the first turn is a left-hander, the pole position is at the head of the left line. If it is a road race with the first turn a right-hander, the pole position is at the head of the right line. The pole is considered the most advantageous position because it permits the pole sitter to race flat-out without fear of ramming any car in front of him.

pop. Fuel blend, methanol, and nitromethane.

press on (British). To persist, with little chance of winning, usually after stopping for time-consuming repairs.

Press On Regardless. The name of a rally conducted annually by the Detroit Region of the Sports Car Club of America. It is a rugged exercise of four nights over 1,200 miles of logging trails, untraveled back roads, snowmobile trails and sand hills in the Lower Peninsula of Michigan.

production. Similar to stock—that is, the way the manufacturer made it in quantity.

promo. Promotion or promotional material.

promoter. An entrepreneur who organizes a race and puts up the prize money. The course may be one that he owns or leases.

proto. Short for prototype.

prototype. 1. A sports car that does not need to conform with the production figures required in homologation. Usually one or few of a kind. 2. Test model of a new car.

pump gas, pump fuel. Gasoline of the same quality available to the public.

push rods. Metal rods operating off the camshaft. They transmit the movement of the camshaft to the valves. A push rod engine (or, frequently, a stock-block engine) is one that has overhead valves but no overhead camshaft.

Q

qualifying. The pre-race speed sessions that determine starting positions in the race. In oval racing (USAC, NASCAR) each driver runs a specified number of laps around the track alone, against the clock. In road racing, the drivers practice for a specified amount of time under race conditions, and all their laps are timed by the scorers.

In both cases the purpose is to form a field from the fastest cars; in both cases, also, the fastest lap times qualify for the pole position.

R

rack and pinion. A design of steering mechanism used in race cars and the best sports cars.

rain tire. In road racing, a tire with soft rubber compound and special tread pattern, designed for traction on wet road surfaces.

raunchy. Slovenly appearance of a car or person; undisciplined conduct.

rev counter. A tachometer, an instrument usually mounted on the panel that shows the driver the number of revolutions per minute the engine is turning.

ride. A job or assignment driving a race car.

road race. A race run on a road course or simulated road course, as distinguished from a race run on an oval track.

roadster. The affectionate designation of a front-engine race car that dominated the USAC Championship Trail and Indianapolis from 1953 to 1963. It was characterized by a low profile, and the engine was offset to the left, with the drive shaft alongside the driver at about hip level. The design was originated in 1952 by Frank Kurtis and was subsequently carried farther by other car builders, notably A. J. Watson.

rocker, rocker arm. A pivoted lever that actuates the valve by transmitting movement from the push rod or cam.

roll bar. A loop or frame of strong tubular steel, securely fixed to the chassis and projecting above the driver's head. If the car turns over, a good roll bar protects the driver from being crushed by the vehicle; it also prevents the driver's body from hitting the ground.

roll cage. Structures of tubular steel, installed inside a stock car or Trans-American sedan. It surrounds the driver, protecting him in the event of a crash or turnover. The structure is welded to the frame and padded with foam rubber.

r.p.m. (usually lower case). Revolutions per minute. A measure of the speed at which the engine is turning.

run out of road. To use up all the road surface during a maneuver and thus go off course.

S

sandbagging. Derived from poker. In practice or in the early stages of a race a crafty driver may not show all the speed he has, thus lulling the opposition into a false sense of security.

sanitary. Steward to the drivers: "I want a nice clean race, no accidents, no rough stuff, no passing on the yellow. I want a sanitary race."

scattershield. Protective steel housing around the clutch and flywheel assembly to prevent broken parts from spewing out onto the track surface.

S.C.C.A. Sports Car Club of America.

scrutineering. In road racing, a detailed inspection of a race car to make certain it conforms with the rules and is safe enough to compete.

scuderia. Italian for stable and, by extension, race team. In French, *équipe.*

shoes. Tires.

shunt (British). A collision.

shut the gate, close the gate. Blocking a driver who is trying to get past on the inside of a turn.

shut-off. The point, before a turn in road racing, at which a driver must slow down by backing off the throttle or braking. Some courses help the driver by posting reference markers—5,4,3,2,1—before the entrance to the turn. Each driver has his own personal shut-off, depending on his equipment, skill and nerve.

slalom. A competition in which drivers maneuver their cars through a twisting course defined by rubber pylons. Drivers run against the clock. Also called *gymkhana, autocross.*

slicks. Wide, flat-surface tires used on the drive wheels of drag racers. Midget and sprint cars also use slicks on paved tracks.

slide. A skid of the rear wheels. In the case of a four-wheel *drift,* the driver is in control. In the case of a slide, there may be some question of control. In a skid, the car is out of control.

slingshot. A type of drag racer in which the driver sits behind the rear wheels.

slingshotting. A technique, usually in stock car racing, for passing a car ahead. In this technique a driver *drafts* (follows closely behind) another driver to take advantage of his slipstream. This preserves his power. At the tactical moment the drafter moves out of the slipstream and, with the reserve power he has been husbanding, slings past the car he has been following.

speed trap. See *trap.*

spin. To lose control of the car and revolve. To *spin out* or *spin off* means to spin and, usually, to leave the course.

spoiler. An air deflector that can be mounted either at the front end or on the rear deck to resist a car's tendency, at high speed, to

217

lift off the ground. By keeping the car in contact with the road the spoiler also improves the adhesion of the tires to the road.

sports car. An agile vehicle that is easily maneuverable, accelerates briskly, brakes positively, handles well. It is instantly responsive, it steers precisely, it gives taut performance. Being tightly sprung, it does not wallow and heave the way a conventional passenger car does. It is usually more expensive than a passenger car.

sporty car. A step removed from a true sports car (above). Looks something like a sports car and has some of the sports car's qualities but is not a sports car. Ask any sports car owner.

stack(s), also **velocity stacks(s).** Horn-like pipe attached to the carburetor or fuel-injection system to draw in air. Sometimes also applied to exhaust system, as in *exhaust stacks.*

stock. The way the manufacturer produced it, with no modifications. (For emphasis, *pure stock.*)

stock block. A mass-produced engine block for a passenger car, usually with valves actuated by push rods. The block is only the beginning of an engine. By the time it has been "prepared" for racing, it is a long way from the assembly line.

stroke. 1. As a noun, the distance a piston travels inside a cylinder. 2. As a verb, to drive slower than the car's capability, usually to conserve the machinery.

supercharger. A blower that forces into the engine more air than the engine could breathe without help. Also see *blown engine, turbocharger, normally aspirated.*

suspension, suspension system. The assembly of springs, shock absorbers, torsion bars, joints, arms, etc., that (1) cushion the shock of the bumps and jolts of the road and (2) serve to keep the wheels in constant contact with the road, thus enhancing the steering and the transmission of power from the engine to the road.

swallow a valve. A valve breaks and falls into the cylinder. That's swallowing a valve.

switchback. A U-turn, or close to it. It may also be called a *hairpin.*

T

tachometer. An instrument, usually mounted on the panel, that shows the driver the number of revolutions per minute at which the engine is turning. Also, *rev counter.*

T-bone. To strike another car broadside.

ten-tenths (British). Maximum effort, driving at the limit. A driver fully extending himself is driving ten-tenths. At a lesser pace he is said to be driving eight-tenths, nine-tenths, etc.

time trials. 1. The speed runs before a race in which starting positions are determined. 2. Motor-sports events in which contestants race solo against the clock, as in gymkhanas.

torque. The twisting force provided by a rotating shaft, measured in foot-pounds. Visualize a stick of wood being turned on a lathe. Imagine grasping that stick of wood and trying to stop its rotation with your hand. The force you will feel is torque.

torsion bar. A rod in the suspension system that, when twisted from a grip at one end, functions like a spring.

tow. Same as *drafting*. That is, the driver "gets a tow" by tucking in behind another car.

transmission. The gear-changing or gear-shifting system through which engine power is applied to the wheels. The purpose of gear changing is to keep maximum engine power applied at all times under all conditions.

trap, speed trap. 1. A timing device, similar in principle to those used by highway policemen, to measure the speed of a race car as it runs through a predetermined stretch. Usually installed on the fastest part of the course, a straightaway. 2. In drag racing, electric eyes set up before and after the finish line to measure the speed of a dragster as it terminates its quarter-mile run.

tread. 1. Width of a car, measured from the centerline of the tires. 2. Pattern on the surface of a tire that touches the ground.

trick. Unorthodox, as in *trick car* or *trick technique*.

tune. To make adjustments that improve engine performance.

turbocharger. A supercharging device driven by exhaust gases from the engine. See *supercharger, blown engine.*

tweak. To engage in fine tuning or mild modification of an engine to coax just a bit more power from it.

tyre. This is the way our English friends spell tire.

U

understeer. Opposite of *oversteer*. The classic illustration is to imagine a car going out of control in a turn and departing the premises, nose first, through a fence. That's understeer. In *oversteer* the same thing happens except that the car goes through the fence stern first.

unreal. Exceptional, great; akin to *boss.*

USAC. United States Auto Club.

V

valve. An engine part that admits the fuel-air mixture into the cylinder or permits the gases to escape after combustion.

velocity stack(s), also **stack(s).** Horn-like pipe attached to the carburetor or fuel-injection system to draw in air.

W

wheel base. The distance between the centers of the front wheels and the rear wheels.

wing. An air foil mounted above the race car to exert downward thrust on the car. The effect is to improve its stability and to enhance the transmission of power from the engine to the ground.

Winner's Circle (also, **Victory Lane**). An area on or beside the track that is cordoned off to receive the winner of the race. This is where he sips the champagne (or—yich!—milk at Indianapolis) and is interviewed on the public-address system; where he poses for the victory photographs. This is where he receives the victory kiss from the beauty queen and the garland of flowers—the first-prize check usually comes afterward.

wishbone. An A-shaped arm, part of the suspension system.

works (British). Factory. What we call a factory team in this country is a *works* team in England.

Y

yellow flag, yellow light. A caution signal warning of dangerous conditions on the track. The rules prohibit improving one's position during a caution period.

APPENDIX B

"Think Group"

FOR INTERNATIONAL RACING to make sense, somebody somewhere had to devise a cosmic classification system and a set of rules to cover all cars everywhere. The system and rules are wrapped up in what is known in the trade as Appendix J, a section of the International Sporting Code of the Federation Internationale de l'Automobile.

Appendix J spells out, in the minute detail that the French master so well, the classification, definition and specifications of cars eligible for internationally recognized competition. The specs cover everything down to the size of seats, doors and windshield. Appendix J arranges classes inside of groups and groups inside of categories—which may be why the French "nuance" is often considered nit-picking here.

The rules are as intricate as the United States tax laws. They are so complicated that disputes over their meaning and intent constitute a subsidiary sport. Appendix J itself is compelled to carry italicized interpretations—*By door should be understood the part of the coachwork opening to give access to the seats.* The International Sporting Code says "Appendix J is certainly one of the most famous and most objected to, if not the best known, of the sporting documents, sometimes even better known than the International Sporting Code, of which it is, after all, part." *

The rules are written in French, the official language of the F.I.A., and disputes are adjudicated on the basis of that language. The English translations emerge in a taffy-like syntax that only a corporation lawyer could love: "Should the manufacturer have provided a greater number of gear box ratios and/or rear axle ratios, he must, to obtain recognition, prove that he has achieved the required minimum production of the car as many times as he has submitted two different gear boxes and two different rear-axle ratios."

The race cars that the spectator sees at Daytona, Laguna Seca, Watkins Glen and Road America are related to Appendix J. At some races the relationship is clear, as in the case of cars designated Formula One, Group 7 or prototype. In others the connection is rather tenuous, as in the case of the Trans-American cars of the S.C.C.A. and the Grand National cars of NASCAR.

* F.I.A. Year Book of Automobile Sport 1970, Green Section, p. 105.

In general, Appendix J can be considered a sort of motherly embrace in which all racing classifications can be included. In North America nearly all single-seaters and all cars competing in world-championship events will conform explicitly with an appropriate section of Appendix J; all the other race cars in our part of the world—late-model sportsman, super-modified, S.C.C.A. production sports cars, American sedans and so on—are North American inventions or adaptations that peep out from the embrace of Appendix J. Nearly every racing country has such "national" racing classifications of its own—the French Monomille, the English F-100, the Argentine Nationale, the Canada Class.

In reality, the groupings of Appendix J are academic to the race spectator. Certainly no promoter ever advertises a race for "Group 2 cars"—nobody would pay to see it. What kind of crowd would attend the Grand Prix of the United States if it were billed as a race for Group 8 cars? But even so, Appendix J does govern racing, and for the record it is summarized here.

In Groups 1 through 6 below, there are 13 classes of engine displacement. The size of the engine affects weight, dimensions, fuel capacity, tires, rollover bars and so on. In Group 7 the cars are arranged in seven "series" according to engine displacement. Group 8 is self-defining into three "formulas" of varying displacement. Group 9, being "Formula Libre," is unlimited in its variety of sizes.

The figures in parentheses indicate the minimum production required in a period of 12 consecutive months.

CATEGORY A

Recognized Production Cars

GROUP 1—Series-production touring cars (5,000), for all practical purposes four-seat cars in showroom condition. "These cars," says Appendix J, "shall compete in an event without having undergone any preparation likely to improve their performance or their conditions of use. The only working authorized is normal maintenance or the replacement [of] parts damaged through wear or accident and the modifications and additions explicitly authorized hereafter. . . ." The

Group 1.

Group 2.

A pair of Corvettes illustrate the difference between Groups 3 and 4. Left, a basic Corvette (Group 3); right, a Corvette highly modified (Group 4) for racing.

modifications that are permitted are quite limited, such as spark plugs, brakes, tires, carburetors.

GROUP 2—Special touring cars (1,000). These also are four-seat passenger cars, but modified far beyond the limits of Group 1 to prepare them for competition. The body must be the same as the original but almost anything else can be modified—manifold injection, gear boxes, cams, pistons, connecting rods, valves, bearings. The modifying is done by machining, finishing, polishing—that is, removal of material but not addition of material. Substitutions are restricted to specifically listed items.

GROUP 3—Series-production grand touring cars (1,000). These are the conventional two-seat sports cars seen on the street, cars such as Alfa Romeo, MG, Fiat, Porsche 914-4, basic Corvette. Modifications are severely limited, precisely the same as those authorized for Group 1.

GROUP 4—Special grand touring cars (500), which are "two-seater cars manufactured on a small series-production scale, and which may be subject to modifications in order to be more particularly adapted to sporting competition." Modifications permitted are extensive—the rules here are exactly the same as those for Group 2.

GROUP 5—Sports cars (25), with a maximum engine displacement of five liters. Despite the designation that implies the kind of sports cars you come across in the neighborhood, these really are high-performance machines that are seldom seen in this country. Usually they appear only in the endurance races of the International Championship for Makes at Daytona, Sebring and Watkins Glen. Examples are Ferrari 512S, Porsche 917, Lola T-70. To distinguish these sports cars from conventional production sports cars or from Group 7 sports-racing cars (below), they are occasionally referred to as "sports-25" cars, since the minimum production required is 25.

Group 5, Ferrari 512S sports car driven by Mario Andretti at Sebring.

CATEGORY B

Experimental Competition Cars
(No minimum production required)

GROUP 6—Prototype sports cars, "experimental competition cars especially manufactured for speed or endurance races. . . ." These are highly tuned machines, with few restrictions, built only for racing. Since the maximum engine size was lowered to 3 liters in 1968, these cars have had to play second fiddle to the 5-liter sports-25's in races

Group 6, Matra 650 prototype at Sebring.

of the International Championship for Makes. Current examples are the Alfa Romeo Tipo 33-3, Matra-Simca 650, Ferrari 312P, Porsche 908. Because no minimum production is required, manufacturers usually produce only two or three cars, sometimes just one.

CATEGORY C

Racing Cars
(No minimum production required)

GROUP 7—Two-seater racing cars, "competition vehicles built exclusively for speed races on closed circuits." The largest of these have no limits on engine size and few restrictions anywhere else; these are the beautifully sculptured cars seen in the Canadian-American Challenge Cup, European hill climbs and, occasionally, in Japan. Those with smaller engines compete in S.C.C.A. and European club racing and throughout the British Commonwealth.

These cars must run on pump gas and must have self-starters. They must have a dual-brake system responsive to one control, the pedal—if one system fails the back-up is automatically actuated.

Group 7, George Eaton's BRM-Chevrolet sports-racing car at St. Jovite.

In Appendix J these are designated "two-seater racing cars," but in North America the custom is to designate them *sports-racing* cars, with a hyphen or slash (/) to distinguish them from the sports cars of Group 5. The makes include McLaren (which won the Can-Am four consecutive years), Chaparral, Porsche, Lola, March, Ferrari, Lotus, a profusion of small-engine English makes and many one-of-a-kinds.

GROUP 8—Single-seat racing cars, with open wheels (no fenders) and open cockpit. These are better known as Formula cars, graded One, Two and Three.

Formula One, with very few restrictions, embodies the most sophisticated and expensive automotive engineering. Formula One cars are the machines that run in the Grand Prix, an international series of 11 to 13 races a year on three continents that count for points toward the World Championship of Drivers. There is also an International

Group 8, a McLaren-Ford Formula One car at St. Jovite. The driver is Denis Hulme, 1967 world champion.

Cup for the winning car manufacturer in Formula One competition. The current Formula One limits engine size to 3 liters displacement if it is normally aspirated—that is, if it has no supercharger. An engine may be supercharged if its displacement is limited to 1,500 cc. (1.5 liters). Minimum weight, 1,166 pounds.

Formula Two and Formula Three are scaled-down versions of Formula One:

Formula Two—A popular class in Europe, frequently run by Grand Prix drivers when they are not engaged in Formula One races. Maximum of four cylinders, 1,300-1,600 cc. displacement, no super-charging. Engine block must be from production model of a car of which 500 units have been produced within 12 consecutive months. Minimum weight 990 pounds. The S.C.C.A.'s Formula B is very similar to Formula Two.

Formula Three—A sort of training ground for Grand Prix drivers, comparable to sprint and sports cars in the United States. Minimum

225

weight 924 pounds. Engine block and head must come from production line of at least 1,000 units in 12 months. Maximum displacement 1,000 cc., rising in 1971 to 1,600 cc., but with certain air-intake restrictions. The S.C.C.A.'s Formula C is similar.

GROUP 9—Formula Libre racing cars, a catch-all for cars "other . . . than those defined by one of the three international formulas." Specifications are left to "the discretion of the promoters and it rests with them to list these specifications as clearly as possible in the Supplementary Regulations of the event, which anyway have to be approved by the National Sporting Authority answerable to the F.I.A. [meaning ACCUS in this country]"

This free-for-all ranges from Indianapolis racers and Grand National stock cars to Formulas Vee and Super Vee. It also includes the old 2.5-liter Tasman Formula used in the New Zealand-Australia series, dragsters and land-speed-record "cars."

Group 9, Formula Vee racers.

Group 9, top fuel eliminator.

Group 9, stock cars.

Group 9, Indy car.

APPENDIX C

The Winner's Circle

WORLD CHAMPIONSHIP OF DRIVERS

YEAR	DRIVER	COUNTRY	CAR
1950	Guiseppe Farina	Italy	Alfa Romeo
1951	Juan Manuel Fangio	Argentina	Alfa Romeo
1952	Alberto Ascari	Italy	Ferrari
1953	Alberto Ascari	Italy	Ferrari
1954	Juan Manuel Fangio	Argentina	Mercedes and Maserati
1955	Juan Manuel Fangio	Argentina	Mercedes
1956	Juan Manuel Fangio	Argentina	Lancia and Ferrari
1957	Juan Manuel Fangio	Argentina	Maserati
1958	Mike Hawthorn	England	Ferrari
1959	Jack Brabham	Australia	Cooper-Climax
1960	Jack Brabham	Australia	Cooper-Climax
1961	Phil Hill	U.S.A.	Ferrari
1962	Graham Hill	England	BRM
1963	Jim Clark	Scotland	Lotus-Climax
1964	John Surtees	England	Ferrari
1965	Jim Clark	Scotland	Lotus-Climax
1966	Jack Brabham	Australia	Brabham-Repco

YEAR	DRIVER	COUNTRY	CAR
1967	Denis Hulme	New Zealand	Brabham-Repco
1968	Graham Hill	England	Lotus-Ford
1969	Jackie Stewart	Scotland	Matra-Ford
1970	Jochen Rindt*	Austria	Lotus-Ford

*Posthumous award. Rindt was killed Sept. 5 while practicing for the Italian Grand Prix. The points he had accumulated up to that time were enough, at the end of the season, to win the championship.

WINNERS OF THE INDIANAPOLIS 500

YEAR	DRIVER	ENGINE	CHASSIS	SPEED
1911	Ray Harroun	Marmon	Marmon	74.59
1912	Joe Dawson	National	National	78.72
1913	Jules Goux, France	Peugeot	Peugeot	75.93
1914	René Thomas, France	Delage	Delage	82.47
1915	Ralph DePalma	Mercedes	Mercedes	89.84
1916	Dario Resta, France	Peugeot	Peugeot	83.26
1917	(World War I—No race)			
1918	(World War I—No race)			
1919	Howdy Wilcox	Peugeot	Peugeot	88.05
1920	Gaston Chevrolet	Frontenac	Frontenac	88.16
1921	Tommy Milton	Frontenac	Frontenac	89.62
1922	Jimmy Murphy	Miller	Duesenberg	94.48
1923	Tommy Milton	Miller	Miller	90.95
1924	Lora Corum	Duesenberg	Duesenberg	98.23
1925	Pete DePaolo	S/Duesenberg	Duesenberg	101.13
1926	Frank Lockhart	Miller	Miller	95.885
1927	George Souders	Duesenberg	Duesenberg	97.545
1928	Louis Meyer	Miller	Miller	99.482
1929	Ray Keech	Miller	Miller	97.585
1930	Billy Arnold	Miller	Summers	100.448
1931	Louis Schneider	Miller	Stevens	96.629
1932	Fred Frame	Miller	Wetteroth	104.144
1933	Louis Meyer	Miller	Miller	104.162
1934	Bill Cummings	Miller	Miller	104.863
1935	Kelly Petillo	Offenhauser	Wetteroth	106.240
1936	Louis Meyer	Miller	Stevens	109.069
1937	Wilbur Shaw	Offenhauser	Shaw	113.580
1938	Floyd Roberts	Miller	Wetteroth	117.200
1939	Wilbur Shaw	Maserati	Maserati	115.035
1940	Wilbur Shaw	Maserati	Maserati	114.277

YEAR	DRIVER	ENGINE	CHASSIS	SPEED
1941	Floyd Davis/Mauri Rose*	Offenhauser	Wetteroth	115.117
1942	(World War II—No race)			
1943	(World War II—No race)			
1944	(World War II—No race)			
1945	(World War II—No race)			
1946	George Robson	Sparks	Adams	114.820
1947	Mauri Rose	Offenhauser	Deidt	116.338
1948	Mauri Rose	Offenhauser	Deidt	119.814
1949	Bill Holland	Offenhauser	Deidt	121.327
1950	Johnnie Parsons	Offenhauser	Kurtis	124.002
1951	Lee Wallard	Offenhauser	Kurtis	126.244
1952	Troy Ruttman	Offenhauser	Kuzma	128.922
1953	Bill Vukovich	Offenhauser	KK 500A	128.740
1954	Bill Vukovich	Offenhauser	KK 500A	130.840
1955	Bob Sweikert	Offenhauser	KK 500C	128.209
1956	Pat Flaherty	Offenhauser	Watson	128.490
1957	Sam Hanks	Offenhauser	Epperly	135.601
1958	Jimmy Bryan	Offenhauser	Epperly	133.791
1959	Rodger Ward	Offenhauser	Watson	135.857
1960	Jim Rathmann	Offenhauser	Watson	138.767
1961	A. J. Foyt	Offenhauser	Watson	139.130
1962	Rodger Ward	Offenhauser	Watson	140.293
1963	Parnelli Jones	Offenhauser	Watson	143.137
1964	A. J. Foyt	Offenhauser	Watson	147.350
1965	Jim Clark, Scotland	Ford	Lotus	151.388
1966	Graham Hill, England	Ford	Lola	144.317
1967	A. J. Foyt	Ford	Coyote	151.207
1968	Bobby Unser	T/Offenhauser	Eagle	152.882
1969	Mario Andretti	T/Ford	Brawner	156.867
1970	Al Unser	T/Ford	P. J. Colt	155.749

Abbreviations:

S/ Supercharged   T/ Turbocharged

*Davis was relieved by Rose.

UNITED STATES AUTO CLUB CHAMPIONS
National

1902—Harry Harkness	1907—Eddie Bald
1903—Barney Oldfield	1908—Louis Strang
1904—George Heath	1909—George Robertson
1905—Victor Hemery	1910—Ray Harroun
1906—Joe Tracy	1911—Ralph Mulford

1912—Ralph DePalma	1940—Rex Mays
1913—Earl Cooper	1941—Rex Mays
1914—Ralph DePalma	1942-45—World War II: No championship
1915—Earl Cooper	1946—Ted Horn
1916—Dario Resta	1947—Ted Horn
1917—Earl Cooper	1948—Ted Horn
1918—Ralph Mulford	1949—Johnnie Parsons
1919—Howard Wilcox	1950—Henry Banks
1920—Thomas Milton	1951—Tony Bettenhausen
1921—Thomas Milton	1952—Chuck Stevenson
1922—James Murphy	1953—Sam Hanks
1923—Eddie Hearne	1954—Jimmy Bryan
1924—James Murphy	1955—Bob Sweikert
1925—Peter DePaolo	1956—Jimmy Bryan
1926—Harry Hartz	1957—Jimmy Bryan
1927—Peter DePaolo	1958—Tony Bettenhausen
1928—Louis Meyer	1959—Rodger Ward
1929—Louis Meyer	1960—A. J. Foyt
1930—Billy Arnold	1961—A. J. Foyt
1931—Louis Schneider	1962—Rodger Ward
1932—Bob Carey	1963—A. J. Foyt
1933—Louis Meyer	1964—A. J. Foyt
1934—Bill Cummings	1965—Mario Andretti
1935—Kelly Petillo	1966—Mario Andretti
1936—Mauri Rose	1967—A. J. Foyt
1937—Wilbur Shaw	1968—Bobby Unser
1938—Floyd Roberts	1969—Mario Andretti
1939—Wilbur Shaw	1970—Al Unser

Stock Car

1950—Jay Frank	1961—Paul Goldsmith
1951—Rodger Ward	1962—Paul Goldsmith
1952—Marshall Teague	1963—Don White
1953—Frank Mundy	1964—Parnelli Jones
1954—Marshall Teague	1965—Norm Nelson
1955—Frank Mundy	1966—Norm Nelson
*1956—Johnny Mantz	1967—Don White
1957—Jerry Unser	1968—A. J. Foyt
1958—Fred Lorenzen	1969—Roger McCluskey
1959—Fred Lorenzen	1970—Roger McCluskey
1960—Norm Nelson	

*First year of USAC sanction; previously, American Automobile Association.

Sprint Car

Mid-West	Eastern
1947—Johnny Shackleford	Ted Horn
1948—Spider Webb	Ted Horn
1949—Jackie Holmes	Tommy Hinnershitz
1950—Duane Carter	Tommy Hinnershitz
1951—Troy Ruttman	Tommy Hinnershitz
1952—Joe James	Tommy Hinnershitz
1953—Pat O'Connor	Joe Sostilio
1954—Pat O'Connor	Johnny Thomson
1955—Bob Sweikert	Tommy Hinnershitz
1956—Pat O'Connor	Tommy Hinnershitz
1957—Elmer George	Bill Randall
1958—Eddie Sachs	Johnny Thomson
1959—Don Branson	Tommy Hinnershitz
1960—Parnelli Jones	A. J. Foyt

After Introduction of Current USAC Point System:

1961—Parnelli Jones	1966—Roger McCluskey
1962—Parnelli Jones	1967—Greg Weld
1963—Roger McCluskey	1968—Larry Dickson
1964—Don Branson	1969—Gary Bettenhausen
1965—Johnny Rutherford	1970—Larry Dickson

Midget

1948—Roy Sherman	1960—Jimmy Davies
1949—Sam Hanks	1961—Jimmy Davies
1950—Bill Vukovich	†1962—Jimmy Davies
1951—Art Cross	1963—Bob Wente
1952—Johnnie Tolan	1964—Mel Kenyon
1953—Leroy Warriner	1965—Mike McGreevy
1954—Jack Turner	1966—Mike McGreevy
1955—Jack Turner	1967—Mel Kenyon
*1956—Shorty Templeman	1968—Mel Kenyon
1957—Shorty Templeman	1969—Bob Tattersall
1958—Shorty Templeman	1970—Jimmy Caruthers
1959—Gene Hartley	

*First year of USAC sanction; previously, American Automobile Association.
†Introduction of current point system.

231

SPORTS CAR CLUB OF AMERICA CHAMPIONS

Professional Series

CANADIAN-AMERICAN CHALLENGE CUP

1966—John Surtees	Lola-Chevrolet
1967—Bruce McLaren	McLaren-Chevrolet
1968—Denis Hulme	McLaren-Chevrolet
1969—Bruce McLaren	McLaren-Chevrolet
1970—Denis Hulme	McLaren-Chevrolet

TRANS-AMERICAN CHAMPIONSHIP

Over 2 Liters	Under 2 Liters
1966—Mustang	Alfa Romeo
1967—Mustang	Porsche
1968—Camaro	Porsche
1969—Camaro	Porsche
1970—Mustang	Alfa Romeo

(Beginning with 1971 season, Trans-American division is over 2.5 liters and under 2.5 liters.)

CONTINENTAL CHAMPIONSHIP

1967—Gus Hutchison	Lotus-Ford
1968—Lou Sell	Eagle-Chevrolet
1969—Tony Adamowicz	Eagle-Chevrolet
1970—John Cannon	McLaren-Chevrolet

UNITED STATES ROAD RACING CHAMPIONSHIP

1963—Bob Holbert	Cobra-Ford; Porsche
1964—Jim Hall	Chaparral-Chevrolet
1965—George Follmer	Lotus-Porsche
1966—Chuck Parsons	Genie and McLaren-Chevrolets
1967—Mark Donohue	Lola-Chevrolet
1968—Mark Donohue	McLaren-Chevrolet

(Discontinued after 1968)

NATIONAL ASSOCIATION FOR STOCK CAR AUTO RACING (NASCAR) DRIVING CHAMPIONS

GRAND NATIONAL

1949—Robert (Red) Byron	Oldsmobile
1950—Bill Rexford	Oldsmobile
1951—Herb Thomas	Plymouth-Hudson

232

1952—Tim Flock	Hudson
1953—Herb Thomas	Hudson
1954—Lee Petty	Chrysler
1955—Tim Flock	Chrysler
1956—Elzie (Buck) Baker	Chrysler-Dodge
1957—Elzie (Buck) Baker	Chevrolet
1958—Lee Petty	Oldsmobile
1959—Lee Petty	Oldsmobile-Plymouth
1960—Rex White	Chevrolet
1961—Ned Jarrett	Chevrolet
1962—Joe Weatherly	Pontiac
1963—Joe Weatherly	Pontiac-Mercury
1964—Richard Petty	Plymouth
1965—Ned Jarrett	Ford
1966—David Pearson	Dodge
1967—Richard Petty	Plymouth
1968—David Pearson	Ford
1969—David Pearson	Ford
1970—Bobby Isaac	Dodge

GRAND AMERICAN SERIES
(Formerly Grand Touring)

1968—Dewayne (Tiny) Lund	Mercury Cougar
1969—Ken Rush	Chevrolet Camaro
1970—Dewayne (Tiny) Lund	Chevrolet Camaro

LATE MODEL SPORTSMAN

1950—Mike Klapak	1961—Dick Nephew
1951—Mike Klapak	Bill Wimble (Co-champions)
1952—Mike Klapak	1962—Rene Charland
1953—Johnny Roberts	1963—Rene Charland
1954—Danny Graves	1964—Rene Charland
1955—Billy Mycrs	1965—Rene Charland
1956—Ralph Earnhardt	1966—Don MacTavish
1957—Ned Jarrett	1967—Pete Hamilton
1958—Ned Jarrett	1968—Joe Thurman
1959—Rick Henderson	1969—Charles (Red) Farmer
1960—Bill Wimble	1970—Charles (Red) Farmer

1948—Robert (Red) Byron
1949—Fonty Flock
1950—Charles Dyer
1951—Wally Campbell
1952—Frankie Schneider
1953—Joe Weatherly
1954—Jack Choquette
1955—Bill Widenhouse
1956—Charles (Red) Farmer
1957—Ken (Bones) Marriott
1958—Budd Olsen

1960—Johnny Roberts
1961—Johnny Roberts
1962—Eddie Crouse
1963—Eddie Crouse
1964—Bobby Allison
1965—Bobby Allison
1966—Ernie Gahan
1967—Carl (Bugs) Stevens
1968—Carl (Bugs) Stevens
1969—Carl (Bugs) Stevens
1970—Fred DeSarro

INTERNATIONAL CHAMPIONSHIP FOR MAKES

From 1953 through 1961 this competition was limited to two-seat sports cars with normal road equipment (lights, windshield wipers, spare tire, etc.), and was informally known as the World Sports Car Championship. Races were required to run a minimum length of 1,000 kilometers (621 miles). The champions were:

1953—Ferrari
1954—Ferrari
1955—Mercedes-Benz
1956—Ferrari
1957—Ferrari

1958—Ferrari
1959—Aston Martin
1960—Ferrari
1961—Ferrari

From 1962 through 1965 the championship was limited to grand touring cars, of which 100 had to be built in 12 consecutive months. Cars had to have normal road equipment. The winners were:

1962—Division 3, over 2,000 cc.—Ferrari
Division 2, 1,001–2,000 cc.—Porsche
Division 1, under 1,000 cc.—Abarth

1963—Division 3, over 2,000 cc.—Ferrari
Division 2, 1,001–2,000 cc.—Porsche
Division 1, under 1,000 cc.—Abarth

1964—Division 3, over 2,000 cc.—Ferrari
Division 2, 1,001–2,000 cc.—Porsche
Division 1, under 1,000 cc.—Abarth-Simca

1965—Division 3, over 2,000 cc.—Shelby American (Cobra)
Division 2, 1,301–2,000 cc.—Porsche
Division 1, under 1,300 cc.—Abarth

234

Appendix J of the International Sporting Code took effect Jan. 1, 1966. In that year there were championships for sports cars (minimum production of 50) and for prototypes (no minimum-production requirements).

> 1966—Sports cars, Division 3, over 2,000 cc.—Ford
> Sports cars, Division 2, 1,301–2,000 cc.—Porsche
> Sports cars, Division 1, under 1,300 cc.—Abarth
>
> Prototypes, Division 2, over 2,000 cc.—Ford
> Prototypes, Division 1, under 2,000 cc.—Porsche

The championship format as it is now known took shape in 1967. There was an eight-race series for prototypes, sports cars and grand touring cars; there was also a separate series for sports cars (of which 50 had to be built in 12 consecutive months).

> 1967—Prototypes, sports cars and grand touring:
>
> Division 1, unlimited—Ferrari
> Division 2, under 2,000 cc.—Porsche
>
> 1967—Sports cars, Division 3, over 2,000 cc.—Ford
> Sports cars, Division 2, 1,301–2,000 cc.—Porsche
> Sports cars, Division 1, under 1,300 cc.—Abarth

The present format has been used since 1968. Sports cars (Group 5) are limited to 5,000 cc. displacement and prototypes (Group 6) to 3,000 cc. Special grand touring cars (Group 4) have no limit on engine displacement. In 1968 the rules governing sports cars (Group 5) required a minimum production of 50 in 12 consecutive months; this was reduced to 25 the following year. In 1968 the F. I. A. also established an International Cup for grand touring cars.

> 1968—Prototypes, sports cars and grand touring—Ford
> International Cup for grand touring—Porsche
>
> 1969—Prototypes, sports cars and grand touring—Porsche
> International Cup for grand touring—Porsche
>
> 1970—Prototypes, sports cars and grand touring—Porsche
> International Cup for grand touring—Porsche

From 1962 through 1967 no single marque was designated world champion—there were only divisional champions. With the revised format, Ford was recognized as the world manufacturers' champion in 1968 and Porsche won the honor in 1969 and 1970.

APPENDIX D

RACING ORGANIZATIONS

ACCUS-F.I.A.

The four principal racing organizations in this country are members of the Automobile Competition Committee for the United States-F.I.A., Inc., 433 Main Street, Stamford, Conn. 06901. They are, in alphabetical order:

National Association for Stock Car Auto Racing, P. O. Box K, Daytona Beach, Fla. 32015.

National Hot Rod Association, 10639 Riverside Drive, North Hollywood, Calif. 91602.

Sports Car Club of America, P.O. Box 791, Westport, Conn. 06880.

United States Auto Club, 4910 West 16th Street, Speedway, Ind. 46224.

Sprint Cars

United States Auto Club, 4910 West 16th Street, Speedway, Ind. 46224.

International Motor Contest Association, 1925 Park Avenue, Des Moines, Iowa 50315.

United Racing Club, c/o Louis Kunz, president, 473 Washington Road, Sayreville, N.J. 08872.

California Racing Association, 17429 Chase Street, Northridge, Calif. 91324.

Big Car Racing Association, 7965 Melrose Drive, Wheatridge, Colo. 80033.

Midget Cars

United States Auto Club, 4910 West 16th Street, Speedway, Ind. 46224.

International Motor Contest Association, 1925 Park Avenue, Des Moines, Iowa. 50315.

American Racing Drivers Club, c/o Ken Brenn, president, 165 Mountain View Road, Warren, N.J. 07060.

Northeastern Midget Racing Association, c/o John McCarthy, president, 9 Trowbridge Lane, Shrewsbury, Mass. 01545.

United Auto Racing Association, c/o Chuck Stebbins, secretary-treasurer, 2321 George Avenue, Joliet, Ill. 60437.

Badger Midget Auto Racing Association, c/o Paul Krueger, secretary, 4005 Major Avenue, Madison, Wis. 53716.

St. Louis Auto Racing Association, 6724 Thurston Avenue, Berkeley, Mo. 63134.

Northwest Midget Racing Association, c/o Bob Putnam, 4716 42d Avenue North, Minneapolis, Minn. 55422.

Bay Cities Racing Association, 4824 Telegraph Avenue, Oakland, Calif. 94609.

United States Racing Club, P.O. Box 1027, Pomona, Calif. 91769

Late-Model Stock Cars

National Association for Stock Car Auto Racing, P.O. Box K, Daytona Beach, Fla. 32015.

United States Auto Club, 4910 West 16th Street, Speedway, Ind. 46224.

Automobile Racing Club of America, 3201 Glenwood Avenue, Toledo, Ohio 43610.

International Motor Contest Association, 1925 Park Avenue, Des Moines, Iowa 50315.

Formula Cars and Small Foreign Sedans

International Motor Sports Association, P.O. Box 805 Fairfield, Conn. 06430.

Drag Racing

National Hot Rod Association, 3418 West First Street, Los Angeles, Calif. 90004.

American Hot Rod Association, 8133 State Line Road, Kansas City, Mo. 64114.

Off-Road Racing

National Off Road Racing Association, 19730 Ventura Boulevard, Suite J, Woodland Hills, Calif. 91364.

International Desert Racing Association, 10870 Lowden Avenue, Stanton, Calif. 90680.

PRINCIPAL NORTH AMERICAN RACING SITES

Start/Finish line ⊢——▶ Direction of race

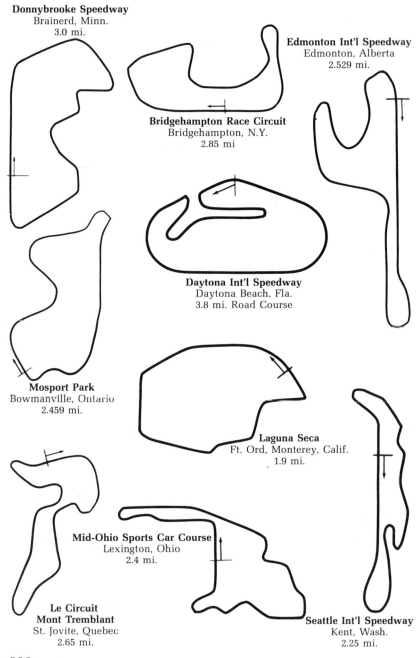

Donnybrooke Speedway
Brainerd, Minn.
3.0 mi.

Edmonton Int'l Speedway
Edmonton, Alberta
2.529 mi.

Bridgehampton Race Circuit
Bridgehampton, N.Y.
2.85 mi

Daytona Int'l Speedway
Daytona Beach, Fla.
3.8 mi. Road Course

Mosport Park
Bowmanville, Ontario
2.459 mi.

Laguna Seca
Ft. Ord, Monterey, Calif.
1.9 mi.

Mid-Ohio Sports Car Course
Lexington, Ohio
2.4 mi.

**Le Circuit
Mont Tremblant**
St. Jovite, Quebec
2.65 mi.

Seattle Int'l Speedway
Kent, Wash.
2.25 mi.

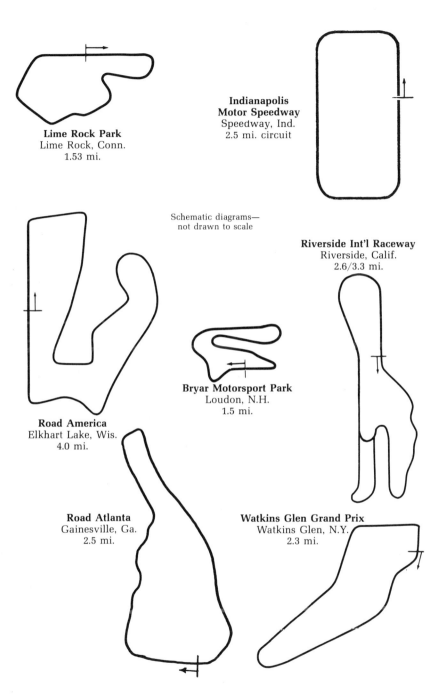

Lime Rock Park
Lime Rock, Conn.
1.53 mi.

**Indianapolis
Motor Speedway**
Speedway, Ind.
2.5 mi. circuit

Schematic diagrams—
not drawn to scale

Riverside Int'l Raceway
Riverside, Calif.
2.6/3.3 mi.

Bryar Motorsport Park
Loudon, N.H.
1.5 mi.

Road America
Elkhart Lake, Wis.
4.0 mi.

Road Atlanta
Gainesville, Ga.
2.5 mi.

Watkins Glen Grand Prix
Watkins Glen, N.Y.
2.3 mi.

Principal North American Racing Sites

Key to Abbreviations

A—Airport road course.
HC—Hill climb.
OD—Oval track, dirt.
OP—Oval track, paved.
PR—Permanent, privately owned road course.
OR—Occasional road course, one that uses public land, such as streets, roads, parks.

Lap distances are omitted from some airport listings because they change from race to race.

Where more than one length is indicated for a road course, it means the promoter has a choice of layouts.

PLACE	NAME	TYPE	LAP DISTANCE (Miles)
ALABAMA			
Birmingham	Birmingham International Raceway	OP	⅝
Huntsville	Huntsville	A	2.2
Montgomery	Montgomery International Speedway	OP	½
Talladega	Alabama International Motor Speedway	OP	2.6
Talladega	Alabama International Motor Speedway	PR	4.0
ARIZONA			
Phoenix	Phoenix International Raceway	OP	1.0
Phoenix	Phoenix International Raceway	PR	2.75
Phoenix	Manzanita Park Speedway	OD	½
Tucson	Tucson Fairgrounds Speedway	OD	¼

PLACE	NAME	TYPE	LAP DISTANCE (Miles)
CALIFORNIA			
Anaheim	Orange County International Raceway	PR	1.8
Fresno	Kearney Bowl	OP	$\frac{1}{4}$
Gardena	Ascot Stadium	OD	$\frac{1}{2}$
Hanford	Hanford Motor Speedway	OP	$1\frac{1}{2}$
Holtville	Holtville	A	1.9
Monterey	Laguna Seca (on Army base, Fort Ord)	OR	1.9
Ontario	Ontario Motor Speedway	OP	$2\frac{1}{2}$
Ontario	Ontario Motor Speedway	PR	3.19
Riverside	Riverside International Raceway	PR	2.5/2.6/3.3
San Jose	San Jose Motor Speedway	OP	$\frac{1}{4}$
Stockton	Stockton 99 Speedway	OP	$\frac{1}{4}$
Vallejo	Vallejo Motor Speedway	OD	$\frac{1}{4}$
Willow Springs	Willow Springs International Raceway	PR	2.0
CANADA			
Bowmanville, Ontario	Mosport Park	PR	2.46
Edmonton, Alberta	Edmonton International Speedway	PR	2.53
St. Jovite, Quebec	Le Circuit Mont Tremblant	PR	2.65
Westwood, British Columbia	Coquitlan	OR	1.8
COLORADO			
Aspen	Aspen Raceways	PR	1.1
Castle Rock	Continental Divide Raceways	PR	2.66
Colorado Springs	Pikes Peak Hill Climb	HC	12.5
CONNECTICUT			
Lime Rock	Lime Rock Park	PR	1.53
Stafford Springs	Stafford Springs Speedway	OP	$\frac{1}{2}$
Thompson	New Thompson Speedway	PR	1.6
Thompson	New Thompson Speedway	OP	$\frac{5}{8}$
DELAWARE			
Dover	Dover Downs International Speedway	OP	1.0

241

PLACE	NAME	TYPE	LAP DISTANCE (Miles)
FLORIDA			
Daytona Beach	Daytona International Speedway	OP	2.5
Daytona Beach	Daytona International Speedway	PR	1.6/3.1/3.81
Fernandina	Fernandina Beach	A	2.8
Hollywood	Miami-Hollywood Speedway	OP	$\frac{1}{3}$
Hollywood	Miami-Hollywood Speedway	PR	1.6
Osceola	Osceola	A	2.3
Sebastian	Sebastian	A	2.23
Sebring	Sebring	A	2.2/5.2
GEORGIA			
Gainesville	Road Atlanta	PR	2.52
Augusta	Augusta Raceway	OP	$\frac{1}{2}$
Faulkville	Savannah International Raceway	PR	2.0
Hampton	Atlanta International Raceway	OP	$1\frac{1}{2}$
Jefferson	Jefco Speedway	OP	$\frac{1}{2}$
Macon	Middle Georgia Raceway	OP	0.55
Savannah	Savannah Speedway	OP	$\frac{1}{2}$
ILLINOIS			
DuQuoin	DuQuoin State Fairgrounds	OD	1.0
Fairbury	Fairbury Fairgrounds	OD	$\frac{1}{4}$
Granite City	Tri-City Speedway	OD	$\frac{1}{2}$
Hinsdale	Santa Fe Park Speedway	OD	$\frac{1}{4}$
Joliet	Joliet Stadium	OP	$\frac{1}{4}$
Rockford	Rockford Motor Speedway	OP	$\frac{1}{4}$
Rockton	Blackhawk Farms	PR	1.8
Springfield	Springfield Speedway	OD	$\frac{1}{4}$
Springfield	Illinois State Fairgrounds	OD	1.0
INDIANA			
Avilla	Avilla Motor Speedway	OD	$\frac{1}{4}$
Clermont	Indianapolis Raceway Park	PR	2.5
Clermont	Indianapolis Raceway Park	OP	$\frac{1}{2}$
Indianapolis	Indiana State Fairgrounds	OD	1.0
Kokomo	Kokomo Speedway	OD	$\frac{1}{4}$
Oxford	Henry's Speedway	OD	$\frac{3}{8}$
Salem	Salem Speedway	OP	$\frac{1}{2}$
South Bend	South Bend Motor Speedway	OP	$\frac{1}{4}$
Speedway	Indianapolis Motor Speedway	OP	$2\frac{1}{2}$
Terre Haute	Vigo County Fairgrounds	OD	$\frac{1}{2}$
Winchester	Winchester Speedway	OP	$\frac{1}{2}$

242

PLACE	NAME	TYPE	LAP DISTANCE (Miles)
IOWA			
Cedar Rapids	Hawkeye Downs	OD	$\frac{1}{2}$
Davenport	Mississippi Valley Fairgrounds	OD	$\frac{1}{4}$
Knoxville	Knoxville Speedway	OD	$\frac{1}{2}$
KANSAS			
Olathe	Olathe Naval Air Station	A	—
Wichita	Lake Afton	OR	1.8
KENTUCKY			
Muldraugh	Otter Creek Park	HC	0.61
LOUISIANA			
Lake Charles	Chennault Air Force Base	A	3.0
MAINE			
Oxford	Oxford Plains Speedway	OP	$\frac{1}{3}$
MARYLAND			
Beltsville	Beltsville Speedway	OP	$\frac{1}{2}$
Cumberland	Cumberland	A	1.6
MICHIGAN			
Cambridge Junction	Michigan International Speedway	OP	2.0
Cambridge Junction	Michigan International Speedway	PR	3.0
Grand Rapids	Berlin Speedway	OP	$\frac{1}{2}$
Grattan	Grattan International	PR	2.0
Jackson	Jackson Motor Speedway	OP	$\frac{1}{3}$
Lansing	Spartan Speedway	OP	$\frac{1}{4}$
Waterford	Waterford Hills	PR	1.5
MINNESOTA			
Brainerd	Donnybrooke Speedway	PR	3.0
Elko	Elko Speedway	OP	$\frac{1}{3}$
MISSOURI			
Jefferson City	Capitol Speedway	OD	$\frac{3}{8}$
Odessa	I-70 Speedway	OP	$\frac{1}{2}$
Sedalia	Missouri State Fairgrounds	OD	1.0
Valley Park	Lake Hill Speedway	OD	$\frac{1}{2}$
Wentzville	Mid-America Raceways	PR	2.86

243

PLACE	NAME	TYPE	LAP DISTANCE (Miles)
NEVADA			
Virginia City	Virginia City	HC	2.0
NEW HAMPSHIRE			
Loudon	Bryar Motorsport Park	PR	1.6
NEW JERSEY			
Trenton	Trenton Speedway	OP	$1\frac{1}{2}$
NEW MEXICO			
Fort Sumner	Fort Sumner	A	2.7
Los Alamos	Los Alamos	HC	1.9
NEW YORK			
Bridgehampton	Bridgehampton Race Circuit	PR	2.85
Fonda	Fonda Speedway	OD	$\frac{1}{2}$
Hamburg	Erie County Fairgrounds	OD	$\frac{1}{2}$
Lancaster	Lancaster Speedway	OP	$\frac{1}{2}$
Syracuse	New York State Fairgrounds	OD	1.0
Watkins Glen	Watkins Glen Grand Prix Circuit	PR	2.3
Windsor	Tuscarora Mountain	HC	1.4
NORTH CAROLINA			
Asheville	New Asheville Speedway	OP	$\frac{1}{3}$
Charlotte	Charlotte Motor Speedway	OP	$1\frac{1}{2}$
Hickory	Hickory Speedway	OP	$\frac{4}{10}$
Lake Lure	Chimney Rock	HC	1.9
North Wilkesboro	North Wilkesboro Speedway	OP	$\frac{5}{8}$
Raleigh	State Fairgrounds Speedway	OD	$\frac{1}{2}$
Rockingham	North Carolina Motor Speedway	OP	1.0
Weaverville	Asheville-Weaverville Speedway	OP	$\frac{1}{2}$
West Salem	Bowman Gray Stadium	OP	$\frac{1}{4}$
OHIO			
Cincinnati	Tri-County Speedway	OD	$\frac{1}{2}$
Columbus	Ohio State Fairgrounds	OD	$\frac{1}{2}$
Cortland	Trumbull County Fairgrounds	OD	$\frac{1}{2}$
Dayton	Dayton Speedway	OP	$\frac{1}{2}$
Lexington	Mid-Ohio Sports Car Course	PR	2.4
Lima	Limaland Motor Speedway	OD	$\frac{1}{4}$
Marietta	Washington City Fairgrounds	OD	$\frac{1}{2}$
New Bremen	New Bremen Speedway	OP	$\frac{1}{2}$
Rossburg	Eldora Speedway	OD	$\frac{1}{2}$
Springfield	Clarke County Fairgrounds	OD	$\frac{1}{2}$

PLACE	NAME	TYPE	LAP DISTANCE (Miles)
Toledo	Toledo Raceway	OP	$\frac{1}{2}$
Warren	Nelson Ledges	PR	2.0
Zanesville	Bellefontaine	HC	0.6
OKLAHOMA			
Oklahoma City	Oklahoma Fairgrounds Speedway	OD	$\frac{1}{4}$
Ponca City	Lake Ponca Park	OR	1.5
OREGON			
Portland	Portland International Raceway	PR	1.8
PENNSYLVANIA			
Hershey	Hershey Stadium	OP	$\frac{1}{4}$
Jennerstown	Jennerstown Speedway	OD	$\frac{1}{2}$
Long Pond	Pocono International Raceway	OP	$2\frac{1}{2}$
Long Pond	Pocono International Raceway	PR	1.79
Mechanicsburg	Williams Grove Speedway	OD	$\frac{1}{2}$
Nazareth	Nazareth National Speedway	OD	$1\frac{1}{8}$
Pittsburgh	Heidelberg Speedway	OP	$\frac{1}{2}$
Reading	Duryea	HC	2.6
Reading	Reading Fairgrounds	OD	$\frac{1}{2}$
Weatherly	Weatherly	HC	0.8
Wilkes-Barre	Giant's Despair	HC	1.0
SOUTH CAROLINA			
Columbia	Columbia Speedway	OD	$\frac{1}{2}$
Darlington	Darlington International Raceway	OP	$1\frac{3}{8}$
Greenville	Greenville-Pickens Speedway	OD	$\frac{1}{2}$
SOUTH DAKOTA			
Edgemont	Igloo Raceways	OR	2.0
TENNESSEE			
Bristol	Bristol International Speedway	OP	$\frac{1}{2}$
Kingsport	Kingsport Speedway	OP	$\frac{4}{10}$
Maryville	Smoky Mountain Raceway	OP	$\frac{1}{2}$
Memphis	Shelby County Raceway	PR	1.7
Nashville	Fairgrounds Speedway	OP	$\frac{1}{2}$
TEXAS			
Beaumont	Motorama Speedway	OD	$\frac{1}{4}$
Bryan	Texas International Speedway	OP	2.0
Bryan	Texas International Speedway	PR	3.0
Galveston	Scholes Field	A	2.8

245

PLACE	NAME	TYPE	LAP DISTANCE (Miles)
Houston	Astrodome (indoor track)	OD	$\frac{1}{4}$
Lewisville	Dallas International Motor Speedway	PR	2.5
Navasota	Moody & Clary Speedway	OD	$\frac{1}{4}$
San Marcos	Camp Gary Air Force Base	A	2.2
Smithfield	Green Valley	PR	1.6
Wichita Falls	Wichita Falls Speedway	OD	$\frac{1}{4}$

UTAH

PLACE	NAME	TYPE	LAP DISTANCE (Miles)
Salt Lake City	Bonneville Raceway Park	PR	1.7

VERMONT

PLACE	NAME	TYPE	LAP DISTANCE (Miles)
Bolton	Bolton Valley	HC	3.0
Manchester	Mount Equinox	HC	5.2

VIRGINIA

PLACE	NAME	TYPE	LAP DISTANCE (Miles)
Danville	Virginia International Raceway	PR	3.23
Hampton	Langley Field Speedway	OP	$\frac{4}{10}$
Manassas	Old Dominion Speedway	OP	$\frac{1}{2}$
Martinsville	Martinsville Speedway	OP	$\frac{3}{8}$
South Boston	South Boston Speedway	OP	$\frac{3}{8}$

WEST VIRGINIA

PLACE	NAME	TYPE	LAP DISTANCE (Miles)
Charleston	International Raceway Park	OP	$\frac{7}{16}$
Summit Point	Summit Point Speedway	PR	1.84

WASHINGTON

PLACE	NAME	TYPE	LAP DISTANCE (Miles)
Kent	Seattle International Raceway	PR	2.25

WISCONSIN

PLACE	NAME	TYPE	LAP DISTANCE (Miles)
Elkhart Lake	Road America	PR	4.0
Hales Corners	Hales Corners Speedway	OD	$\frac{1}{4}$
Madison	Capitol City Speedway	OP	$\frac{1}{2}$
West Allis	Wisconsin State Fairgrounds Speedway	OP	1.0
West Allis	State Fair Park	PR	2.0

Conversions, Equivalents and Some Basic Racing Arithmetic

LINEAR MEASUREMENTS

1 centimeter = 0.4 inch	1 inch = 2.54 centimeters
1 meter = 39.37 inches	1 foot = 30.48 centimeters
1 meter = 3.3 feet	1 foot = 0.3 meter
1 kilometer = 0.62 mile	1 mile = 1.61 kilometers

---

1 km = 1,000 m, 1 m = 100 cm
1 mile = 5,280 feet

WEIGHT

1 kilogram = 2.2 pounds (avdp)	1 pound (avdp) = 0.45 kilogram
1 tonne (metric) = 2,200 pounds	1 U.S. ton = 907.18 kilograms

---

1 tonne = 1,000 kg, 1 kg = 1,000 grams
1 U.S. ton = 2,000 pounds

CAPACITY

1 cubic centimeter = 0.061 cubic inch	1 cubic inch = 16.4 cubic
1,000 cubic centimeters = 61 cubic inches	centimeters
1 liter = 61 cubic inches	1 quart (liq) = 0.95 liters
1 liter = 1.057 quarts (liq)	1 U.S. gallon = 3.8 liters (liq)

---

1 liter = 1,000 cc, 1 U.S. quart = 32 fluid ounces,
1 U.S. gallon = 4 quarts

MISCELLANEOUS

6 U.S. gallons = 5 Imperial (British) gallons
1 mile per hour = 1.467 feet per second

How to Calculate Piston Displacement

Piston displacement, also called engine displacement, measures the size of an engine. It does not measure power, though it is a rough guide. Piston displacement is derived from measuring that portion of the cylinder that is "swept" by the piston. In this country displacement is expressed in cubic inches or, in racing slang, "cubes." The abbreviation c.i.d. for "cubic inches displacement" is commonly used. In most other countries displacement is calculated under the metric system—liters or cubic centimeters (1 liter equals 1,000 cubic centimeters). Cubic centimeters are abbreviated cc., commonly spoken as "see-sees."

Manufacturers' specifications usually include the bore and stroke. Bore is the diameter of the cylinder, stroke is the distance the piston travels between the top and bottom of the cylinder. Piston displacement is calculated by this formula:

BORE X BORE X STROKE X 0.785 X NUMBER OF CYLINDERS

Take, as an example, a 8-cylinder engine with a bore of 4.08 inches and a stroke of 3.44 inches:

$$4.08 \times 4.08 = 16.6464, \text{ or } 16.65 \text{ rounded out}$$
$$16.65 \times 3.44 = 57.276 \text{ or } 57.28 \text{ rounded out}$$
$$57.28 \times 0.785 = 44.96480 \text{ or } 44.97 \text{ rounded out}$$
$$44.97 \times 8 = 359.76 \text{ or } 360 \text{ rounded out}$$

The engine, therefore, has a piston displacement of 360 cubic inches.

Foreign-made cars often incorporate the engine size into the name—Datsun 2000, Fiat 850, BMW 2002, Opel GT 1900 indicate the size in cubic centimeters; larger engines are designated in liters, as in Jaguar 4.2.

How to Compute the Winner's Average Speed

(1) Multiply the length of the race (miles) by 3,600 (number of seconds in an hour).

(2) Divide this product by the winner's time, computed in seconds. The result is the average speed in miles per hour.

Example: In a race of 225 miles the winner's time is 2 hours 27 minutes 15.3 seconds (or 8835 seconds).

$$225 \times 3600 = 810,000$$
$$810,000 \div 8835 = 91.8 \text{ miles per hour}$$

Index

References to illustrations are printed in boldface.
References to footnotes are abbreviated *ftn.*

250

254

255